The Great New York City Trivia & Fact Book

The Great New York City Trivia & Fact Book

B. KIM TAYLOR

Cumberland House
Nashville, Tennessee

Published by Cumberland House Publishing, Inc., 431 Harding Industrial Park Drive, Nashville, TN 37211-3160.

Cover design by Joel Wright
Cover photographs by

Library of Congress Cataloging-in-Publication Data

Taylor, B. Kim, 1960-
    The great New York City trivia & fact book / B. Kim Taylor.
    p. cm.
    Includes bibliographical references (p.).
    ISBN 1-888952-77-6 (alk. paper)
    1. New York (N.Y.)—Miscellanea. I. Title.
F128.3T39 1998
974.7'1—dc21   98-5221
                                                                      CIP

Printed in the United States of America
1 2 3 4 5 6 7—04 03 02 01 00 99 98

For Bill and Spencer

Contents

Acknowledgments

Many thanks to my agent, Sheree Bykofsky, and to Ronald Pitkin and Leslie Peterson at Cumberland House for their enthusiasm and patience. Also, special thanks to Tom Allon at NCI Communications, to Gene DeRose at Jupiter Communications, to Larry Johnson, Eric Capstick, Jeff Prant, and Barb Kimball-Walker for their artful photographs, and to David Lockwood and Joey Lieber for thinking of me long ago when searching for writers on the topic of New York City.

It's impossible to imagine a more helpful and knowledgeable source of information about city specifics than Frank Vardy at the city's Planning Department and Census Bureau.

I am also indebted to numerous authors who have written scholarly histories of New York City, including two of New York City's early residents of the upper-middle class: businessman Philip Hone, who kept a diary of local events from 1830 to 1850, and lawyer George Templeton Strong, whose diary of local events stretched from 1851 to 1874. Prolific writer Louis Auchincloss edited their diaries and gathered them together in *The Hone & Strong Diaries of Old Manhattan,* which is illustrated with Currier & Ives prints and early photographs of the city.

The documentation of New York City's rich history wasn't complete until Luc Sante published *Low Life* in 1991, which thoroughly detailed the numerous rigged card games played in gambling houses, the variety of opium dens, the lives of street urchins and preteen gangsters, the unbelievable shantytowns and slums, and the colorful life found on the Bowery in Old New York. Reading *Low Life* is akin to stepping into a time-traveling machine and then finding yourself in a dangerously exciting and grimy part of Manhattan, and I'm grateful for the glimpse of history afforded by Sante's murky tour of the underground.

A special mention of gratitude must go to my husband, Bill, and my son, Spencer, who savored the city without me while I worked on this book. They're my favorite Manhattanites, and I dedicate this book to them with love.

INTRODUCTION:

*A City Halfway Between America
and the World*

*New York City is a place halfway between America
and the world.*

-GEORGE BERNARD SHAW

George Bernard Shaw was able to define what most people sense about New York City: It's located in America yet it is distinctly and wonderfully different in character from any other American city. New York City's unique, defining charm is that it offers a dazzling variety of everything—a cultural smorgasbord for the entire globe. Manhattan is a small, precious stretch of land that runs only 13 miles long and is less than three miles wide yet is home to 1.5 million people and host to over four million daily commuters. The population of Manhattan exceeds the populations of Vermont (511,456) and Wyoming (469,557) combined, and it comprises only 22.6 square miles. Including all of the city's five boroughs, New York's population is approximately 7.3 million.

Manhattan has used more marble in churches, building lobbies, and facades than all of Rome. It boasts as many French restaurants as Paris. It offers more museums and art galleries than London and has over one thousand skyscrapers—more than any other city in the world.

New York City is also a city of amazing contradictions. It is the oldest continuous city in the nation, yet it's perched firmly at the forefront of nearly every conceivable business enterprise. It offers unimaginable luxury and splendor yet contains pockets of poverty and homelessness; well-heeled professionals ride the subways each morning with homeless panhandlers, the elderly share park benches with children, and people from all socioeconomic levels and religious and ethnic backgrounds coexist peacefully (for the most part) throughout the city. New York contains an abundance of life, which is on display seemingly around the clock, and may be one of the few places in the country where you can purchase a carton of milk at 3:00 A.M. without a car.

New York City is also one of the last great walking cities in America, and all of it is accessible. Each neighborhood has its own unique personality, ethnic subtext, or particular feel, and neighborhoods can change dramatically in as little as five years. Portions of the city alter constantly, but the city's Landmarks Preservation Commission has ensured that New York's most magnificent and unusual buildings, parks, and landmarks will remain intact and preserved.

French-speaking Protestant Belgians settled at the southern tip of New York City in 1624, followed by Africans in 1625. Then came the Dutch, English, Scottish, Welsh, French, Spanish, Portuguese, German, and Irish settlers. Soon the entire globe seemed headed for the New World. Throughout the years New York City has been the entranceway to America for the majority of the country's immigrants, and immigrants continue to define and enhance the city today.

What set New York City apart from other American settlements right from its inception was that it was a place where people went to earn a fortune or learn a trade; religion was never as important as commerce, and that remains true now. New York City's successful history of commerce and trade encompasses everything from the growth of Wall Street to Bazooka gum, from new technology in Manhattan's burgeoning "Silicon Alley" to the Bronx's homemade Ghetto Cookies, and from fresh bread to fresh fashion.

The link between politics and crime—as well as politics and greed—is woefully obvious in New York's history. Early directors of New Amsterdam such as Wouter Van Twiller often favored taverns over offices and allotted to themselves enormous chunks of prime land on which to build impressive family estates; two hundred years later, Tammany Hall followed suit. But New York City had also the benefit of noble, colorful politicians such as Fiorello La Guardia, honest Tammany Hall Mayor George McClellan Jr., Theodore Roosevelt, Governor Cuomo, John Lindsay, vice-squashing Mayor Giuliani, and many other insightful, unsullied political visionaries. The city, typically enough, also had an early cross-dressing English governor named Lord Cornbury who flounced around lower Broadway in lipstick, rouge, and sweeping Scarlett O'Hara-style dresses.

New York City's history of education and public health underscores its spirit of innovation in both realms. At least 16 of New York City's physicians have won Nobel Prizes for, among other things, the isolation of antibiotics, finding a way to preserve whole blood for blood banks, and demonstrating that DNA transmits hereditary factors. The first birth control clinic was opened in Brooklyn, and the first ambulance service was developed at Bellevue Hospital.

New York City is practically synonymous with theater, television, and newspaper, magazine, and book publishing. There were as many as 10 major daily newspapers in the city in 1841; now there are three, with dozens of foreign-language newspapers offered as well. So many people have chased their dreams to New York City over the decades (and centuries) that the notion has now become a cliché. New York City was home to Mark Twain and Jimi Hendrix, Sherwood Anderson and Beverly Sills, Malcolm X and Mother Hale, Tito Puente and the Ramones, George Washington and Al Sharpton, Jerry Seinfeld and Boss Tweed, Typhoid Mary and Walt Whitman, Edgar Allan Poe and Margaret Sanger, Theodore Roosevelt and Mary Tyler Moore, Andy Warhol and Salvadore Dalí, Katharine Hepburn and Madonna. Millions can attest to the fact that when you love New York City, no other place will do.

The Great New York City Trivia & Fact Book provides a timeline of how, and sometimes why, the city developed into what it is today, encompassing all of the city's quirks, foibles, legends, crimes, fads, movements, improvements, wars, sports, people, business endeavors, landmarks, and trivia that have permanently become part of its character.

Cheers from the Big Apple.

The
Great
New York
City
Trivia
& Fact
Book

New York City: Gateway to the East

CHAPTER 1

Apple Origins & Basics

In Darkness Dwells the People Which Knows its Annals Not.

ULRICH B. PHILLIPS

When I was a boy, the Battery was way uptown.

ROBERT BENCHLEY

New York is a catastrophe—but a magnificent catastrophe.

LE CORBUSIER

New York City originated as New Amsterdam, in the state of New Netherland, in the mid-1600s and (for the most part) prospered into the sprawling metropolis it is today through a combination of reform movements, comprehensive city planning initiatives introduced in the nineteenth century, nonpartisan municipal commissions, and the ceaseless lure of commerce. New Amsterdam denizens attended primarily to regulating port industry and trade, controlling or isolating noxious industry, and providing defense.

New Amsterdam initially looked like a rural imitation of a Dutch city, with a two-story windmill near the southern tip of Manhattan, a major canal that ran through the middle of the town, and a smattering of three-story homes boasting lush gardens and fruit trees or farmland. Although New Amsterdam was reminiscent of Holland, the majority of the city's first immigrants were not Dutch, but were instead refugees from Holland: Protestants, Walloons, and the Africans. Dutch citizens were too content and economically comfortable in Holland to want to stake a claim in a new country's unchartered territory.

Deer, fox, and bears romped across Manhattan in dense forests that stretched as high as 80 feet. Dozens of streams and ponds in the village provided perch, beaver, and trout for the colonists and Indians, and as colonists dug dirt for the foundations of their homes, they slowly filled in the river's edge at the Hudson and East Rivers, and eventually created what is now called Battery Park City.

Only about 40 percent of New York City was mapped by 1898; due to astounding population growth and a booming economy, the role of government was increased when the boroughs were consolidated in 1898, and the rest of the city was then mapped out. After the boroughs were consolidated, Brooklyn was the fourth largest city in the United States, so New York City's population doubled to nearly three and a half million. Park planning was then instigated, a citywide water system was devised, Central Park was built, a rapid transit system was erected, legislation was passed to regulate tenement housing, and New York became one of the world's most impressively organized and sophisticated cities.

The Algonquin Indians who first settled in Manhattan dubbed it *Manna-Hata,* meaning "Hill Island" or "Island of the Hills." Other terms for Manhattan attributed to the Algonquins include "People of the Whirlpool" and (the still popular) "Place of Intoxication." It is generally believed that Norsemen were the first Europeans to actually sight Manhattan Island—a place so lush and overflowing with grapevines that the Norsemen called it "Wineland."

1524

The pirate and explorer credited with discovering New York Harbor was the Florentine Giovanni da Verrazano, commonly known as John the Florentine, then employed by Francis I of

France. His ship was blown off its course by a storm as he waited for Spanish ships to plunder for salt and silver, which is how he serendipitously discovered New York Harbor. He was so pleased with Manhattan's beauty and the many cordial Indians who resided there, that he kidnapped an Indian boy to take back to France and attempted to abduct an 18-year-old Indian girl as well.

Francis I was embroiled in a war with Spain when Verrazano discovered Manhattan, and since France had little capital or time to found foreign property, Verrazano's discovery in North America was largely ignored. As a result, the French name given to Manhattan by Verrazano in honor of the royal family of France, "Angoueme," never stuck.

1602

The Dutch East India Company (Vereenigde Oostindische Compagnie, or VOC)was founded in Holland.

1607

An anonymous English voyager entered the mouth of the Hudson River, sailed around the area interacting with the Indians, and then drew up a map of the area. When Henry Hudson arrived two years later, it is presumed he had a copy of that map to guide him.

1609

English mariner Henry Hudson was employed by the Dutch East India Company to search for the northeast trading passage to China. He received $320 for this task. His crew, half Dutch and half English, sailed from Texel, Holland, in an 80-ton ship called the *Half Moon*. In the area where the crew slept, these three brass tablets were nailed to the wall:

1. *Honor Thy Father and Mother*
2. *Good Advice Makes the Wheels Run Smoothly*
3. *Do Not Fight Without Cause*

On September 2, the *Half Moon*'s crew anchored on what is now Sandy Hook after five months of bitter quarreling and having narrowly averted a mutiny on numerous occasions.

This is a very good land to fall with, a pleasant Land to see.
HUDSON'S CLERK, ROBERT JUET OF LIMEHOUSE, ENGLAND

*This day the people of the Countrey [sic] came aboord of us,
seeming very glad of our company, and brought greene Tobacco,
and gave us of it for Knives and Beads. They goe in Deere
skins loose, well dressed. . . . They desire Cloathes, and are very
civill. They have great store of Maiz, or Indian Wheate, whereof
they make good Bread. The countrey is full of great and tall
Oakes. The Lands were as pleasant with Grasse and Flowers,
and goodly Trees . . . and very sweet smells came from them.*
ROBERT JUET, ON THE ALGONQUIN INDIANS AND MANHATTAN

Hudson's crew introduced European goods to the Algonquins, as well as alcohol and firearms.

1609

Sources of water in New York City were wells, ponds, and
springs—the origin of Spring and Canal Streets' names. The primary source of water was a 48-acre pond near Franklin and
Pearl Streets.

1624

New York City was called New Amsterdam, the state of New
York was called New Netherland, and the Dutch West India
Company had been granted a trade monopoly in the state. The
first boatload of settlers arrived in the New World in 1624;
Manhattan's first settlers were French-speaking Walloons
(Belgians) and Netherlanders. The emigrants sailed from
Holland in March; at the start of the voyage there were 30 fam-
ilies, but by the time the ship reached Manhattan there were 34.
As the vessel had traveled by the warm waters of Madeira, the
West Indies, and the Canary Islands, love had blossomed.

Thirty houses for 270 inhabitants were built in the two years
after New Amsterdam's first settlers arrived.

A typical Manhattan apartment complex prior to the arrival of the Dutch and European architectural influence.

Q: What were houses built from?
A: Bark, reeds, and hewn planks.

Q: Why were the first settlers Walloons when the Dutch West India Company was Dutch?
A: Walloons, or Protestant Belgians, had migrated north to Holland to escape regions of Belgium ruled by Catholic Spain.

Q: What did many settlers call Manhattan?
A: "Manate."

SOME THINGS NEVER CHANGE

Just as today, early settlers in New Amsterdam complained of noise, traffic, congestion, cost of living, quantity of drinking and carousing, menace of fire, and the different cultures of minority groups. The Dutch settlers differed from their Puritan English counterparts in Massachusetts and Connecticut in that they were less inclined to enforce stringent principles of ethics in politics and more inclined to tolerate perceived religious or cultural eccentrics and nonconformists.

1625

The first settlers sent letters abroad to their families, describing the rich flora and fauna of the New World and the tall corn and vast stock of fish and game, which prompted another party of Walloons to sail for New Netherland in January of 1625. They sailed in a ship called *Oranjeboom* (Orange Tree) and arrived in New Amsterdam in late March. The number of passengers who sailed was not recorded, but 11 of them died and 20 became ill with the plague in Plymouth, England, while waiting out a storm in a harbor. Within a couple of months six families and a few single settlers arrived to join the small settlement at Manhattan's southern tip, bringing the total number of people in the settlement to 45.

1626

Peter Minuit bought the island of Manhattan from the Indians for 60 guilders, which translates into 24 twentieth-century American dollars. At the edge of Columbia University's Baker Field, a large rock features a plaque proclaiming that the site is where Minuit bought the island. Thirteen miles away at the southern tip of Manhattan, a flagpole in Battery Park contains an inscription that claims the transaction occurred there. No one can claim for certain which spot in Manhattan is the correct one, but the official capital of New Amsterdam (also called Fort Amsterdam) was the region located on the island's southern tip.

1626

Fort Amsterdam's first black settlers, 12 Angolan men, arrived as slaves. The Dutch did not officially engage in the slave trade, so the men were most likely taken from Portuguese ships bound for Brazil from Angola and were viewed as indentured servants for the Dutch West India Company. They were eventually given land of their own and freed from servitude, but the Dutch West India Company continued to import slaves to work in the prosperous fur trade and to build public works. Slaves or indentured servants could sue or testify against other citizens and own property.

The first black landowner's home was on Minetta Lane in

Greenwich Village. Greenwich Village would be home to most of Manhattan's black population for the next two centuries (along with what is now the Soho area).

1635

A few settlers were living in Breuckelen, now known as Brooklyn (named after a village in the Netherlands), and in Midwout, now called Flatbush. The Flushing section of Queens was named after the port city of Vlissingen in the Netherlands; the pronunciation of Vlissingen sounds like Flushing.

1638

The first Anglo-Saxons arrived in New Netherland from New England, still in search of the elusive freedom for which they had left England. Captain John Underhill, Salem's John Throgmorton, religious and political dissenter Lady Deborah Moody, and religious dissenter Anne Hutchinson were among the first Anglo-Saxons to move to New Netherland.

1639

Manhattan Indians Ranaque and Tackamuck only wanted "two guns, two kettles, two coats, two adzes, two shirts, one barrel of cider, and six bits of money" for the 500 acres between the Harlem and Bronx Rivers north of Port Morris.

1643

There were 18 different languages spoken in New Amsterdam; in addition to the Dutch, there were German, African, Scandinavian, Walloon, and French Huguenots residing in the town. Transcripts illustrate New Netherland's early melting pot by mentioning a Polish Lutheran resident, and the marriages of an Irish Catholic man to a Protestant Walloon widow and a Portuguese Catholic woman to a non-Catholic Dutch army officer.

Colonial traders were among the first South Asians in New York City, but the first significant influx of Indian immigrants to the city didn't occur until after 1695.

1644

Manhattan's population dwindled from 300 to 100 inhabitants between 1642 and 1644. Many settlers returned to Holland because of the threat of Indian attacks.

1648

Manhattan's first pier was built in the East River south of State Street. It remained the town's only landing until another was built in 1649.

1653

Between 700 and 800 inhabitants called New Amsterdam.

A 13-foot wall made of logs that stretched from the East to the West Rivers separated the wilderness from the town. The wall contained two gates: a land gate at Broadway and a water gate at Pearl Street. The wall was erected because Cromwell in England declared war on the Dutch Republic in 1653, and the residents of New Amsterdam were wary of the British in nearby New Haven, Connecticut. The wall was torn down in 1699 to accommodate the growth of the city, which is how Wall Street got its name.

1654

The first Jewish settler, an Ashkenazi (northern European) Jew, Jacob bar Simson, arrived from Amsterdam on August 22 in the Dutch ship *Pereboom* (Pear Tree). On the ship, bar Simson served as a guardian for about 25 orphans whom the Dutch West India Company had sent as young settlers, and worked as a manual laborer in New Netherland. Two weeks after he arrived, 23 Sephardic (Spanish and Portuguese) Jews arrived from Recife, Brazil, and bar Simson joined them for the first Rosh Hashanah services conducted in America.

1658

The city's first street pavement was cobblestone, laid on Stone Street between Whitehall and Broad on Manhattan's southern tip. Stone Street was originally named Brouwer Street (Brewer in

Dutch) because a brewery operated on the site. The brewery horses raised so much dirt and dust from the ground that nearby homes were coated. The area's residents demanded that the city pave the street; the city paved it and the residents paid the cost.

1664

The Dutch lost the new colony, which was ruled by the Dutch West India Company, to the English after they threatened New Amsterdam with ship guns. New Amsterdam then became New York City.

PINEAPPLE GREETING

Around the turn of the nineteenth century, buildings in New York City were adorned with cast-iron or concrete pineapples, oak leaves, pinecones, and acorns. The pineapple was usually found on the posts of the stoops of Federal and Greek Revival row houses in Greenwich Village and the regions south of the area.

Although Caribe Indians welcomed Columbus to Guadeloupe in 1493 with a pineapple, the tradition may actually date back to when New York City-based sea captains, returning home from southern climates, left pineapples on their stoops to let neighbors know they were back. Pineapples were considered a sign of hospitality in New York City (and in Charleston and England as well). Acorns and oak leaves were considered a sign of strength, and pinecones were perceived as ancient symbols of rebirth.

The city's most obvious uses of these decorations are: the fences on the stairways by Bethesda Fountain in Central Park, the information clock in Grand Central Terminal, Charlton Street, 56 West 10th Street, 83-85 Sullivan Street, 64 West 12th Street, 473-87 Hudson Street, and 1 East 75th Street.

1664

Approximately one-third of the houses in Manhattan in 1664 were taverns. This fact is partially the reason why some communities along the Atlantic seaboard regarded Manhattan as the "capital of the devil."

1664

The population was 1,500.

1667

Houses varied in size and were one, two, or three stories high and were made of wood or red, black, or yellow brick brought from Holland as ship's ballast. The settlers kept lush vegetable gardens and grew fruit trees. On most of the island Indians and settlers hunted deer, fox, and bear and caught beaver, trout, oysters, and perch in scores of small streams and ponds. Forests on the island grew to 80 feet high.

1676

A canal ran up the middle of New Amsterdam to Broad Street and Exchange Place. As in Holland, pedestrians crossed the canal by footbridge and walked next to it on sidewalks, but the canal grew increasingly polluted with litter with each passing year. In 1676 the canal was filled with fresh dirt to form the 72-foot-wide Broad Street.

1683

Q: What is the oldest burial site in Manhattan?
A: The First Sheareth Israel graveyard at 55 St. James Place. Burials at the site span from 1683 through 1825. New York City legislation outlawed burial within Manhattan in 1851.

Q: How many unclaimed burials are there each year in the 1990s, on average, in New York City's potter's field on Hart Island?
A: 2,650.

1697

Street lighting was introduced in New York City. An ordinance was passed that required "every seventh householder, in the dark time of the moon, cause a lantern and candle to be hung out of his window on a pole, the expense to be divided among the seven families." Aldermen were expected to enforce the lighting code.

1709

English-style taverns with elaborate signs and names like "The White Lion," "The St. George," and "The Black Horse" predominated in the city. A typical tavern featured a fireplace in the center of the room to cook hot lunches and for heating purposes. Most customers, all men, drank porter and ale, but rum, brandy, and Madeira were also favored. Dinners were usually served cold and visitors from other cities could usually find accommodations in a small room on a tavern's second story. Many taverns were used as entertainment centers for lectures, animal shows, bear baitings, cockfights, and rat killings. Sailors seeking employment went to a tavern called Sign of the Pine Apple near the docks at the East River.

Early Manhattan at Greenwich Street below Thames Street. Rush-hour traffic wasn't quite the problem it is today.

1710

The first recorded Germans arrived in New York City—3,000 of them—to manufacture tar for the British Royal Navy. Many remained in New York City, and some ventured to the Catskills, but most headed for Pennsylvania, where they came to be known as "Pennsylvania Dutch."

1746

African immigration reached its historical peak, representing 20.9 percent of the city's residents.

1750

The number of skilled Irish merchants and Irish indentured servants in the colony grew because of trade with various Irish ports. Most of the Irish in the colony were not Catholic, as there was a rigid penal code against Catholics enforced in the city until 1784.

1764

New York City was ranked by the British as second in importance only to Philadelphia. The city was wealthier and more populous than Boston, accommodating 25,000 inhabitants in the area below what is now City Hall, which ranked seventh in terms of population within the 13 colonies.

1775

The northern boundary of Manhattan was a winding creek that connected the Harlem River on the east with the Hudson River on the west. The Dutch called the creek *Spuyten Duyvil,* which means "in spite of the devil," because an early settler named Anthony Van Corlaer had drowned there in an attempt to warn northern settlements that the British were coming. Van Corlaer had been drinking rum, couldn't find a boat to get him across the river, and decided to swim. The creek was eventually rerouted in 1895 "in spite of the devil."

1778

Manhattan contained two substantial ponds, marshlands, numerous streams, and a craggy, swampish coastline. Manhattan's largest body of water was the Collect Pond (which came from the Dutch word *Kalchhook*) on Lime Shell Point, which covered what is now the area between Baxter, Franklin, Worth, and Lafayette Streets. It was abundantly stocked until the mid-eighteenth century, at which point it was almost devoid of fish and quickly filling up with litter. It was finally drained in 1808, and the city's first slum replaced it.

1790

The city's first official census was conducted. It revealed that New York City's population of 33,131 was second only to the population of Philadelphia. Inhabitants were mostly English, Dutch, African, Scottish, Irish, German, French, and Welsh.

1790

There were 2,500 Germans in the city, two German Lutheran churches, a German reform church, a Moravian church, and a German society.

1790

The city's first sidewalks, made of brick and stone, were laid on Broadway between Vesey and Murray Streets and were barely wide enough for two people.

1797

The severe problem of air pollution was addressed by law. Peter T. Curtenius operated an ironworks factory that produced Franklin stoves, kettles, pots, and assorted other items, and the factory drenched the city in black smoke. Soap factories were another source of irksome air pollution, as were glue manufacturers, starch makers, vellum makers, and tallow chandlers. Law deemed that no manufacturer could produce unclean air or foul smells anywhere within the city south of Grand Street, west of Mulberry, or east of the Hudson River. Soap and candle manufacturers protested so stridently that they were exempt from the law as long as they maintained inoffensive operations.

There were many smaller, mom-and-pop-type operations that continued to produce pollution, as the law only applied to the larger manufacturers.

WEATHER OR NOT

- Snowflakes in the city pick up soot, dust, bits of iron, copper, nickel, or lead.
- Weather can be remarkably varied from borough to borough: thunderstorms and fog tend to be most severe around Jamaica Bay and the Lower New York Bay area, which can receive as much as 2 inches more rainfall than midtown Manhattan.
- Brooklyn is the coldest borough during the day because of the sea breezes; Staten Island and the Bronx are colder at night.
- Queens is the warmest borough, sometimes as much as 5 degrees warmer than other boroughs.
- Manhattan is the windiest borough in terms of gusts of wind, but Brooklyn is the most consistently windy. The Bronx and central/northern Queens are tied for snowiest borough.
- The average amount spent on snow removal each winter is $9 million, but the city spent over $50 million during the winter of 1993-94.
- The surface temperature of an average New York City street during a hot summer day is 150 degrees. An egg begins to cook at 145 degrees.
- Dark asphalt streets are the hottest in New York City.
- The average annual temperature in the city is 54.5 degrees.
- The annual average percentage of time the sun shines during daylight hours in Manhattan is 59%.

1801

Elgin Garden, which opened in 1801, was the city's first botanical garden. It spanned 20 acres and was located where Radio City Music Hall and Rockefeller Center now stand. The garden was funded by Dr. David Hosack—the physician who attended to the dying Alexander Hamilton after his duel with Aaron Burr. Medical science emphasized the therapeutic properties of plants at the time, and the garden was intended to be a place of study for medical students as well as a place of contemplative pleasure for the public. By 1824 only a small portion of the garden remained. The Channel Gardens in Rockefeller Center currently occupy the remains of the Elgin Garden.

1811

Before 1811, Sixth Avenue was known as West Road.

1815

Between 1815 and 1915 approximately 33 million people immigrated to the U.S. from all over the world, and three quarters of them entered through the port of New York City. Most were Irish and German Catholics.

1823

The city's first German neighborhood and commercial center took shape in the area extending from Pine Street to Pearl Street southeast of City Hall.

1825

The first gas pipeline (for gas made from coal) was laid in May; it extended up Broadway from the Bowery to Canal Street, and was built by the New York Gas-Light Company.

1829

Canal Street was primarily where the city extended to the north, although clusters of people had settled in Chelsea and Greenwich Village.

1830

New York City's population increased from 240,000 to 391,000 between 1830 and 1840 as a result of rapid industrialization and immigration.

1832

The route of America's first horse-drawn streetcar line ran from Prince Street to Union Square; 250 horse-drawn cars carried passengers along established routes, along with 200 hackney coaches.

TRAFFIC PATTERNS

- There are 12,700 traffic lights in New York City. A traffic signal light bulb, on average, burns for 333 days.
- The average daily traffic volume in New York City is 2.3 million.
- The number of people in New York City who drive to work in a

car pool is 271,503. Approximately 765,151 drive to work alone. At least 10,000 vehicles per day move onto First Avenue, headed for the F.D.R. entrance ramp.

- In 1997, 180,000 people were delayed in cars for an average of 15 minutes due to a parade on 6th Avenue between 44th and 58th Streets that lasted 3 hours. Ten thousand extra pounds of carbon monoxide were produced by the delay. Accruing lost leisure time at $5 an hour, the total cost of congestion for motorists delayed by a parade is $225,000.
- The percentage of roadways in poor condition in New York City that improved between 1985 and 1997 is 19.5%. In New York State the figure is 3.3%.
- The advertising budget for New York's custom license plates is $2 million; New York had the nation's first license plate gift certificate. There are 2.5 million pairs of license plates made annually at the Auburn Correctional Facility—the only place in New York State where license plates are made.
- Approximately 72% of drivers use seat belts in New York, as compared with 64% of the drivers in New Jersey. The figure for the United States is 67%.

1835

The city's most devastating and widespread fire began at 9:00 A.M. on December 16 (in zero-degree weather) inside the Comstock & Adams dry-goods store at the corner of Hanover and Pearl Streets. The fire razed everything south of Wall Street and east of Broadway; no less than 674 mostly wooden buildings on 20 blocks in Manhattan burned, and the financial loss was estimated to be $20 million. Firefighters battled the blaze for 19 hours with engines from Brooklyn and Jersey City. The fire required 1,900 firemen, including 400 from Philadelphia.

The fire led to a demand for the reorganization of the volunteer fire force or its replacement with a paid force, and to the introduction of horse-drawn engines equipped with steam pumps.

1836

The first passenger train, Long Island Railroad, ran on April 18 from New York City to Greenport. Long Island Railroad is the country's third oldest railroad and is the largest commuter railroad in the nation to date.

1839

Since 1830, 200,000 Irish had arrived at the port of New York City.

1840

More than 24,000 Germans lived in New York City. An additional 100,000 arrived over the course of the next 20 years with mass transatlantic migration. A new German neighborhood was established east of the Bowery, just north of Division Street, which stretched to the East River. This area was the major German-American center in the country for the remainder of the 1800s.

1843

The area on the Upper West Side between 59th and 110th Streets was covered with farmland. The region was known as "bloemendael," which was Dutch for "vale of flowers."

1844

Water flowed for the first time from upstate reservoirs to New York City.

1844

The city's first Greek immigrant, Basil Constantin, arrived in New York City in July. Within 10 years there were several Greek merchants in the city importing currants and exporting cotton and wheat.

Q: What was the distinction of the city's first Greek student, Christodoulas M. L. Evangelides, who graduated from Columbia University?
A: He was the subject of a poem by William Cullen Bryant.

1844

The city's worst shantytown at the time existed at the far end of 42nd Street in an area called Dutch Hill. The shantytown was comprised of Irish squatters who worked as traveling quarrymen.

1845

The community of Latin Americans in New York City grew rapidly with expanded trade in Latin America and the Caribbean, although there had been residents from Spain and its possessions in the city in the earliest times. Between 1845 and 1870, however, the number of Latin Americans increased from 508 to 2,062, with the majority of them from Spain, Cuba, and the Spanish-speaking West Indies. The Latin-American population in New York City continued to grow after the Spanish-American War when the U.S. acquired Puerto Rico.

1845

The potato famine in Ireland, which lasted from 1845 to 1847, led to an increase in Irish immigration to the city.

1849

The Croton Reservoir could hold 660 million gallons of water, and the Murray Hill Water Distributing Reservoir was located where the New York Public Library now stands at 42nd Street and Fifth Avenue.

1850

The streets of New York were paved with stones called "Belgian Blocks." Enormous sailing ships that carried fur, rum, tobacco, and other luxurious necessities to Europe frequently returned empty and the square stones were loaded aboard as ballast; most of the stones were dumped into the harbor as landfill, but a small portion was used as paving material.

1851

The Hudson River Railroad tracks were laid on the Upper West Side, which opened the area—previously comprised of farmland and small Dutch cottages—for development.

1852

The number of homeless children roving the streets of the city in 1852 was approximately 10,000.

1853

A sumptuous meal was comprised of clam fritters, colonial carpetbagger steak stuffed with oysters, Indian pudding, and chocolate icebox cake.

1853

The function of the tavern changed from being a multipurpose place for meeting and socializing, eating, watching entertainment, and finding employment to being a "poor man's club" or a place of refuge for the working class. Long, narrow bars replaced tables, and free lunches were served to factory workers; patrons rarely sat down. In the evenings, men played cards, billiards, and shuffleboard in taverns and read newspapers provided by the establishment. Some customers even received mail at their favorite saloons.

1855

New York City attained the highest population in the hemisphere with 622,924 people in residence. An official immigration center was established at Castle Garden, which was located off the southern tip of Manhattan in an unused fortification.

1856

Makeshift campgrounds for the homeless existed in alleyways and courtyards around tenement buildings, as 40,000 men were out of work in New York City.

1857

The world's first passenger elevator was installed in the five-story Haughwout Building at 488-92 Broadway by Elisha Graves Otis. The steam-powered elevator rose 40 feet a minute and cost $300 to build. The elevator worked for 50 years.

Q: Where was the Otis Elevator Company established in 1854?
A: Yonkers, New York.

1858

The first recorded Chinese immigrant, Cantonese Ah Ken, arrived in New York City and opened a cigar store on Park Row. He resided on Mott Street. Eight years later another Cantonese man, Wah Kee, moved to Manhattan from San Francisco to open a vegetable and curio store at 13 Pell Street. By 1880 large numbers of Chinese settlers had flowed into the city.

Q: What percentage of Chinese residents in New York City presently live in Chinatown?
A: 30%.

Q: What percentage of the people who live in Chinatown in 1997 are Chinese?
A: 75%.

1869

New York City's first apartment house was erected at East 18th Street near Irving Place.

1870

A subway, propelled with wind from a large fan, was built in secret under Broadway between Warren and Murray Streets by patent attorney Alfred Ely Beach. The car was especially elegant: it had a 120-foot waiting room adorned with a fountain, settees, paintings, frescoes, a stocked aquarium, and a grand piano. The car seated 22 people, and was propelled at 10 miles per hour. When the car reached its destination, it tripped a wire that reversed the fan, literally "sucking" the car back to the starting point.

Above-ground transportation in 1870 was so heavily congested with carriages, carts, horses, pedestrians, and horse-drawn buses that a trip from Wall Street to 20th Street usually took an hour. William "Boss" Tweed, then running the city from Tammany Hall, had a rival plan for mass transportation—the elevated railway—which is why Beach had to build his subway in secrecy. Beach obtained a permit to construct a small pneumatic tube for shooting mail and packages beneath the streets and began to dig underground at night with a dozen other men. A *New York Herald* reporter, curious about the sagging sidewalk on part of Broadway, investigated the sag and published a story that exposed the operation. The subway was completed a month after the article ran, and the public loved it. For a year, four hundred thousand sightseeing passengers rode the subway for 25 cents. When Beach was ready to build the line to Central Park, Tweed made sure that the governor vetoed bills that would permit him to extend the subway. Beach continued to fight for the subway until he ran completely out of money.

1878

The first Arab-speaking residents of the city arrived from Syria and Lebanon, most of them Christian. By the end of the century the area around Rector and Washington Streets in Lower Manhattan became known as Little Syria.

1880

There were more than 270,000 German residents in New York City. Germans were more religiously diverse than other immigrants to the city.

Q: What were the various religions practiced by the city's German immigrants in the 1880s?
A: Calvinism, Lutheran, Catholicism, Judaism, Protestant, and crusading German Atheists.

1880

There were only 69 Greek residents in the city.

1880

Between 1880 and 1919 more than 23 million people immigrated to the U.S., with 17 million of them entering through New York City. The two largest groups were the Russian Jews and the Italians, and most remained in New York City.

1881

New York City was ranked first as the location with the most German-speaking residents in America.

1883

The Brooklyn Bridge opened. Twelve pedestrians were trampled to death during a panic created when an anonymous person erroneously yelled into the crowd that the bridge was collapsing.

MEN OF STEEL

The unprecedented use of steel for the mighty Brooklyn suspension bridge, which spans the East River, was the inspiration of builder-engineer John Augustus Roebling. He knew it would ensure greater strength and durability.

In June of 1869 Roebling was killed when a ferry knocked him from a piling on the waterfront. His son, Washington Roebling, oversaw the remaining construction of the bridge and solved many of the bridge's structural defects. Washington Roebling was crippled in 1872 while working on the bridge's western caisson but continued to supervise operations through a telescope from a room nearby, with his wife serving as relay messenger to workers and site managers.

Q: What did John Augustus Roebling invent?
A: Wire cable.

1883

The first sliding fire pole, which appeared in New York City at 209 Elizabeth Street, was made of mercifully splinterless brass.

POLESTERS

By 1997 there were 314 fire stations in New York City and sliding down fire poles was still the quickest way to get from the bed to the fire truck in all of them (a lot of firefighters take the stairs too). Most of the city's fire stations are over 100 years old.

1884

The last major earthquake in New York City occurred on August 10. There are no building regulations specifically meant to prevent earthquake damage in the city and at least two fault lines run across Upper Manhattan.

1888

The city's first blackout occurred, toppling overhead power lines and shutting off lights for three hours.

1895

The Harlem River was straightened, rendering the term "Island of Manhattan" incorrect.

1898

Shantytowns existed all around and through Central Park, Harlem, and the West Side through the 40s. The uptown shantytowns were called "the Goats" and were considered places of exile for indiscreet or insubordinate policemen.

1900

Twenty-two percent of the city was Irish by descent or by birth.

1900

The German population reached its peak of 748,882, and Yorkville (on the Upper East Side at 86th Street and Third Avenue) had the largest population of Germans in the city. Astoria in Queens had the second largest.

1900

Half of the more than 7,500 Latin Americans in New York City were emigrants from the Caribbean.

1900

There were 6,321 Chinese residents living in Chinatown in Lower Manhattan.

1901

Sixth Avenue was paved between 1900 and 1910 and overshadowed by an elevated train.

TWO-WHEELED COMMUTERS

• Approximately 3,000 people belong to Transportation Alternatives, a group trying to reduce dependence on cars. The members commute to work on bicycles.
•10,000 people in New York City are bike messengers, foot messengers, and clerical workers in the courier industry. Messengers are paid $2.50 to $3 per delivery.

1902

An estimate from the turn of the century posited that an average of 2.5 million pounds of manure and 60,000 gallons of urine was deposited on city streets each day.

1904

The three-tiered excursion steamer *General Slocum* caught fire shortly after it had departed from an East Third Street pier carrying 1,335 passengers bound for a picnic at Huntington Bay. Most were German children from a Sunday school. Of the 1,335 passengers, 1,051 died and 124 were injured. When the *General Slocum* reached 125th Street, a boy in the city noticed smoke on the bow and told a nearby ticket-taker. The ticket-taker ignored him.

> *We are doomed, I know it, I feel it.*
> MRS. PHILIP STRAUB, AS SHE DEBARKED THE *GENERAL SLOCUM*
> WITH HER THREE CHILDREN

The fire on the ship originated in a paint storage locker and quickly devoured the lower deck. After the disaster the steamboat inspection system was thoroughly revised when it was found the boat's sand buckets were empty, the fire hoses didn't work, and the life jackets were ripped and useless. Two petty thieves were breaking rocks on Riker's Island when they saw the smoking steamboat in the water. They grabbed a nearby rowboat and were able to save 15 lives before guards caught up to them and returned them to their rock pile.

1904

The city's first electric-powered subway line began running in October between City Hall and 145th Street. The fare was five cents.

NEW YORK UNDERGROUND

- There are 469 subway stations in New York City; 109 of them have working public restrooms.
- There are 4,379 subway cars; 2,111 of them have speedometers.
- The average number of transactions at subway stations per week is 1.1 million; the average number of people who ride the subway each year is 1 billion.
- An average of 80 women go into labor on New York City subways each year.
- There were three serious subway grate injuries in New York City in the 10-year period between 1985 and 1995; one person was killed in a grate accident.
- The average number of subway accidents per year in the city is 13, but 160 people were injured in a subway crash in 1991 at Union Square that ranked as the worst subway crash in New York City's history.
- The average number of subway escalator injuries per year is 185. Most escalator accidents occur at the Lexington Avenue & 53rd Street Station each year; the Lexington Avenue and 59th Street Station ranks second.
- Opera music is played over the subway's public address system at the Lincoln Center stop.
- At 95 decibels, the Union Square Station is ranked as the worst in terms of noise.
- Transit Authority officials spent $1.47 billion between 1982 and 1997 trying to reduce noise in the subway system. Average inside noise levels in the TA's older subway cars is in the high-80 decibels. The noise level of newer subway cars is 80 decibels. The noise level of express trains as they pass through local stops is 100 decibels; the noise level 1,000 feet away from a jumbo jet during takeoff is 100 decibels.
- An average of 340,000 people walk to work each day in New York City.

1907

An agreement was negotiated between the U.S. Department of State and Japan to end direct migration between the U.S. and Japan.

1908

Subway service was extended to Brooklyn.

1910

There were 545,000 Italian residents in New York City. By the time World War I started, Italian immigrants had sent about $750 million back to Italy.

1910

About 41 percent of New York City's population was immigrants.

1911

The Triangle Shirtwaist factory fire on March 21 killed 146 immigrant women, mostly Italian and Jewish, in less than 15 minutes and is considered one of the worst fires in New York City's history. The factory operated from the top three floors of the Asch Building at the northwest corner of Washington and Greene Streets. When the fire broke out on the eighth floor around 4:30 P.M., workers on the ninth floor couldn't escape because the exit doors were locked. The back fire escape collapsed, firefighters were hindered by the bodies of those who had jumped, fire truck ladders only extended up to the sixth floor, and life nets broke when three or four people jumped at once. The owners of the company were charged with manslaughter, later acquitted, and ordered by a judge to each pay $75 to the families of 23 victims who had sued.

Later in the year the city established the Bureau of Fire Investigation, which granted the fire department power to further improve factory safety conditions. The tragedy cemented burgeoning grassroots support for the organization of workers in the garment district, particularly for the International Ladies Garment Workers Union.

1919

There was no farmland left in Manhattan.

1920

A typical Manhattan speakeasy in the 1920s was located in a midtown brownstone with a basement entrance. Approximately 30,000 speakeasies operated in New York City during Prohibition.

> *The Big Apple. The dream of every lad that ever threw a leg over a thoroughbred. There's only one Big Apple. That's New York.*
> JOHN FITZGERALD, IN HIS DEBUT NEWSPAPER COLUMN FOR THE *NEW YORK MORNING TELEGRAPH* ON FEBRUARY 18, 1924.

Q: What did tramps and hoboes call New York City in the 1920s and 1930s?

A: The Big Onion.

THE ORIGIN OF "THE BIG APPLE"

New York City's nickname, "The Big Apple," was thought by many to be a jazz term from the 1930s but it actually originated as a horse-racing term in the 1920s. A New York City-based racing writer named John FitzGerald heard the term from stable-hands in New Orleans and took it back to the city. Mayor Patten Adams of Columbia, South Carolina, remains convinced that New York City stole the term from a Columbia-based nightclub called Fat Sam's that featured a dance craze called "The Big Apple." In 1997 the City Council voted to rename the intersection of West 54th Street and Broadway "Big Apple Corner" in honor of John FitzGerald.

1920

Almost 40 percent of the city's population was foreign born. Russian Jews comprised the largest foreign-born group, numbered at 480,000. Italians were the second largest foreign-born group with 391,000 city residents.

1921

Roosevelt Island was originally called Blackwell's Island for the family that owned it. In 1921 the name was changed from Blackwell's Island to Welfare Island because of the city hospitals and the psychiatric institution located there. Welfare Island was changed to Roosevelt Island in 1973; it didn't seem right to developers to construct high-rent apartments on a place called Welfare Island.

1924

Laws restricting immigration were enacted in response to a depression after World War I, the "red scare," and the fear of an impending new wave of immigration. A limit of 150,000 was imposed for all countries outside of the Western Hemisphere, which discriminated against Italians and other southern and eastern European immigrants. The law also ensured continued exclusion of Asians.

1929

The Great Depression hit. The largest shantytowns during the Depression were located in Central Park and at 72nd Street near the Hudson River.

1930

The population decrease on the Lower East Side was 50 percent.

1930

A quarter of the immigrants to New York City in the 1930s were Jews escaping Nazism.

1930

Italian residents accounted for 17 percent of the city's population, which was the highest concentration of Italians in the country.

1932

There were 17 shantytowns in Central Park, the largest occupied by 450 men.

1935

There were 21,000 homeless living in city shelters.

1935

In December, 122 tenement apartments opened on the Lower East Side and 3,800 people applied for them. Eighty-one of the apartments didn't have toilets and 20 didn't have windows in all of the rooms.

1938

Passenger regulations like "No Smoking. No Spitting. No Littering" were first posted in the subways. "No Radio Playing" was added around 1975, but the introduction of the Sony Walkman in 1979 rendered the addition unnecessary.

THE NEW YORK BUS SYSTEM

- There are 3,500 to 3,700 buses, 3,000 bus shelters, and 19 bus depots where buses are stored and maintained in New York City.
- 15% of aspiring bus drivers fail their training period.
- 80% of city buses are equipped with wheelchair lifts.
- The Transit Authority pays delis $50 to allow drivers to use their washroom facilities en route.
- A city bus travels 3,000 miles before requiring a maintenance inspection.

1943

Puerto Ricans were the largest Latin-American group in the city, accounting for 46 percent of the total Spanish-speaking population. By 1960 they would comprise 81 percent.

1945

A B-25 plane smashed into the seventy-ninth floor of the Empire State Building on July 28, killing 14 and causing only minor structural damage to the building.

1950

There were 450,000 first- and second-generation Irish in NYC.

1961

Due to political turmoil and economic difficulties in the Middle East, Arabs and Israelis began moving to the city.

1965

Manhattan, the Bronx, and part of Brooklyn experienced a blackout at the height of rush hour on November 9. Approximately 800,000 people were trapped in subways, and power wasn't restored for more than 13 hours; there was remarkably little civil disorder.

1965

Q: The Hart-Celler Act of 1965 dramatically affected immigration to New York City. What did it deem illegal?
A: Immigration discrimination based on national origin. Equal quotas of 20,000 were set for each country in the Eastern Hemisphere, and for the first time there were limitations set on emigration from the Western Hemisphere.

1970

Whites in New York City comprised 63 percent of the total population, compared to 52 percent in 1980 and 35 percent by 1997. Immigrants accounted for 18 percent of the city's population.

1973

Weeping willows were planted in tenement gardens built atop vacant lots in the East Village, and they thrived in spite of the tree's notorious thirst for water. Since the Lower East Side was originally built on a landfill over streams and wetlands, the trees may have tapped into long-buried water sources.

1975

A DC-10 airplane crashed and burned at Kennedy Airport after colliding with gulls following takeoff. There were nearly 4,000 recorded incidents of birds damaging aircraft at Kennedy International Airport between 1975 and 1995. Federal officials deal with the problem by shooting the birds, and as many as 10,000 have been shot in a year. Recent experiments proved that hawks and falcons can scare off gulls nesting near runways—dropping the total number of birds shot each year to 2,000. There was a 75 percent decrease in birds striking airplanes after the use of falconry as a weapon in 1995. The only colony of laughing gulls known to nest in New York State is located at Kennedy Airport.

Q: How many wildlife biologists are presently on staff at New York City's Port Authority?
A: 1.

Q: How many annual New York City Airport arrivals are there?
A: Approximately 35.8 million.

1980

The Chinese population in New York City was the largest in the country, surpassing that of San Francisco.

1980

The 1,005,304 people of Italian descent in New York City were the largest national group, accounting for one-seventh of the city's population and one-twelfth of the country's Italian population.

1981

By the time the Soviet Union ceased granting exit visas, approximately 100,000 Soviet Jews had settled in New York City.

1982

New York State designated Battery Park as part of Harbor Park, a group of historic waterfront sites.

1983

Home delivery of seltzer was reintroduced by companies like the Bronx-based Havana Dry and Gimme Seltzer of Long Island City. The Canada Dry Bottling Company, based in Queens, distributed seltzer under four different brand names: Kirsch, Good Old Times Seltzer, Cott, and Hoffman's. New York City had the largest seltzer market in the country, with more than fifteen million cases consumed annually.

1985

Q: Where were the three Chinatowns located in NYC?
A: Canal Street in Lower Manhattan, Flushing, and Bay Ridge.

Chinatown south of Canal Street near Mott Street. To enter Chinatown is to step into a different world.

1986

The last two of fourteen water treatment plants opened on the Hudson River at 137th Street in Manhattan and in Brooklyn's Red Hook section. The system was able to handle the 1,600 million gallons of daily sewage carried through 6,200 miles of pipe.

1987

There were 25,000 homeless in New York City.

1989

The Salvation Army had 1,820 soldiers, 156 officers, and thirty-five halls in the New York metropolitan area.

1989

The first subway station on Roosevelt Island opened. Before that time, access to Manhattan from Roosevelt Island was limited to the tram.

1990

There were 71,301 marriages in New York City, 10,000 more than a decade earlier. The year with the most marriages was 1941 with 76,086.

1990

Between 1990 and 1994, 23,700 immigrants from the Dominican Republic settled in the Washington Heights section of Manhattan, 19,100 immigrants from China, Taiwan, and Hong Kong settled in Chinatown, and 10,200 immigrants from the former Soviet Union settled into Brooklyn's Gravesend-Homecrest section.

1990

The last census was taken in the city before the turn of the century. There were 18,087,000 residents and over 90 languages spoken in the metro area.

1990 CENSUS: IMMIGRATION STATS

- There were 1,783,511 people in New York City's Latin American community.
- New immigrants in the 1980s and 1990s were mostly from Ecuador, Colombia, El Salvador, and the Dominican Republic.
- The city's non-Hispanic black community accounted for about 25.2% of the population.
- The Indian population had increased from 5,032 in 1970 to 42,367 in 1990.
- There were 61,184 Polish residents in the city, compared with 238,339 in 1930.
- There were 79,701 residents from the Soviet Union, compared with 442,431 in 1930.

1991

Mandatory recycling laws took effect for each household in New York City.

Q: How many pounds of residential and institutional garbage are currently collected each day in New York City?
A: 26,400,000.

1993

Thirty-three percent of the city's residents were foreign-born; their children counted as an additional 20 percent of the population—making foreign residents a 53-percent majority of the city's population.

1994

Fifty-two percent of the first-class mail was delivered on time in Manhattan. By 1997 the figure had improved to 76 percent.

Q: What is the current national average?
A: 85%.

1994

Sixty judgments were entered in divorce court on Valentine's Day. The reason most cited for a desired divorce was remarriage plans.

1995

Fifty tenants were found living in one Chinatown basement on Market Street by New York City firefighters, and 40 tenants were found by firefighters in a basement on Canal Street.

Q: How much did each of the 50 tenants on Market Street have to pay for rent each month?
A: $60.

1996

In January the blizzard of '96 brings New York City to a grinding halt.

1996

Felix I was first introduced. Felix I is a high-tech sidewalk sweeper used in Times Square. It weighs 800 pounds, runs on a diesel engine, costs $20,000 ($25,000 for a model that can be ridden), and is made in Scotland. The machine is named after the persnickety, neat character Felix in *The Odd Couple,* and it sucks dirt from curbs. It also throws hot water for deicing and disinfecting and degreases the Restaurant Row sidewalk area. The model is cheaper and more effective than a plow and can cut a nine-foot-wide path through 4.5 miles of sidewalk in three hours.

THE ODD COUPLE

The Vatican shares a problem with Times Square, one that Felix I has tackled successfully in both locales: too much urine on the sidewalk. Felix also pulverizes bottles and trash.

Q: Whose voice is on the Felix I machine, saying, "Move it!"?
A: Tony Randall's.

1997

Gum is removed from New York City sidewalks with a 2,000-pounds-per-square-inch steam hose.

Q: How deep are New York City's sidewalks?
A: 4 inches.

Q: Which is the most heavily traveled two blocks of sidewalk in Manhattan?
A: Broadway between Zabar's at 80th Street and Barnes & Noble at 82nd Street.

1997

About a dozen fire stations in New York City still have Dalmatians. The average number of serious fires in New York City per year is 3,700.

Q: What percentage of firefighters in New York City are female?
A: 3%.

Q: What percentage of the firefighters in New York City are white males?
A: 93.4%.

THE PEOPLE OF NEW YORK CITY

Average size of New York City households citywide ....2.5 people
Percentage of New York City residents with college degrees 42%
Percentage of Manhattanites born outside of New York State 56%
Percentage of Manhattanites who did not graduate from high school 24.7%
Percentage of Manhattanites over 75 years of age 6.1%
Percentage of Manhattanites with limited mobility 3%
Rank of Manhattan in most densely populated counties in the U.S. 1
Percentage of New York City residents who move there from the city's surrounding regions 16.7%
Percentage of Manhattan births per year to unmarried women 48.4%
Number of deaths per year of New York City residents 70,000
Percentage of New York City immigrants under the age of 27 in the 1990s 50%
Median age for New York City residents 36

Increase in immigration to New York City from the
former Soviet Union between 1987 and 1997 . . . . .900%
Percentage of New York State welfare recipients who
live in New York City 75%

1997

Approximately 4,160 Japanese people come to New York City
annually on student visas.

Q: What part of Manhattan has the most Japanese residents
under the age of 30?
A: The East Village.

1997

New York City is ranked second nationally of the cities with the
highest percentage of bilingual Hispanic adults.

Q: What city is ranked first?
A: San Antonio, Texas.

1997

Fifty-two percent of Hispanics in New York City are bilingual,
and 62 percent of Hispanics in San Antonio are bilingual.

1997

The Transit Authority attempted to instill a sense of subway eti-
quette in New York riders by having announcers or placards
politely request that passengers wait before boarding a train, step
aside once in the train, and refrain from elbowing other passengers. The program was adapted from Hong Kong's subway
behavior modification program. The official name of the program in New York City is: "Step Aside, Speed Your Ride."

*The classic terrible is 72nd Street on the 1,2,3. There are
parts of the morning rush hour there that are like the burning
of Atlanta in* Gone With The Wind.
GENE RUSSIANOFF, STAFF ATTORNEY FOR THE ADVOCACY GROUP
STRAPHANGERS CAMPAIGN, TO THE *NEW YORK TIMES*

THOSE YELLOW CABS

- In 1997, 1.1% of licensed taxi drivers were female; in 1966 about 10% of the city's cab drivers were women.
- There are 12,053 licensed cabs in the city.
- 200 million million people are transported by cab in New York City each year.
- The average age of a New York City cab is 4 years.
- The average number of fares a driver picks up each day is 30.
- The average number of miles a driver travels is 141.
- The average number of hours per day they drive is 12, compared to 8 hours in 1978.
- The average amount in fares and tips that a driver grosses per day is $190.
- As of 1992, 80 course/study hours are required for prospective cabbies who know little English. 40 hours are required for those comfortable with English but unfamiliar with New York City.
- The name for the round yellow lights to the left of the license plate on the bumper of a cab is "Trouble lights." All New York City cabs were required to have them as of November 1994 in order to alert police and pedestrians to the fact that the driver needs help.
- The Taxi and Limousine Commission was established in 1971.
- New York City cabs lost their individual company names in 1987.
- New York State began requiring a driving test for prospective cab drivers with licenses from other countries in 1989.
- The number of new licenses granted each year varies from around 400 to thousands.
- Less than 50% of new cab drivers remain on the job for 5 years.
- A 1968 New York City code states that the exterior of all cabs "shall be painted yellow, or any shade thereof." The previous code had allowed cab companies to choose their own color, but the variety of colors made it difficult for people to distinguish licensed cabs from gypsy cabs. Any shade of yellow, from a pale lemon hue to a deep golden yellow, can be used on a cab.
- The Taxi and Limousine Commission is experimenting with different car models for use as cabs. The Chevrolet Caprice and Ford Crown Victoria are the most commonly used cars in 1997. The Ford Explorer, Honda Odyssey, and Isuzu Oasis are under consideration for use as city cabs.
- The average number of annual violations issued to cab drivers for excessive noise is 273.
- The fine for a taxi driver who refuses to make multiple stops when requested to do so is $200 to $500.

Q: What percentage of taxi license applicants in 1996 failed the English proficiency test?
A: 36%.

Q: What percentage of new cab driver applicants are immigrants?
A: Over 90%.

Q: What percentage of new cab drivers are from Pakistan or India?
A: 50%.

Q: What percentage are American-born?
A: 10.5%.

Traffic signals in New York are just rough guidelines.
DAVID LETTERMAN

New York is the only city in the world where you can get deliberately run down on the sidewalk by a pedestrian.
RUSSELL BAKER

A car is useless in New York, essential everywhere else. The same with good manners.
MIGNON MCLAUGHLIN

1998

On January 2, a water-main break on Fifth Avenue between 19th and 20th Streets created chaos and held up traffic for over a week in the Flatiron district. A cavernous, 30-foot crater more than 10 feet deep was created by the water-main break, and a car parked near the break was partially "swallowed" into the hole while a gas fire raged nearby. There were at least 11 other water-main breaks in the city between 1994 and early 1998.

A day isn't complete without a hotdog or soft pretzel from one of hundreds of concession stands around the city.

CHAPTER 2

The Business of New York City

I like thinking big. I always have. To me it's very simple: if you're going to be thinking anyway, you might as well think big. Most people think small, because most people are afraid of success, afraid of making decisions, afraid of winning. And that gives people like me a great advantage.

DONALD TRUMP

Since New Amsterdam was a port town, New York City began as an auspicious place for trade and commerce; since it was so remarkably populous, it was also an ideal place for merchants to ply a trade. The early colonists sold bread, beef, pork, wood, flour, soap, milk, skins, and household staples, and bartered for wampum with the Indians. Ships laden with goods from foreign ports found interested buyers in New York City, and colonists were bound together not by language or religion or custom, but by the mutual desire to accumulate wealth or, at the very least, to enjoy a comfortable existence.

Merchant associations were formed in the mid-eighteenth century. The city's first bank, the Bank of New York, opened at Wall and William Streets on June 9, 1784, with $500,000 in capital. The bank granted the federal government its first loan in 1789, which was an advance of $200,000. The city has remained an important financial and banking center ever since.

With the exception of agricultural pursuits, New York has been the chosen site for almost every conceivable business venture on earth. New York has evolved from a manufacturing center into a more service-oriented city, catering to a growing demand for information and comfort; it's this spirit of flexibility and appropriate change that contributes to New York's reputation as one of the world's foremost business cities.

It's difficult to imagine a type of business venture that hasn't flourished in New York City throughout its history: real estate firms, hospitals, law firms, universities, business franchises, candy factories, shoemaking, the fashion industry, publishing, filmmaking, commercials, advertising, television stations, theaters, importing and exporting, dance troupes, restaurants, gyms, transportation companies, Wall Street brokers, temples, synagogues, churches, and new media firms have all achieved resounding success in New York City; not to mention thousands of psychoanalysts and psychiatrists, and society's more illicit undertakings.

1625

The city's first office building was built of stone with a reed-thatched roof on Whitehall Street between Bridge and Pearl Streets. It was used and owned by the Dutch West India Company.

1625

Cattle and a few milk cows were introduced to New Amsterdam in 1625. Dairy products were sought after but scarce in Manhattan for many decades to come, especially cheese, which was used to barter.

1626

The city's first mill was built at 20-22 South William Street and it doubled as a religious meeting place on Sundays. The mill was built by Francois Molemacher (which means "millmaker"). It featured one horse that turned in a circle to power the machinery. The machinery ground pine bark for tanning.

1630

Indians sold Staten Island to the Dutch. Trade flourished between the Indians and the Dutch, with Indians offering pelts, wampum (cylindrical blue and white shell beads), and food for European textiles, glass beads, and tools made of brass, copper, and iron. Although illegal, many colonists still sold guns, ammunition, and alcohol to the Indians.

1631

New Amsterdam's first ship construction was undertaken by two Belgian shipbuilders who managed to convince Director General Peter Minuit that the ship would exemplify New Netherland's fine timber and New Amsterdam's superb craftsmanship. Minuit financed the venture with money from the Dutch West India Company. The ship, one of the biggest in the world at the time, entailed an enormous overrun. Called *New Netherland,* it displaced 800 tons and toted 30 large guns to ward off pirates. The directors of the Dutch West India Company were irate over the eventual size of the construction bills and the sheer expense of running the ship, and part of the reason for Minuit's ensuing dismissal as director general was his financing the ship.

For the next three centuries, the construction of boats and ships would be a major New York City industry.

A MAIDEN VOYAGE

Most ships were built at the foot of Maiden Lane and then launched into the stream where maidens washed the family laundry.

1641

Although one of every four business establishments sold liquor and beer, the city's first official tavern was opened at the corner of Whitehall and Stone Streets by Philip Geraerdy and was called "At the Sign of the Wooden Horse."

Q: Why was it called "At the Sign of the Wooden Horse"?

A: While serving as a militiaman, Geraerdy had been convicted of absence from guard duty and sentenced to ride a wooden horse on parade while carrying a pitcher of beer in one hand and a sword in another. The horse had a very sharp spine—which is how the act of riding it served as punishment.

1647

The first apple orchard was planted by Governor Peter Stuyvesant on his Bowery farm. His apples and grafts from the trees were shipped up the Hudson River to apple growers upstate and New York eventually became noted for its delicious apples. Residents upstate were called "appleknockers" because boys or men usually picked apples for girls or women to gather into baskets below the trees.

1648

Scottish merchants and traders from other countries would price-cut local property-owning merchants by visiting in ships from time to time and disposing of goods at any price simply to unload them. Legal protection was granted to local merchants on September 18, barring visitors from conducting business on shore unless they had resided in New Netherland for three consecutive years and had built "in this city New Amsterdam a decent dwelling, each according to his circumstances and means."

1650

The first candy makers in the city were Dutch bakers-turned-confectioners who sold sugarplums, sugar wafers, and macaroons to the wealthy.

1655

Sales tax was first imposed in the city on August 6 and applied only to the slave trade. The tax was 10 percent on the price of purchase for each slave carried beyond the jurisdiction of New Netherland, and the law was signed by Director General P. Stuyvesant.

1656

Food was sold by vendors in open markets instead of in stores, and the first documented food market opened on Pearl Street.

1656

The first price-fixing law was established on October 26 by Governor Peter Stuyvesant and his council. The law pertained to the price of bread and ordained that all bread bakers would bake at least twice a week both white and coarse bread for "Christians or Barbarians (Indians)" at a standard weight and price. A previous law had forbidden the sale of white bread since only the Indians had enough wampum to purchase it. Bread prices were fixed at eight stivers for a double two-pound white loaf, and 14 stivers for a double eight-pound coarse loaf. The single loaves were half the stivers. A stiver was worth about two cents.

1664

The highest point in town was a two-story windmill used to grind grain into flour and used for a meeting place.

1670

The forerunner of all of New York's impressive commodity and stock exchanges began in 1670 when a merchants' exchange was organized by Colonel Sir Francis Lovelace, a British governor who had taken command two years earlier. Dutch and English craftsmen, traders, importers, and merchants agreed to meet on a bridge over a canal at Bridge Street (then Brugh Street) on Fridays between 11 A.M. and noon.

1686

In the city's early days currency from any country was welcome. Dutch coins continued to circulate long after New Amsterdam became New York in 1664.

1695

A man named Smith began a ferry service from the foot of Maiden Lane to the farming communities of Long Island. Farmers began selling produce on the site, which was dubbed "Smith's Valley."

1699

The fur trade diminished in volume, underscoring the need for a new economic staple.

1701

Wampum ceased to be used a medium of currency in the colony.

1708

There was a 150-percent increase between 1708 and 1715 in the number of locally owned ships. The flow of capital into shipping benefited the city's local artisans, shopkeepers, taverns, and innkeepers.

1709

The provincial government issued paper currency for the first time, which increased the amount of money in circulation and bolstered commercial life in the city.

1714

The number of ships clearing the ports of New York City averaged 64 vessels and 4,330 tons annually, surpassing the number for any previous year.

1720

Within the business community, New York's richer residents were of English stock (as opposed to those of Dutch descent) since extensive contacts in Britain were necessary for establishing trade and obtaining credit.

1721

An average of 215 ships cleared the ports of New York City annually carrying 7,464 tons.

1722

New York developed extensive trade with the British West Indies and captured a sizable share of the Chesapeake tobacco trade away from Boston and British carriers.

1730

Promissory notes were in common use and legally established, although the practice of "writing obligatory" notes had not yet been supplanted. Commercial transactions moved away from a barter economy and toward a credit-based economy.

1737

New York's imports increased 46.3 percent from the last year.

1742

Iron plantations first appeared in the providence of New York: the Ancram Works on Livingston Manor and Stirling Ironworks in Orange County.

1754

Politicians and businessmen often met to seal deals at the Merchants' Coffee House on Broad Street and at the Black Horse Tavern on Exchange Place and William Street. Drovers and butchers ironed out cattle prices at the Bulls Head Tavern on the Bowery north of Canal Street.

1763

With the end of Seven Years' War ended came the end of NYC's prosperity. Merchants' turnovers were halved. Merchants were further outraged by the Sugar Act the following year, which ensured British control over the American sugar market.

1765

Rural communities in New York flourished, but the economic situation in New York City remained depressed until 1775 due to nonimportation, curtailed smuggling, and a short supply of currency. Additionally, a large concentration of British soldiers resulted in increased unemployment.

1768

Horse carriages could be hired for a 14-mile circuit of Manhattan. Other excursions included a transit of the fields directly to the north of the city or a trip to Flatbush and Jamaica or Kingbridge in Upper Manhattan.

1770

Residents could send their laundry out to washerwomen; barbering was usually contracted out as well. In polite society "visiting cards" similar to modern-day business cards were used regularly, and the reciprocation of a social visit was mandatory.

1773

The Joseph Rose House was erected at 273 Water Street. Rose was a mariner who became a distiller in 1785 and used the house for his operations. His son then ran an apothecary at the address from 1796 to 1807. In 1860 the building became a saloon for clients that a missionary publication in 1868 called "the most depraved and infamous" in Manhattan.

1774

Builders in colonial New York City worked for "masters" and were lumped under the heading of "mechanics." They led resistance efforts against the British and were sometimes associated with the Sons of Liberty. They formed the General Committee of Mechanics in 1774, which led to unions and trade societies.

1775

The Bowne & Company printer and stationer opened at 39 Queen Street, now the corner of Pearl and Fulton Streets. It is the oldest New York firm still doing business under its original name, and its operations are now nationwide.

1776

Some New Yorkers reaped enormous wealth from transatlantic trade and wartime supply contracts during the American Revolution. The confiscated estate of Loyalist Oliver de Lancey (1718-85) was estimated to be worth 115,000 English pounds after the revolution.

1777

Artisans and independent craftsmen created products to compete with merchants' imports, and to protect their trade they united and began instigating riots.

1779

Ice cream was called "everyman's dessert" and colonists loved it. A man named Joseph Coree made fresh ice cream in his dairy shop at 17 Hanover Square and delivered it to local residents.

1781

Effingham Lawrence formed the first pharmaceutical firm in the city, which survived into the twentieth century as Schieffelin and Company. By 1786 there were five druggists listed in the city directory. Medicine was produced in small labs connected to drugstores and some firms eventually specialized in producing just one particular medicine in bulk. Pharmacies derived their medicines from plants, and herbal remedies included: ipecac, jalap, sarsaparilla, and balsam.

PHARMACEUTICALS-R-US

When quinine was discovered to treat malaria in 1820, John Currie set up a factory to manufacture quinine sulfate.

Q: What type of bark is quinine derived from?
A: Cinchona bark.

In the mid-1850s New York was the national center for the pharmaceutical industry. Foreign drug companies were attracted to the city by its port; the German firm Merck established an agency in the city in 1890. Some of the firms in the city after World War I were Pfizer, Squibb, Warner-Lambert, and Bristol-Meyers, but manufacturing, research, and development eventually moved outside of the city.

The estimated 1997 market for drugstores in New York City is $2.7 billion. Fifty percent of the drugstores in New York City are not part of a large drugstore chain, compared with 33% of the independent drugstore market in most other parts of the United States.

Q: Which pharmacy in New York City has the largest inventory of single-remedy medicines?
A: Bigelow's Chemists. There are 700 different remedies there.

Q: What is Bigelow's other distinction?
A: It is the oldest drugstore still operating in the city; it opened in 1838.

1785

The first mechanized tattoo shop was opened at 11 Chatham Square by Samuel F. O'Reilly. He invented the electric tattoo machine after noting that Thomas Edison's electric engraving pen could be modified to place ink into skin quickly and efficiently. The bawdiness of the Bowery area near Chatham Square was the perfect atmosphere for a tattoo parlor to thrive in.

1790

Samuel Hopkins of Philadelphia was granted the first patent in the nation in New York City on July 31. The patent was issued for a process for making and purifying potash, which was used in soapmaking, and it bore the signatures of President Washington, Secretary of State Thomas Jefferson, and Attorney General Edmund Randolph.

1796

The Tontine Coffee House at the corner of Wall and Water Streets became the headquarters of the New York Insurance Company, precursor of the New York Stock Exchange. The company's board of directors had 21 members who assigned values to ships, slaves, houses, and belongings. They formed a "tontine" or financial arrangement in which each member received a share of profit that increased as the number of participants was reduced by death. The tontine's first president was Archibald Gracie, whose home on the East River later became the official residence of the mayor—which is why the mayor's home in New York City is (still) called Gracie Mansion.

1799

Q: Who was head of the Manhattan Company—the company with exclusive rights to supply water to New York City?
A: Aaron Burr. The Manhattan Company founded Chase Manhattan Bank with its surplus water funds.

1805

New York City was the largest concentrated urban market in the country. The city was a major seaport and financial center, and had the largest population as well.

1817

The New York Stock Exchange, which currently accounts for about 85 percent of all transactions in the securities listed on it, was organized on March 8 when a group of 28 brokers adopted a constitution and created formal membership rules. The original name was the New York Stock and Exchange Board—the present name dates to 1863. At first, the Big Board's business consisted mainly of insurance and bank stock. Railroad securities began to dominate in the 1830s and 1840s and continued to dominate until the end of the century. Only a few dozen brokers attended the early exchange.

1818

New York's oldest law firm for 176 years was Lord, Day, & Lord, Barrett Smith. Daniel Lord opened his law practice in 1818; the practice closed on September 30, 1994, along with three other midsize New York City law firms.

1822

The Fulton Fish Market opened at the South Street Seaport.

As now, local eateries did a brisk business in Manhattan; beef and seafood were common fare.

1822

The Blue Boar Tavern on William Street was known as a national employment center for carpet weavers.

1825

A 40-acre farm near 72nd Street and Fifth Avenue cost about $40,000. By 1875 the same farm was assessed at $9 million. Land prices multiplied with stunning speed throughout the 1800s.

1828

Specialty shops opened to sell produce, baked goods, meat, dairy products, fish, spirits, coffee, and tea. These were the forerunners of the city's chain grocery stores.

1828

The first roasted chestnut vendor appeared on Duane Street in Tribeca.

Q: What was the ethnic origin of the first chestnut vendor?
A: French

1830

The Manhattan Gas-Light Company was incorporated to supply the remainder of Manhattan with gas. The first private residence to use gas was the home of Samuel Treadwell at 29 East 4th Street, which is now known as the Old Merchant's House landmark. The New York Gas-Light Company and the Manhattan Gas-Light Company merged into what is now Consolidated Edison.

1831

John Stephenson introduced a horse-drawn carriage called an omnibus, and a year later introduced horse-drawn streetcars that ran on tracks. He was among one of the many manufacturers of private carriages and manufactured carriage components. The city's most internationally lauded manufacturer of elegant private carriages for the wealthy at the time was Brewster and Company.

A HORSE OF ANOTHER CARRIAGE

New York City was the leading manufacturer of horse-drawn vehicles in America from 1820 until the 1870s, when many companies moved west for inexpensive land and more affordable raw materials.

1836

The price of a house on the 200 block of Broadway was $25,000.

1844

"Hokey-Pokey men" first sold homemade, hand-dipped ice cream from small wagons pulled by goats.

1845

George Relyea and two partners opened the first detective agency in America at 48 Centre Street on October 16. The firm offered to apprehend criminals in other cities; since New York City was the only major city with a police force, criminals who fled the city limits were usually not pursued. Detective agencies were initially met with public distrust, as some detectives actually worked with thieves. Wealthy families would often hire detectives to research their children's suitors; marital investigations were popular too.

1845

Ye Waverly Inn at 16 Bank Street in Greenwich Village began operating as a tavern; it then became a bordello, a carriage house for the wealthy, a teahouse visited by Robert Frost and Edna St. Vincent Millay in 1920, and currently operates as a restaurant.

YE WAVERLY INN

The owners, customers, and staff at Ye Waverly Inn have believed for decades that the inn is haunted because of mysterious occurrences and the strong feeling of a "presence" in Room 16. The fireplace at the inn often rekindles itself; irons and other fireplace tools have moved in and out of the fireplace. Lights have been turned on and off without explanation, computer keys have switched, doors have opened and closed, a glimpse of a man in a top hat and waistcoat was seen in a mirror, and the sound of something heavy being dragged up the back stairs has been heard. Ghost tales have circulated there for decades, and dozens of people have seen the specter in turn-of-the-century habiliment.

The White Horse Tavern, located a few blocks away, is also said to be haunted and is reported to have been the place where poet Dylan Thomas died.

Q: How much did it cost to buy a glass of beer and a bowl of soup?
A: 5 cents.

1850

New York City was the center of the needle trades and garment industry, and merchants from across the country and abroad traveled to the city to purchase dry goods for distribution. Women went to the city specifically to shop for both imported and domestic consumer goods.

1852

There were 25 milk companies in New York City, employing 1,200 people and using 800 horses.

1855

Eighty-six percent of the city's laborers and 74 percent of its domestic servants were Irish. More than 11,000 Irish people were artisans in the clothing industry, and there was a growing Irish middle class in the city by 1855, many of them small business owners.

1857

The city's first Greek restaurant opened. It was called The Peleponnesos.

1857

Joseph C. Gayetty of 154 West 33rd Street manufactured the first roll of toilet paper in the world. Cream-colored and made of hemp, the paper was advertised as "Gayetty's Medicated Paper—a perfectly pure article for the toilet and for the prevention of piles."

Q: How much did 500 sheets cost?
A: 50 cents.

1857

The city offered what could be the best real estate bargain in history: it sold the site of St. Patrick's Cathedral to the church for $1.

1858

One-third of America's exports and two-thirds of its imports were handled in New York City.

1865

A branch of the national Pinkerton Detective Agency was formed in the city. The company refused to accept rewards, which was reassuring to a wary public, and it soon became the leading detective agency in the nation. Detectives were used to catch streetcar conductors who kept the nickel fares, to infiltrate unions and dissuade workers from striking, and to report gamblers and alcoholics to employers. Pinkerton detectives even led raids and apprehended gang leaders before the development of federal and state law enforcement agencies in the early 20th century.

1866

The large influx of German immigrants led to the establishment of many breweries in New York City. George Ehret, a German immigrant, opened the Hell Gate Brewery in 1866 that by 1879 was the largest brewery in the United States.

1868

Membership on the New York Stock Exchange became a salable property right, with seats selling for $4,000. By the late 1980s seats sold for $1.1 million.

1869

Candy manufacturing became a salient industry in New York City where the sugar industry was concentrated and where a demand for the product was increasing. Immigrant Henry Heide formed a business under his own name and produced Jujyfruits, Jujubes, and Red Hot Dollars along with a variety of chocolates and hard candies. Milton Hershey had a candy firm in New York City before moving his operations to Pennsylvania.

1869

Dr. Brown's Soda was founded in New York City.

Q: How many Dr. Brown flavors are there?
A: 6: celery, black cherry, cream soda, root beer, orange, and ginger ale.

DOCTOR BROWN'S QUIZ

Match the correct Dr. Brown flavor with the New York City illustration on its can:

1. Orange	A. Statue of Liberty
2. Root Beer	B. Brooklyn Bridge
3. Cel-Ray	C. The Astor Hotel
4. Ginger Ale	D. The Central Park carousel
5. Black Cherry	E. Grand Central terminal
6. Cream Soda	F. An ice cream parlor

Answers: 1. E; 2. F; 3. B; 4. C; 5. D; 6. A

1870

Frederick August Otto Schwarz moved to New York City to open the Schwarz Toy Bazaar at 765 Broadway. He and his three brothers prospered in the toy business by importing toys from Europe, and in 1880 he moved his store across from Union Square. He settled his store, then called F .A. O. Schwarz, uptown at 745 Fifth Avenue in 1931. In 1986 the store moved across the street to 767 Fifth Avenue, and in 1988 a children's bank was opened at the store by the First Women's Bank.

Q: Which two films featured scenes in F .A. O. Schwarz?
A: *Miracle on 34th Street* and *Big*.

Q: What is the most expensive toy in F. A. O Schwarz?
A: A $20,000 life-size stuffed bear.

1870

The licorice-flavored chewing gum Black Jack, manufactured by the American Chicle Company, first appeared on the market. Chewing gum was invented in New York City (perhaps an explanation for why there is so much of it on city sidewalks), by Thomas Adams in 1870. The first brand was called "Adams New York Gum No.1," replacing chewable paraffin wax, and it was made from licorice flavoring and chicle, a form of sapodilla tree sap chewed in the Yucatan and Guatemala. In 1899 Adams joined forces with six other gum manufacturers and became the American Chicle Company on 44th Street in Manhattan. In 1923 the company moved to Long Island City and manufactured "Dentyne" and "Chiclets," and in 1981 the company left New York City altogether. Black Jack gum was manufactured until the 1970s, although it is periodically reintroduced for nostalgia's sake.

1871

The New York Stock Exchange's call market was replaced by the current continuous-auction market.

TEA & SYMPATHY
AN ENGLISH RESTAURANT

Menu items include:

- Irish back bacon
- bangers and mash
- Stilton and walnut salad
- Yorkshire pudding and roast beef
- Welsh rarebit
- sherry trifle
- tweed kettle pie
- lemon barley water
- Scotch egg
- Myers sausage

1872

F. W. Woolworth's "five-and-dime" stores helped introduce the concept of shopping for fun and merely browsing. Before then, merchandise in stores was not on display for browsing. Customers usually entered a store knowing exactly what they wanted and could bargain over the price.

1873

The Oleo-Margarine Manufacturing Company opened in Manhattan and produced buttery-tasting oleomargarine.

1874

As a result of a severe depression for builders (partially a conse-quence of competition from immigrants) century builders formed the Committee of Safety to demand more public works projects. Workmen and the police often brawled at rallies, which resulted in the Tompkins Square Riot in January of 1874. Building trade unions adopted stringent entry requirements, high initiation fees, and strict rules of apprenticeship. City trade unions went on strike when contractors employed nonunion members; they wielded strength for at least another century.

1877

Cornelius Vanderbilt died. As a young man he borrowed $100 from his mother to buy his first boat; he eventually garnered a fortune as a shipping and railroad magnate. In 1995, 126 relatives gathered in the city to mark what would have been his two-hundredth birthday.

1877

The city's first private telephone was installed at 89 Fifth Avenue.

1877

New York City boasted more than 120 breweries. Germans in New York City often congregated in beer halls, beer gardens, and saloons, and some of the beer halls featured live entertain-ment (usually a theater troupe) and meeting rooms.

1878

The Metropolitan Telephone and Telegraph Company was formed when a central switching office opened in Manhattan to serve 271 customers. New York Telephone wasn't organized until 1896, when it absorbed the Bell operations for the city.

1880

The electric streetlight first appeared in New York City at Broadway and 23rd Street, illuminating an ad for homes on Long Island. It was turned off each night at 11:00 P.M. In 1880 the entire stretch of Broadway from 14th to 26th Streets was lit with electricity provided by the Brush Electric Illuminating Company. At the same time, Thomas Edison was perfecting the light bulb with the intention of supplying light to homes and stores, and selling stock in the Edison Electric Illuminating Company.

1880

New York City's telephone directory contained 2,800 names.

1882

On September 4, Thomas Edison turned on the lights at Broad and Wall Streets in the office of his wealthiest customer, J. Pierpont Morgan.

1882

James Butler opened a grocery store on Second Avenue. By 1934 he had 1,100 stores, 200 of which grossed $15 million annually.

1882

The Gansevoort Market on Gansevoort Street in Greenwich Village opened with farmers from neighboring states peddling their goods. Author Herman Melville worked as a customs inspector on a pier in the vicinity. Most of the meatpacking activity in the area still occurs between midnight and dawn, and the area is unprotected by the Greenwich Village Historic District, which does not extend north of Gansevoort Street or west of Washington Street.

1885

There were 10,000 drinking establishments in the city, one for every 140 residents.

1885

Boxing matches at Harry Hill's Saloon on Crosby and Houston Streets attracted both the wealthy and the poverty-stricken. The saloon called Jimmy the Priest's attracted sailors and was the inspiration for the saloon in one of Eugene O'Neill's plays.

Q: Which play?
A: *The Iceman Cometh.*

1886

The volume of shares traded on the New York Stock Exchange exceeded one million for the first time on December 15. By the turn of the century industrial securities had been traded.

NEW YORK BANKS

- There are approximately 1,319 bank branches in New York City, averaging 1 branch for every 5,610 people—except for Manhattan, where the average numberof people for 1 branch is 2,408.
- The only black-owned bank in New York City is the Carver Savings Bank on 125th Street near Lenox Avenue.

1887

Bloomingdale's department store opened on 59th Street and Third Avenue. The store soon expanded west to Lexington Avenue.

1888

Sussman Volk (a.k.a. Reb Sussel) opened a delicatessen at 88 Delancey Street and the first pastrami sandwich was served in New York City. Food stores selling specialty items such as pickles, cured meats, flavored sodas, and special breads had sprung up all over Manhattan between 1850 and 1888; many offered ethnic specialties from Germany and Central Europe. By 1900 there were 60 delicatessens on the Lower East Side specializing in the cuisine of Jewish Europeans, featuring lox, whitefish, bagels, bialys, and kosher foods. By 1997 there were 6,000 delicatessens in New York City. *Essen* means "to eat" in German.

Q: What are 4 of the city's most famous delis?

A: Katz's Delicatessen, the Second Avenue Kosher Delicatessen, Carnegie Delicatessen, and the Stage Delicatessen.

Q: What was the slogan for Katz's Delicatessen during World War II?

A: "Send a Salami to Your Boy in the Army."

The borough of Queens offers many culturally diverse restaurants, often within mere feeet of each other, for adventuresome diners.

1889

The city's first milk depot that pasteurized milk for poor infants was opened by Henry Koplik.

1892

A tourist guide informed visitors that "all America goes to New York for its shopping." Dry-goods emporiums were the forerunners of department stores in the city. Rowland Macy and A. T. Stewart in New York City transformed the dry-goods emporium into the department store by taking advantage of better speed and dependability in transport and communication—

which in turn affected the ease of production and distribution. By the 1890s dry-goods emporiums were known as department stores. The next generation of prominent American dry-goods merchants included many German Jews: Adam Gimbel, Herbert Marcus, Morris Rich, Abraham Abraham, Samuel and Jacob Lit, Isidor and Nathan Straus, and Fred and Ralph Lazarus. A one-price policy that barred haggling and a money-back guarantee were adopted for the department store, and administrative layers based on a model of a corporation moved the dry-goods business squarely into the department store era.

1892

The largest department stores in the city in 1892 were R. H. Macy and Siegel-Cooper, each employing thousands of young, primarily single women as shopgirls. By the late 1880s, the stores that rendered New York City the shopping and fashion capital were all located between 10th and 23rd Streets, bound by Broadway and Sixth Avenue. Some of the stores included: Bonwit Teller; Brooks Brothers; B. Altman; Best & Company; Greenhut; Lord & Taylo;, Stern Brothers; Tiffany & Company; J. Sloan, Herns, Crawford & Simpson; O'Neill's; Arnold Constable, James McCreery & Company; McCutcheon; and Ehrich Brothers.

The area between 14th and 23rd Streets on Sixth Avenue was known as the Ladies' Mile because of the finely garbed women who shopped there. The architecture and mercantile display in the area were so fantastic that the location became a magnet for retail trade and shoppers.

1895

Ten thousand people could shop comfortably in the James McCreery & Company store at the southwest corner of Sixth Avenue and 23rd Street.

1896

The first bagel was made in New York City in a cellar at 15 Clinton Street on the Lower East Side.

NYC: BAGEL CAPITAL OF THE EAST

Bagels were originally made and consumed by the city's community of Eastern European Jews. Introduced from Philadelphia, they were made with malt rather than sugar and were boiled and then baked to achieve a crispy outer shell and a soft inside. The bagel trade was passed from father to son through apprenticeships, and by the 1950s the bagel's appeal extended beyond the city's Jewish neighborhoods.

The bagel originated in fourteenth century Germany with hunters; after a hunter had bagged a boar or stag, a lump of dough was boiled and fashioned into the shape of a *Steigbugel*, or stirrup, and used to adorn the meat. The word *bagel* derives from Yiddish, however, and means "small arc" (*beig* means "bend" in Yiddish).

1896

Leo Hirshfield introduced the Tootsie Roll. By 1900 there were 108 candy factories in New York City.

1900

Nearly 500 Latin Americans who resided in the Lower East Side and in Chelsea owned tobacco factories.

1901

New York City boasted the largest port in the nation and offered much employment on the waterfront. The city was also a center for light manufacturing and the garment industry. Italian and Jewish families often sewed garments at home and young Italian and Jewish women worked in sweatshops or factories, supervised by Italian and Jewish foremen and tailors.

1901

Two-thirds of the Jewish immigrants were skilled workers, compared with 20 percent of other groups, and practiced butchery, carpentry, shoemaking, and tailoring.

1902

Philip Morris, a British tobacco and food processor firm, opened its first American branch in New York City on Broad Street, and became a publicly traded American firm in 1919. The company headquarters were moved to a 26-story building on Park Avenue and 41st Street in 1980. The Philip Morris Company is currently the largest industrial corporation in New York City.

Q: In what year was the "Marlboro Man" introduced?
A: 1955.

Q: Name two food companies that Philip Morris owns.
A: Kraft and General Foods.

1904

R. H. Macy moved to Herald Square on 34th Street because of changes on 14th Street and an expanding subway and rail service on 34th Street. The Gimbel brothers followed five years after by opening a store on 32nd Street, and Fifth Avenue eventually became known as the primary department store thoroughfare. Lord & Taylor and B. Altman moved to Fifth Avenue.

1905

The first Italian pizzeria in the city, Gennaro Lombardi's, opened on Spring Street in Manhattan.

NEW YORK CITY COMMERCIAL RENTAL PRICES—A COMPARISON

Q: The most commercially expensive street in New York City?
A: Fifth Avenue from 49th to 57th Streets

Q: The most commercially expensive street in the world?
A: Fifth Avenue from 49th to 57th Streets

Q: The second most commercially expensive street in the world?
A: The Ginza District, Tokyo

Q: The third?
A: East 57th Street between 5th Avenue and Madison Avenue

Q: The fourth?
A: Champs Elysée, Paris

Q: The fifth?
A: Madison Avenue in New York City

• The average price, per square foot, to rent commercial space on Fifth Avenue between 49th and 57th Streets is $375, compared with Tokyo's Ginza District at $370 and the Champs Elysée at $275.
• The city of New York owns about 3,500 addresses in Manhattan. Columbia University owns about 250, New York University owns 80, and Trinity Church owns 80.

1907

Taxicabs became popular when vehicles powered by 800-pound batteries were replaced with gas-powered ones. Slow-moving battery-operated cars had been in use since 1899. The newer gas-fueled vehicles were equipped with taximeters to halt fare-gouging. Five thousand taxi drivers went on strike in 1907 for better wages and the right to unionize. Within two years there were six major taxi fleets in New York City, and inspectors were appointed by the city government to monitor cabs.

1909

Greek-owned Manhattan businesses included:

• 151 bootblack parlors
• 113 florists
• 107 restaurants and lunchrooms
• 70 confectioneries
• 62 retail fruit stores
• 11 wholesale produce dealers

There were 24 Greek fraternal organizations in the city. Greeks did not live in contained ethnic areas in the city but were scattered throughout the boroughs. It wasn't until 1965 that Astoria, Queens became the Greek center for the city.

1910

The secretary from the New York Philharmonic Society visited businessman/philanthropist Andrew Carnegie at his mansion and requested $60,000 to meet the society's annual deficit. Carnegie promised to match half of that amount if the secretary found other people willing to donate $30,000. "Surely there are other people who like music enough to help with their own money," he said. The next day the secretary was back at the Carnegie mansion, announcing that he had raised the $30,000. Carnegie congratulated him on a job well done and wrote out a check for $30,000. As he handed the check to the secretary, he said, "Would you mind telling me who gave you the other half?" The secretary said, "Not at all. Mrs. Carnegie."

1911

An ardent socialist visited Andrew Carnegie and lectured to him at length about the evils of capitalism and the need for fair distribution of wealth. Carnegie called his secretary and asked for two figures: the total value of his assets and possessions, and the latest estimate of the world's population. After a quick calculation, he told his secretary, "Give this gentleman sixteen cents. That's his share of my wealth."

1912

Hellman's mayonnaise was introduced by the same name at a deli on West 84th Street and Columbus Avenue.

1913

F. W. Woolworth wanted to build the tallest building in the city to represent his corporate headquarters and to serve as an advertisement for his chain of five-and-ten stores. He disliked buying on credit so he paid for the construction of the building with $13.5 million in cash. The Woolworth Building was completed on Lower Broadway in 1913 and stood 800 feet tall with 60 floors. It was the tallest building in the world for 16 years, until it was eclipsed by the Chrysler Building in midtown. Woolworth's marble-lined executive offices were on the 24th floor, and a corbel of F. W. Woolworth counting nickels and dimes is located on the wall of the lobby.

1914

The New York Stock Exchange closed for six months due to World War I.

1916

The Federal Reserve Bank of New York in Lower Manhattan at Liberty and Nassau Streets, which is a Florentine neo-Renaissance palazzo fortress fashioned after the Palazzo Strozzi of the fifteenth-century Florentine banking family, first began accepting gold from other nations.

A POT—OR TWENTY—OF GOLD

The Federal Reserve Bank of New York is the largest of the 12 banks in the Federal Reserve System, acting as the banker for the United States government. The New York City branch conducts all foreign exchange trading on behalf of the Federal Reserve System and holds gold from 80 countries and organizations valued at $117 billion, which is the world's largest store of gold. The gold at Fort Knox is worth about half as much.

Q: What percentage of the world's monetary gold is stored in NYC?
A: Approximately 40%.

The gold is stored five stories underground in a vault that is 76 feet below the street and 50 feet below sea level, accessible only by elevator. Twelve thousand tons of gold are housed in 122 cells and security can seal off the building within 30 seconds. Each gold brick weighs 27 lbs, and each brick is valued at $153,000. There are over 700,000 bricks in the bank. When one country pays a debt to another, rather than ship gold from country to country, the bullion can be moved from cell to cell. Scales used to weigh the gold bars are so sensitive that they weigh to the nearest one-one-hundredth of a troy ounce, or one-third the weight of a dollar bill.

Q: Why is this gold kept in America?
A: At times of unrest, especially at the onset of World War II, it was safer here than in Europe. The New York branch is the branch in America that has the most dealings with foreign nations.

1916

Nathan Handwerker opened a hot dog stand on Surf Avenue in Coney Island called "Nathan's." The business mushroomed, the outcome of low prices, a comfortable atmosphere, and the popularity of hot dogs. There are now approximately 62 outlets nationwide, and the original stand in Coney Island sells about one million hot dogs a year.

MAKING CONCESSIONS

The annual 1997 rent for the hot dog and soda concession stand on the north side of the Metropolitan Museum of Art is $296,200. The rent for the concession on the south side of the museum is $316,200. These museum spots are ranked second in the city's largest revenue producers. The city only received $80,000 for 60 concession stands in and around Central Park in 1997.

Concession Stand Rents:

Fifth Avenue and 72nd Street	$52,000
Washington Square Park (6 carts)	$84,000
Fifth Avenue and 60th Street	$90,500
Carl Schultz Park, Upper East Side	$12,519
Riverside Park	$16,145
Marcus Garvey Park, Harlem	$1,100

1922

There were over 1,100 candy factories operating in the city.

1923

The police department took control of taxi licensing in response to the excess of citizen complaints about dirty, dangerous, and uninsured taxicabs. Cabs were often used in holdups, bootlegging operations, and burglaries, so the police department was happy to intervene. There were 16,000 licensed cabs in the city in 1923.

1923

There were 275 businesses and 150 professionals (physicians, dentists, and lawyers) listed in the Guia Hispana, a guide to Latin-American-owned businesses and services.

NYC'S DEARLY DEPARTED

- There are 130 cemeteries in the city.
- Approximately 15% of the funerals in the city are cremations; the national rate is 21%.
- In 10% of cremations in New York City, ashes are split up to accommodate relatives in various parts of the country.
- Only 17% of funerals are planned in advance.
- There are approximately 100 black funeral professionals in New York City.
- Houston-based Service Corporation International (SCI) owns 24 funeral parlors in the city; employees earn commissions.
- The Domenick De Nigris monument-building firm in the Bronx produces 10,000 monuments annually (in 18 colors of stone) for all ethnic and religious backgrounds. Most clients in 1997 preferred to customize their monuments.

1925

Women first became taxicab drivers and the Taxicab Commission was formed.

1926

NBC, the National Broadcasting Company, was founded in New York City as the nation's first coast-to-coast network by businessmen representing the Radio Corporation of America, General Electric, and Westinghouse. In 1932 RCA, led by David Sarnoff, bought out Westinghouse and General Electric. In spite of the depression, NBC thrived and the network moved to Rockefeller Center in 1931. Experimental television broadcasts began in 1932; by 1939 it began regular television service.

Q: What was the network's first television broadcast?
A: President Franklin D. Roosevelt opening the World's Fair.

1926

The T. O. Dey company opened to sell handmade shoes and boots. By 1997, there were 20 custom shoemakers on staff, creating 2,500 shoes and boots annually. Sixty to 75 percent of the custom-made footwear is sold to people with serious foot problems.

CUSTOM-MADE: THE OFFERINGS OF NEW YORK

Custom-cut butcher block . . . . .Empire Restaurant Supply
Ski cases to order . . . . .Louis Vuitton
Women's bathing suits . . . . .Keiko
Women's jeans . . . . .Selected Levi's outlets in Manhattan
Men's shirts . . . . .Alexander Kabbaz
Children's clothing . . . . .Miss Pym
Women's hats . . . . .Lola Millinery
Children's furniture . . . . .Portico Kids
Shoes . . . . .Vincent and Edgar
Boots . . . . .E. Vogel
Gloves . . . . .LaCrasia Gloves
Wallpaper . . . . .Richard's Interior Design
Beds . . . . .Frederick Bed Center
Humidors . . . . .Jay Kos
Fishing rods . . . . .Manhattan Custom Tackle
Bicycles . . . . .Bicycle Renaissance
Corsets, girdles, bustles . . . . .Barbra Matera Ltd.

1927

Zito's Bakery opened in Greenwich Village.

LOAFING AROUND

The price for a loaf of Zito's bread in:
1927 . . . . .5 cents
1943 . . . . .50 cents
1958 . . . . .80 cents
1985 . . . .$1.10
1993 . . . .$1.25
1997 . . . .$1.50

1929

Before the stock market crashed late in 1929, 275 new seats were created on the New York Stock Exchange. On "Black Tuesday," October 29, over 16 million shares were traded on the NYSE—a record that stood for 40 years. By the end of the trading session the Dow-Jones Industrial Average had declined over 23 percent from the preceding week. When the DJIA reached its nadir in the summer of 1932, it was one-tenth its 1929 value.

Q: Street vendors sold apples during the depression. How much did an apple cost?
A: 5 cents.

1930

The King Kullen grocery store was opened in August by Michael Kullen at 171st Street and Jamaica Avenue in Queens. This was considered to be the first grocery store in the country because customers helped themselves to groceries. There was ample parking for customers, and a wide assortment of food replaced extensive store furnishings and decorations. By 1997 supermarkets accounted for approximately 63 percent of retail food sales in New York City.

Q: What is the current largest grocery chain in the city?
A: A & P.

A grocery shopper in 1997 paid 20 percent more for groceries in Manhattan than in the other boroughs.

1931

Italian immigrant Generoso Pope owned the largest business supply firm in the country. There were 10,000 Italian grocery stores and about 10,000 ice and coal dealers.

1933

Due to the depression, the number of taxicab drivers in the city increased to the point where there were 75,000 part-time drivers operating 19,000 cabs. The average weekly pay dropped from $26 in 1929 to $15.

1934

Tavern on the Green opened on the site of a sheepfold at 67th Street and Central Park West on October 20. It was built by the order of Parks Commissioner Robert Moses and featured stained glass windows—including one by Louis Comfort Tiffany—and views of the gardens in Central Park. The restaurant closed for a two-year renovation after Warner LeRoy acquired the lease in 1974, and the restaurant reopened with 45 new chandeliers, 14 new sand-carved mirrors, and two new rooms: the Crystal Room and the Terrace Room. The restaurant serves an average of 2,000 people a day.

Q: How many cooks are employed at Tavern on the Green?
A: 52.

Q: How long does it take a crew of 7 full-time workers during the winter to put 400,000 tiny lights on the trees at Tavern on the Green?
A: 3 months.

Q: How is the Tavern on the Green connected to the New York City Marathon?
A: It marks the finish line.

1935

Before 1935, children who had reached the age of 14 were legally allowed to drop out of school to work full time. After 1935, children were required to first reach the age of 16.

1936

Confectioner Philip Silverstein introduced the Chunky Bar.

Q: Why did he name the candy bar Chunky?
A: It was named after his granddaughter, who was chubby as an infant.

Other candies manufactured in New York City in 1936: Bonomo's Turkish Taffy, Mike & Ikes, Hot Tamales, Now and Laters, Hopalongs, Joyva Halvah.

1938

Topps Chewing Gum Company was formed to manufacture baseball cards and chewing gum.

Q: What did the company call its gum?
A: Bazooka.

1939

Authentic French cuisine was introduced in the U.S. at the French pavilion of the World's Fair. Shortly after, the maitre d' at the restaurant of the pavilion, Henri Soule, opened a lush French restaurant called Le Pavilion on East 55th Street—which inspired a flurry of other French restaurants and French cooking schools to open in the city.

MATCH THE RESTAURANT WITH THE DISH

1. Sasso
2. Red Tulip
3. The Stanhope

4. Coconut Grill
5. Passage to India
6. Katz's Deli
7. Senor Swanky's Crepe Sauce
8. Tavern on the Green

9. Judson Grill
10. Chanterelle Dipping Sauce

11. Telephone

A. Chino Latino Kabobs
B. Beet Gnocchi
C. Moroccan-Style Barbecued Salmon
D. Hortobagyi Palascinta
E. Grilled Frankfurters
F. Potato Ravioli in Vegetables
G. Asparagus & Smithfield Ham
H. Sweet Potato Fries w/ Maple
I. Chicken Karahi
J. Toasted Pistachio-Butterscotch Semifreddo Dome
K. Stilton Cheese Fritters

Answers: 1.B, 2.D, 3.G, 4.H, 5.I, 6.E, 7.A, 8.C, 9.J, 10.F, 11.K

1940

A sandwich in the Horn & Hardart Automat was 15 cents and a piece of cake was 25 cents.

1941

In 1941 NBC obtained a commercial television license from the Federal Communications Commission for WNBT-TV in New York City, which was the first commercial television station in the world.

1942

Daniel Carasso and Juan Metzger founded Dannon Yogurt in the Bronx. In the 1970s the company began using skim milk instead of whole milk.

1944

The Coach Leather Company was founded as a family-run workshop in a Manhattan loft. Between 1987 and 1997 the sales growth for the Coach Leather Company were tenfold.

1950

The Masonic Supply Company opened. Between 1950 and 1997 all of the company's sales were obtained without advertising. Ninety-five percent of the business has been mail-order, with the largest portion located in Western Europe. The price for a walnut gavel at Masonic Supply Company in the Flatiron Building is currently $20.

1955

The McDonald's Corporation was founded. By 1997 there were 183 McDonalds restaurants in New York City, 56 located in Manhattan, with 40 of them delivering food before 8:00 P.M. The McDonalds computer clearing-house for orders can simultaneously handle 17 callers.

1961

The dominant force in the New York Stock Exchange was the institutional market, comprising trust funds, private pension funds, insurance companies, mutual funds, and open-end investment companies.

1962

Coffee drinkers compromised 74.7 percent of the city's population, compared with only 53.8 percent in 1997.

COFFEE KLATCH

- There are over 50 independent coffee roasters in New York City.
- New York is ranked first of the locations with the most long-standing coffee roasters in the country. There are 350 New York City-based cafe listings in the Java Journal database.
- The average daily coffee consumption among men is 2.11 cups, among women it's 1.64 cups.
- 56.8% of the city's population drinks coffee to relax and 39.3% drinks coffee for energy.
- The estimated required price to open a coffeehouse in Manhattan is $200,000.

1964

Jacqueline Onassis's 14-room apartment on Fifth Avenue cost $200,000. By 1995 it was worth $9,500,000.

1964

A Flintstones lunch box in 1964 was $1.98, including a thermos. The same Flintstones lunch box from 1964 is currently selling for $200 at Alphaville in New York City—without the thermos. The additional cost of the thermos is $50.

1967

The bridal store Kleinfelds opened in Brooklyn. It had been a furrier store prior to 1967. By 1997 there were 30 bridal consultants on staff, 1,500 bridal gowns for sale, $30 million in annual sales, and typically 325 scheduled appointments for bridal consultants on Saturdays.

1968

Shah Bagh was the first restaurant to open in Little India on East Sixth Street, which now features 27 Indian restaurants. Mitali East, which opened in 1973, is the oldest restaurant on the strip, as Shah Bagh didn't last long. Most of the area's 300 employees come from Sylhet in northeastern Bangladesh. Haveli, with 185 seats, is the largest restaurant on the strip and Rupali, with 31 seats, is the smallest. Milon Bangladesh has the largest light display with 6,000 flashing bulbs.

Q: How much was a dish of curried chicken at Shah Bagh in 1968?
A: $1.25. Now the dish is around $5.95 in Little India.

Q: How much does a clay oven for tandoori cost?
A: $7,000 to $8,000.

1969

There were 131 Fortune 500 companies located in the city.

Q: How many were located in New York City in 1997?
A: 29.

BRINGING HOME MANHATTAN'S BACON

Median income of Battery Park and Tribeca $47,445
Median income of Soho and Greenwich Village $39,592
Median income in the Lower East Side and Chinatown . . .$20,007
Median income on the Upper West Side $40,852
Median income on the Upper East Side $53,000
Median income in Harlem $20,775
Median income in the Flatiron District $43,150
Citywide average income $41,741

1970

McSorley's Old Ale House on East Seventh Street was the last tavern in the city to finally admit women. The bar's slogan was "Good ale, raw onions, and no ladies."

1971

The New York Stock Exchange was incorporated as a nonprofit corporation.

1975

A rule mandating fixed commissions for stock transactions was repealed, leading to the growth of discount brokers and negotiable commissions from full-service brokers.

TRADING PLACES

The New York Stock Exchange spent over $1,000 million throughout the 1980s on new technology to increase the volume of trading that can be handled to over 1,000 million shares per day. By 1995, 90% of all orders were processed electronically with the trade confirmed in seconds and an instantaneous record of transaction made available to investors around the globe.

1977

During a real estate slump in the city, the Canadian firm of Olympia & York bought eight office buildings at distressed prices. When the market later improved, the value of the buildings quadrupled.

1978

Singles bars began proliferating in the city, especially on the Upper East Side, as a result of the nation's shifting sexual mores. The most lauded was Maxwell Plums.

Q: Which Diane Keaton movie was centered around singles bars in New York City?
A: *Looking for Mr. Goodbar.*

1980

- 26% of the construction workers in the city were Italian.
- 10% of the city's Italian immigrants were professionals, mainly teachers.
- 40% of the city's Italian immigrants had administrative, retail, and technical occupations.

1985

Chinese businesses began moving into the Little Italy area, directly north of Chinatown. Between 1985 and 1997 there was a 30 percent increase in Chinese business moving into Little Italy.

1987

A stock market crash followed an extended "bull" market. On October 20, 608 million shares were traded with an approximate value of $21,000 million. The Dow-Jones Industrial Average declined by over 500 points. The decline was the result of transactions executed by computer when prices reached a certain level, so "trading collars" were implemented to stabilize the market. Special controls take effect, for example, when the DJIA declines by 50 points from the closing level of the preceding day.

The Times Square Stock Exchange ribbon reveals the fate of millions.

PHOTO BY ERIC CAPSTICK

1990

New York Telephone employed almost 50,000 people, and handled almost 106 million telephone calls a day through nearly 100 million miles of cable.

Q: How many requests for numbers, per 7.5-hour shift, does a New York City directory assistance operator currently handle?
A: 1,000.

Q: What is the average length of time it takes to handle a call?
A: 30 seconds.

1991

In 1991 metal swings were first replaced with rubber swings in New York City parks and 36 swings were chewed up by dogs within a year. Nontoxic oils like eucalyptus and citrus were used in 1994 to deter dogs from chewing swings.

Q: How much does it cost the city to buy a tire swing?
A: $250.

Q: How much is a plain swing?
A: $50.

Q: How much does it cost the city to buy a manhole cover?
A: $50 to $75 each. They are manufactured in China and India.

1991

A sushi robot began operating in New York City, but sushi robots have been used in Japan since 1977. The fastest chef in the city can turn out 200 to 300 pieces of sushi per hour but a sushi "robot" can turn out 1,200. The cost for handmade sushi is $1.50 or more and the cost for machine-made sushi is 50 to 70 cents. A sushi robot costs $86,000.

Q: How many robot-made pieces of sushi, on average, are sold each weekday in Manhattan?
A: 100,000.

NEW YORK CITY'S ENORMOUS RESTAURANTS

Number of people America in the Flatiron district can
accommodate at once 350
The Motown Cafe 350
Brother's Bar-B-Que on 77th and Broadway 425
The Crab House in Chelsea 500
The All Star Cafe in Times Square 700
Lundy's in Brooklyn 800
The Tavern on the Green 800
The Bryant Park Grill 1,420

1992

The city's first telephone dial-a-parlor opened for business. Manhattan-based Dominican Communications now owns 50 telephone parlors in the United States.

Q: What is the current estimated total number of telephone parlors in the New York metropolitan area?
A: 700.

1992

There were 12 fully enclosed, old-fashioned outdoor public phone booths left in New York City.

1995

A portion of Manhattan on Broadway between 23rd Street and Tribeca became known as "Silicon Alley" because of the proliferation of multimedia businesses there. At least 10,000 people in NYC were employed in the business of new media and multimedia.

1995

The now-closed Area Code Cafe was visited by 2,600 patrons in one weekend. The owners leased 30 phone lines from NYNEX for $1,000, but one of the kinks the owners hadn't ironed out before opening was blocking access to phone-sex lines.

1995

New York City employees paid approximately $150 million in union dues. It cost New York City $17 million annually to pay city employees their salaries while they were on release time to tend to union business. An average of 282 city employees were paid full salaries while they served their unions.

1995

The Department Of Environmental Protection spent $45 to $50 million replacing outdated sewer and water mains. There are 6,000 water lines in New York City; the oldest pipes are 157 years old. A ruptured main, leaking for eight hours under Times Square, cost the city subway system $1 million in damages.

Q: How many Olympic-size swimming pools could be filled with the amount of water leaked?
A: 10.

Q: What is the average number of water main breaks in New York City each year?
A: 600.

Q: How many gallons of water a minute can a gushing fire hydrant spill?
A: 1,000.

Q: How many fire hydrants are in New York City?
A: 100,000.

1996

The Metropolitan Transit Authority garnered $23 million in revenues from advertising, about 40 percent of which came from subway advertisements. The cost for ads that take up half a subway car and were posted in 570 cars for a month was $75,000. Calvin Klein purchased all of the space in 570 cars for one month, and Swatch U.S.A. purchased all the space in 900 cars for three months.

1996

The estimated total annual amount of restaurant business in the city was between $6.5 and $6.7 billion. The cost of a restaurant meal in the city decreased 13 percent over a five-year period (as it did in Los Angeles as well).

1996

Drummer Ralph Rolle and dancer Marisol Figueroa of the East Bronx created a mail-order cookie business called Ghetto Cookies from their apartment in the Bronx River Houses. Their customers, largely garnered through word of mouth, place orders from as far away as Japan, England, California, and Mississippi. They bake 100 dozen cookies a day in five varieties.

1996

Over 400,000 cans were collected in a warehouse by We Can, representing $20,000 in nickels to the homeless. We Can redeemed 245 million bottles before 1996 and has recycled over 21,616 tons of solid waste. It has paid over $11 million in deposits to collectors.

Q: What is the commodity price for a ton of recycled newspaper?
A: $160.

PAPER TRAIL

There are 1,100 tons of newspaper and cardboard recycled daily in the city; 300,000 tons are recycled annually. The amount of projected revenue for the city in a fiscal year from the sale of recycled newspaper is $18 to $20 million. New York City ranks the highest of the cities in the U.S. with the most aggressive recycling programs.

1997

The Fulton Street Fishmarket's sales were approximately $1 billion. The Fulton Street market is the largest market for fish in the nation with over a million pounds of fish weighed nightly. There are approximately 60 wholesalers at the market, employing 800 people.

1997

Urban Organic delivered 16 to 20 different types of produce to 1,500 homes in New York City each week, and employed 22 full-time workers. Annual sales were $2.1 million, and the weekly price for fruit and vegetables for two was $27.

1997

Chinatown's largest restaurant, Jing Fong, is the size of a football field. In early 1997 authorities discovered that waiters at the restaurant were only being paid $1 an hour and could not keep all of their tips.

1997

El Restaurant de los Taxistas is a converted yellow school bus that serves homemade Dominican dishes for $4 at 172nd Street and Inwood Avenue in the Bronx. Customers stand at counters inside of the bus, although there is one seat to be had: the driver's seat.

1997

The Korean-American Nail Association in New York City represents 1,500 salons and 5,000 manicurists.

Q: What percentage of nail salons in New York City are Korean-owned?
A: 85%.

To visit, as distinct from living in it, is to miss something fundamental: the poignancy of irreversible change, which gives depth and resonance to life in this most volatile of cities.
JOHN RUSSELL

Q: How many Japanese tourists visit New York City each year?
A: Approximately 350,000.

THE TOURIST TRADE

The percentage of annual domestic tourists in New York City from:

The South 25%
The Northeast 63%
The Midwest 7%
The West 5%

The percentage of annual international tourists in New York City from:

Western Europe 36.7%
Canada 33.4%
The Far East 12.8%
South and Central America and the Caribbean 10.8%

2017

By 2017 there will be no unsold cemetery plots in NYC.

Q: How do Europeans tackle the space problem for burials?
A: People can rent graves for 5 years, after which the body is cremated.

The headquarters of the United Nations Organization, occupying fifteen acres, presides over the East Bank.

PHOTO BY ERIC CAPSTICK

CHAPTER 3

Everything Is Politics

I like the rough impersonality of New York, where human relations are oiled by jokes, complaints, and confessions—all made with the assumption of never seeing the other person again. I like New York because there are enough competing units to make it still seem a very mobile society. I like New York because it engenders high expectations simply by its pace.

U.S. SENATOR BILL BRADLEY

Colonial politics in New York City were extremely partisan, with loose alliances formed around economic and social groups, families, and business factions. Early politicians were expected to be landowners and in good community standing, but since land was readily attainable and status was loosely interpreted, the early politicians were a more diverse lot than those found in England. Before the 1760s, important issues were rarely addressed, candidates could often run virtually unopposed, and voter turnout hardly ever exceeded 50 percent of the population. Merchants and the wealthy dominated the mayoralty and the Common Council, with members of prominent families such as the de Lanceys, the Beekmans, the Livingstons, and the Van Cortlandts defining important local issues. Artisans and shopkeepers were also included in the council to keep it more democratic and to ensure public interest in the elections.

After the American Revolution, the state appointed and removed city mayors; all appointees were landowners. Tammany Hall members persuaded the legislature to appoint men who rented property and to utilize the ballot system; by 1833 the city's mayor was voted in by popular election.

In 1849 Theodore Roosevelt pointed out (with distaste) that two-thirds of the ward meetings were held in saloons. By 1853 the City Council had clearly earned its nickname: "The Forty Thieves." Tammany Hall politicians ensured control by exerting influence over the city's immigrant population, particularly the Irish, but by 1885 the political muscle of the Tweed Ring began to weaken.

Mayor James J. Walker created a new foundation for partnership between the state and the city in the 1920s; housing and working conditions in the city were improved, and Walker forged a democracy dedicated primarily to aiding the poor and the city's working class for the first time. Backed by funds provided by the New Deal, Mayor Fiorello La Guardia initiated a broad scope of public works in the 1930s and 1940s, which included building new college campuses (City University of New York), municipal hospitals, and extensive public housing.

After the Second World War, city politicians saw the slow, steady decline of the political club and a growing emphasis on the actual candidate. Television, newspapers, magazines, and political consultants became political tools, and candidates grew more adept at using them with each subsequent decade. Mayor Koch epitomized the city during his three terms that stretched from 1977 to 1989, although he was politically marred during his third term by corruption in city agencies uncovered by a particularly Democratic political base along more conservative lines.

What people remember is that I gave them a sense of pride.
They were so dejected based on two mayors that had sent us
into bankruptcy. And I gave them back their pride.
MAYOR ED KOCH TO A REPORTER FOR *TOTAL TV* IN 1977

When Mayor David N. Dinkins was elected in 1989, black voters were the city's largest component of the Democratic electorate. Mayor Rudolph Giuliani, a Republican, was elected in 1993 and surprised city residents by endorsing Democrat Mario Cuomo for governor instead of Republican candidate George Pataki.

New York City experienced the entire spectrum of the political experience: the most liberal of the liberals, the most conservative of the Democrats, the most liberal of the Republicans, remote and ineffective mayors, corrupt and self-serving politicians, dedicated mayors with a broad vision, mayors that left little impact on the city, and mayors that forever altered the way the city functioned and appeared.

Reader, suppose you were an idiot; and suppose you were a member of Congress; but I repeat myself.

Fleas can be taught nearly anything that a Congressman can.

It could probably be shown by facts and figures that there is no distinctly native criminal class except Congress.
    THREE FROM MARK TWAIN, WHILE RESIDING IN NEW YORK CITY

1624

Cornelius Jacobsen May, commander of the ship *Nieu Nederlandt,* was appointed as the first director of New Nederland.

1625

May was swiftly replaced by Willem Verhulst. Leading members of the New Netherland Company who happened to be present in the new colony either as settlers or as voyagers were to serve the director as advisory council.

1626

Peter Minuit (a German by birth, a Frenchman by name, and a Dutchman by residence and citizenship) became the first popularly elected governor in Fort Amsterdam by a council of the settlers. Minuit returned to the Netherlands for confirmation of the post, received it, and then returned to Fort Amsterdam in May of 1626. Minuit assembled Indian chiefs and their wives and negotiated to buy the island of Manhattan from the Indians for 60 guilders in goods—$30 at current exchange rates. The amount at that time was enough for a roundtrip transatlantic passage. After the sale of the island, Minuit began the construction of 30 houses, gristmills, a warehouse, a blacksmith house, sawmills, and a mill to grind bark for tanning.

1627

Minuit initiated trade talks with the English colony at Plymouth, Massachusetts.

1631

The Dutch West India Company fired Governor Minuit for being too generous in granting trading privileges to the company's investors; the company's trade monopoly was threatened. Also, Minuit had bankrolled the building of an 800-ton boat called the *New Netherland* with company funds, and the boat was perceived as a poor investment. Minuit was rendered jobless at the age of 51, but soon took a job with the Swedish West India Company, bought an enormous tract of land in Delaware for the company from the Indians in exchange for a copper pot, and established a colony of Swedes and Finns near Wilmington. Minuit died in 1638 on a ship at sea during a storm.

Q: What does the word *minuit* mean in French?
A: "Midnight."

1633

Wouter Van Twiller, a heavyset man with a crew cut, was the fifth director general of New Netherland and ruled from 1633 through 1637. He started out as a clerk in the Dutch West India Company's Amsterdam warehouse, married a niece of an influential Amsterdam citizen who owned property up the Hudson River from Manhattan, and arrived in Manhattan in April of 1633. As director general (or governor), he deeded to himself several hundred acres of prime tobacco farmland in Greenwich Village that belonged to the Dutch West India Company. Then he bought three islands and a share in 15,000 acres in Brooklyn, and he and three of his associates appropriated to themselves between 10,000 and 15,000 acres of land on Long Island. Van

Twiller was the first New World governor to corrupt public office for his personal gain.

The town's public prosecutor, Lubbertus van Dincklagen, objected to Van Twiller's greed, so Van Twiller sent him back to Holland as a prisoner and refused to grant him the three years' pay that was his due. When van Dincklagen arrived in Amsterdam, he informed on Van Twiller, who was dismissed by the Dutch West India Company in 1637. Van Dincklagen then became Manhattan's assistant director general, and the Dutch West India Company took back most of the land Van Twiller had granted to himself.

Q: What happened to Van Twiller?
A: He stayed on in Manhattan, savoring life as the island's wealthiest citizen.

GOVERNOR'S ISLAND

Governor's Island was called Nuttin Island because of the spectacular nut, oak, and hickory trees that flourished there. Wouter Van Twiller purchased Nuttin Island from the Algonquin Indians and it was soon dubbed Governor's Island.

1640

Governor Willem Kieft, who succeeded Wouter Van Twiller, began as Manhattan's first reformer. He issued numerous proclamations against the rampant smuggling and illegal trade that went on in the colony. Colonists who resented the Dutch West India Company's monopoly on trade actively searched for ways to work around its regulations. Kieft attempted to reform the morals of the town by ordering sailors to stay on their ships by night, but sailors paid little attention to the order and continued to drink throughout the night in saloons. Kieft prohibited "fighting, lewdness, rebellion, theft, perjury, calumny, and all other immoralities," but his proclamations went unheeded. Kieft tried to issue passports to keep out foreigners, but his attempt was ignored. A wealthy Frenchman from Rouen named Michel Picquet denounced Kieft as "a betrayer of his country, a villain, and a traitor," and he offered to shoot the director general if no one else would do it.

GOVERNOR KIEFT'S WAR

In 1641, Kieft sent an army detachment to Staten Island to investigate the theft of a pig that had been stolen by Dutch criminals on their way to Delaware. Kieft's troops attacked a Raitan Indian community in the mistaken belief that the Indians had robbed the farmer of his swine. This sparked what became known throughout the seventeenth century as "Governor Kieft's War," which was part of a much wider struggle between the Europeans who had invaded the northeastern region and various Indian tribes—tribes that were often at war with one another as well. Eleven Indian tribes waged war on the small settlement in Manhattan. The Indians of Long Island, Hackensack, and Westchester had been friendly to the Dutch, but after Kieft's attack, they began to kill isolated farmers and to take wives and children as captives. Between 1662 and 1664, 1,600 Indians were killed and the number of settlers had dwindled from 300 to 100, with many returning to Holland.

1641

Heads of families in New Amsterdam chose a council of twelve men to advise the governor-general.

1642

The Stadt Herberg (or City Tavern) was built at 71-73 Pearl Street by Governor Willem Kieft. It served as a tavern and the town's first inn. Although leased out by the city as a tavern, government officials conducted business on the building's upper floors within quick walking distance of the bar. When New Amsterdam was granted municipal government in 1654, the tavern was renamed Stadt-Huys or City Hall. After it fell into disrepair in the 1690s, it was sold to a merchant named John Rodman in 1699 and was soon demolished.

1647

Peter Stuyvesant was sent to Manhattan by the Dutch West India Company to replace Kieft. Stuyvesant had been director of the company's colony on Curacoa and had lost his leg during the Dutch attack on the Portuguese island of St. Martin. He was the first strong leader in the colony, and his administration was efficient and respected.

> *The consciences of men ought to remain free and unshackled. This maxim of moderation has always been the guide of the magistrates in this city; and the consequence has been that people have flocked from every land to this asylum. Tread thus in their steps, and we doubt not you will be blessed.*
> THE DIRECTORS OF THE DUTCH WEST INDIA
> COMPANY TO PETER STUYVESANT, 1654

Washington Irving considered Peter Stuyvesant a good candidate for some political spoofing in his A History of New York, IV.

1648

Stuyvesant fought with the colonists over taxes, political participation, morality, personal responsibility, the administration of justice, and land purchases from the Indians. He fought with the company over religious tolerance, the need for a schoolmaster, the behavior of the local clergy, and fur trade regulations. These problems stemmed from the lack of legitimacy in public institutions and the population's political diversity.

The people..[of the colony] have actually not only not prevented the raising of the Parliament's flag by some English freebooter, but also permitted it to be done. . . . their [the English] immigrating and having favors granted to them must therefore be restricted henceforth, that we may not nourish serpents in our bosom, who finally might devour our hearts.
THE NEW NETHERLAND COMPANY TO PETER STUYVESANT IN 1653

Let us then—we here in this country and you there—employ all diligence . . . [so] that the wolves may be warded off from the tender lambs of Christ.
THE CLASSIS OF AMSTERDAM TO PETER STUYVESANT, IN RESPONSE TO THE KNOWLEDGE THAT VARIOUS RELIGIOUS DENOMINATIONS WERE FLOURISHING PRIVATELY IN NEW AMSTERDAM IN 1656

The Dutch eat us out of our trade at home and abroad; they refuse to sell us a hogshead of water to refresh us at sea, and call us 'English Dogs,' which doth much grieve our English spirits. They will not sail with us, but shoot at us, and by indirect courses bring their goods into our ports, which wrongs not only us but you in your customs.
A PETITION TO OLIVER CROMWELL FROM MORE THAN 100 ENGLISH SHIP CAPTAINS IN 1658

1665

The first mayor of New York City, Thomas Willett, was appointed by the English governor Richard Nicolls. For a century and a half, the mayor was then appointed annually by the governor of New York State. Early mayors had limited powers and sat on the Common Council.

1665

The English victory over New Netherland resulted in harsher laws: any public assembly of more than three Africans or Indians was considered illegal and curfews were set for each group.

1665

The English jury system, a trial by a jury of twelve peers, was established in New York.

1668

Colonel Francis Lovelace replaced Colonel Richard Nicholls as governor of New York. Lovelace remained governor until 1673, concerning himself with Indian relations, boundary disputes, insurrection in the Delaware country, the possibility of Dutch reconquest, and rebellion in New Jersey.

1668

Cornelius Steenwyck served as mayor from 1668 until 1670 (and again in 1683-84). He used his position as mayor and prominent merchant to obtain significant benefits for the Dutch.

1673

The Dutch recaptured New Netherland, holding it for 15 months.

1674

New York was restored to the English in November by the Second Treaty of Westminster.

1677

Stephanus Van Cortland was appointed mayor. He was the first mayor actually born in New York; from 1777 until 1691, most of the city's mayors were of Dutch descent.

1683

Governor Colonel Thomas Dongan was New York's first Roman Catholic governor; he arrived on April 25 in the company of a Jesuit priest. The mostly Protestant population was initially wary of him, but his fairness, honesty, and politeness won most residents over to his side. He was appointed by the Duke of York, a convert to Catholicism who owned the province. The Duke instructed Dongan to ensure a generous measure of both political and religious liberty for New York residents—hoping the political liberty would make them more amenable to paying taxes, and religious liberty would create the opportunity for Catholicism to emerge as the colony's major faith. Dongan promptly created a Charter of Liberties and Privileges that provided for a popularly elected General Assembly, forbade taxation without the Assembly's consent, established trial by jury, and granted freedom of worship to all Christians.

Since this was more than the Duke intended, when he became King James II in 1685, he signed the charter but never returned it to New York. King James instructed Dongan not to interfere if the French sent down an expedition from Quebec to exterminate the Indians, but Dongan warned the Indian tribes. He also negotiated with the Indians and neighboring colonies to create New York's borders, and established charters for New York City and Albany.

1688

King James fired Dongan, who then retired to his 5,100-acre estate in Staten Island. He had to take refuge in New England when William and Mary replaced King James and anti-Catholic sentiment set in. Dongan eventually returned to England, replaced his brother as Earl of Limerick, and lived to be 81 years old.

1691

Jacob Leisler, a German clergyman's son and the only governor of New York ever to be hanged, was led to the gallows at Broadway and Chambers Street on May 16. Leisler was persuaded by a majority of residents who called themselves the Committee of Safety to assume governorship of New York City in 1688 until William and Mary—who had just replaced King James II—sent replacements from England. Leisler assumed the role of governor with ease and managed to keep the peace throughout a turbulent time of riots and upheaval. When a new lieutenant governor, Richard Ingoldesby, and new governor, Henry Sloughter, were sent from England to take charge of New York City, one of Leisler's enemies, Nicholas Bayard, persuaded the new guard that Leisler was a rebel, a traitor, and a murderer who should be put to death.

Sloughter did not want to execute anyone and refused to carry out a sentence. However, while drunk at a party, Bayard and others persuaded Sloughter to sign the death warrants. At the execution scores of townspeople looked on, weeping, shrieking, and pleading for mercy. When Sloughter died two months later, Leisler's enemies claimed he was poisoned and Leisler's mourners claimed he committed suicide out of remorse. Six doctors examined Sloughter during New York's first autopsy and determined that he had died of alcohol poisoning.

I forgive my enemies as I hope to be forgiven and I entreat my children to do the same.
                    JACOB LEISLER'S LAST WORDS BEFORE BEING HANGED

1702

Edward Hyde, known as Lord Cornbury, became governor; he governed from 1702 to 1708. He was a cousin of England's Queen Anne, a former army officer, the father of seven children, and he had been a member of Parliament for 16 years. Lord Cornbury confused colonists at a welcoming banquet by speaking extensively about the loveliness of his wife's ears and inviting each male guest to touch them. Then Cornbury irked colonists by hosting a lavish ball and charging guests at the door.

NEW YORK'S FIRST (KNOWN) TRANSVESTITE GOVERNOR

Once settled into office, Lord Cornbury began dressing in his wife's frocks and using her rouge and perfume. Thus turned out, he would stroll about the fort he commanded, prompting snickers and guffaws. He would occasionally venture out into the streets in his wife's attire. He was arrested once on Broadway by a patrolling watchman who mistook him for a prostitute, and Cornbury giggled at the watchman and pulled his ears. Cornbury sat for his official office portrait in a gorgeous dress with lace in his hair, holding a fan. When asked why he dressed like a woman for the portrait, he said he enjoyed resembling his cousin, Queen Anne.

The cross-dressing didn't bother the colonists, who were an open-minded, tolerant group. If anything, they found Cornbury delightful and amusing. What did bother people, however, was Cornbury's habit of borrowing money from just about everyone and never paying it back, as it was difficult to refuse the governor.

1708

Lord John Lovelace was appointed governor of New York on December 18. He was not among the former and future governors distracted by political tugs-of-war with the assembly, which increasingly controlled funds from the 1690s through the 1760s.

1709

Peter Schuyler was appointed president of the council on May 6. He was appointed to the same position twice more before 1720.

1719

Fraunces Tavern was built as an elegant residence for the prosperous Huguenot merchant Stephen de Lancey and his family (de Lancey gave the city its first clock). The tavern was purchased in 1762 by tavernkeeper Samuel Fraunces, a black West Indian, who established it as one of the most lauded dining and drinking places in the city. George Washington was a frequent guest and the tavern was a meeting place for revolutionaries, traders, and merchants. The Sons of Liberty met there to plan New York City's own Tea Party in 1774. Fraunces's young daughter Phoebe worked as Washington's housekeeper, and Fraunces served as a private in the Revolutionary Army. After being taken prisoner by the British, Fraunces cooked for an English general and stole food for hungry prisoners. While Fraunces was away at war, his wife and daughters ran the tavern; they frequently overheard valuable military information while serving their British customers drinks.

Congress voted Fraunces its gratitude and 200 pounds "in consequence of his generous advances and kindness to American prisoners and secret services," and the New York State legislature honored him as well. Fraunces provided the dinner when Washington met Sir Guy Carleton in 1783 to negotiate a peace treaty. In 1783 Washington chose the tavern as the site of his farewell address to the officers of the Continental Army.

After the war, when New York City was the nation's first capital, the tavern was rented to the new government to house the offices of the Departments of War, the Treasury, and Foreign Affairs.

Q: Why did Fraunces sell the tavern in 1789?

A: To serve as steward of Washington's presidential household. When the nation's capital was moved from New York to Philadelphia, Washington took his dear friend Fraunces with him—as well as Fraunces's entire family. Fraunces remained the president's steward until 1794, dying the following year.

In 1904 the Sons of the Revolution in the state of New York purchased the tavern and returned it to its previous colonial appearance. The second and third floors of the tavern comprise the Fraunces Tavern Museum, which opened in 1907.

Q: For whom is the tavern's Clinton Room named?

A: George Clinton, the first American-born governor of New York. He hosted a dinner party at the tavern in 1783 to celebrate the departure of the British from New York.

1732

Colonel William Cosby was appointed governor of New York. He viewed the colonies as offshoots of England and firmly enforced trade laws. To offset the power of the assembly, he freely granted patronage, land tracts, contracts, and judicial appointments.

1754

George Washington wrote his brother after his first experience in battle: "I heard the bullets whistle, and, believe me, there is something charming in the sound." When the letter was later published in England, King George II remarked, "He would not have found the sound so charming if he had been used to hearing more."

1756

The Seven Years' War began and the British made New York City their headquarters. The city prospered throughout the duration of the war.

1760

Cadwallader Colden was appointed president of the council on August 4. He was appointed to the same position four more times before 1775.

1765

The Stamp Act was imposed, which mandated the use of stamps on all legal and commercial documents. The colonies created a Stamp Act Congress that met in New York City, and popular revolutionary leaders created a network throughout the colonies and called themselves the Sons of Liberty.

The Sons of Liberty, comprised of small merchants and artisans, was committed to action. In October 1765 they led their first revolt, destroying carriages and sleighs that belonged to the enforcer of the Stamp Act, Lieutenant Governor Cadwallader Colden, and a grand estate rented by Major Thomas James, the man who had trained the guns of Fort George on the city.

1766

In May the Sons of Liberty rioted, destroying a new theater considered a blatant luxury in a time of public distress and upheaval.

1768

The elections of 1768 and 1769 underscored a division in the assembly between the landholding Livingstons and the merchant-class de Lanceys, men who gained the support of the Sons of Liberty by disparaging the Livingstons for supplying British troops. The presence of British troops in the city created competition for jobs, as the troops were permitted to seek work while off duty.

1772

Alexander Hamilton came to New York City to study at King's College, now known as Columbia University. He organized and became captain of a city artillery company at the onset of the American Revolution. He later served as lieutenant colonel on George Washington's staff. When he married Elizabeth Schuyler in 1780, he was connected to the state's most powerful families.

1773

On May 5 the king of England signed an act giving the East India Company a monopoly on the tea trade in the American colonies.

Free men are not to be governed by power and force."
JOHN THURMAN WARNING AN ENGLISH FRIEND IN 1775

1776

In July the Loyalists captured 1,300 of Washington's soldiers in what is now Brooklyn's Flatbush area during the American Revolution. The remainder of Washington's army retreated to Brooklyn Heights and escaped at nightfall by crossing the East River. In September Washington retreated to what is now Harlem, and two fires raged out of control in Manhattan due to a water shortage, destroying over 300 buildings (including one-third of the city's housing). The British occupying force then easily took control of Manhattan, Staten Island, Long Island, and southern Westchester County.

In November Washington tried to reclaim New York City but was defeated at Fort Washington and 2,800 Continental soldiers were captured. Washington withdrew from British-controlled New York City, to which Loyalists and slaves then fled, as it was considered safe, impregnable, and the best bet for freedom.

After the Declaration of Independence was signed on July 4, New Yorkers toppled a statue of George III. New York City remained under British control.

1776

Nathan Hale was captured out of uniform and arrested on September 21 for spying on the British in New York City. Hale, a Yale graduate, was made a captain for the Revolutionaries in 1776 under Major General William Heath. Hale traveled throughout Manhattan taking notes on various British fortifications.

Q: In what language did he write the notes?
A: Latin.

Hale was held at Provost Jail near City Hall Park and was deemed guilty of spying. He was hanged near Chambers Street.

Q: What were his purported last words?
A: "I only regret that I have but one life to lose for my country."

Photo by Eric Capstick

If you must give your life for your country, New York City is a good place in which to give it.

1777

Thirty-eight thousand Loyalists in New York City organized into a militia for the British, but this guard was never deployed against the American army.

1781

The Associated Loyalists created their own board of directors that included Benjamin Franklin's son William, who had been governor of New Jersey, and refugees from areas under revolutionary domain. For four months they conducted raids across the Hudson River and into Westchester and New England, but were forced to disband after one of their captains, Richard Lippincott, angered both British and Americans by hanging a prisoner, Joshua Luddy, whom he had agreed to swap.

ESCAPE FROM NEW YORK CITY

New York City was the primary location for detaining prisoners of war. They were held in public buildings, old warehouses, and on 11 notorious prison ships. Eleven hundred prisoners were kept on a ship called the *Jersey*; aside from the soldiers, many prisoners were simply privateers captured at sea. An estimated 11,000 revolutionaries died on prison ships in New York City.

1782

Sir Guy Carleton (1724-1808) became the British commander of New York City. The subsequent surrender of Lord Cornwallis at Yorktown meant that Carleton had to evacuate British troops and Loyalists and transfer power in New York City. Consequently, many Loyalists fled to Britain to escape punishment under the laws passed by the newly independent state. Black Loyalists who could not escape were re-enslaved. All New York City residents—as well as the entire southern district—were forced to pay a special tax to help cover the cost of the war.

1784

Alexander Hamilton, then a prominent lawyer, successfully defended British merchant Joshua Waddington in a case that helped establish the principle of judicial review. Hamilton also helped create the Bank of New York.

Hamilton was a strident advocate of a strong central government, and wrote at least 51 papers in the Federalist in favor of ratifying the Constitution in New York.

1785

Predating the Democratic Party was the Democratic organization Tammany Hall, which was formed around 1785.

1789

New York City became the nation's capital for one year.

1789

By May most congressmen had settled into New York and a daily routine. Congress generally met from 11:00 A.M. until 3:00 or 4:00 P.M. Members did not necessarily remain on the floor, particularly during routine business when quorum requirements were ignored. Senator Richard Lee of Virginia chose to live "all the way in Greenwich Village," which was considered out of town.

1789

When the new federal government assembled, Alexander Hamilton became its first secretary of the treasury and supported policies favorable to business in New York City. These policies helped establish New York City as a financial center.

Democratic Republicans, a political coalition that formed against the ideals of Alexander Hamilton, found support from former Governor George Clinton, wealthy landowner Robert Livingston, and farmers upstate. The party grew in popularity by 1800 and helped elect Thomas Jefferson.

1796

Chief Justice John Jay was elected governor of New York.

1804

Alexander Hamilton died in a duel with Aaron Burr in Weehauken, New Jersey, on July 11. Hamilton had helped to thwart Burr's run for presidency in 1800 and his run for governor of New York in 1804.

Meetings consisting of some half a dozen scurvy pothouse politicians.
WASHINGTON IRVING, IN KNICKERBOCKER'S *A HISTORY OF NEW YORK, IV,* IN 1901

1814

Joseph Bonaparte bought extensive acreage in New York State for his brother, the emperor Napoleon. A few years later,

Napoleon's nephew, Joseph, built several sprawling houses in New York City to hold his uncle's art collection and to serve as a possible refuge for Napoleon.

In politics, absurdity is not an impediment.

The great difficulty with politics is that there are no established principles.

Two from Napoleon Bonaparte

1820

The Common Council elected the mayor of New York City for the first time. Stephen Allen was elected.

1825

Martin Van Buren helped establish the Democratic Party in New York City. It was challenged by the Workingmen's Party in the 1820s and 1830s, and then by the Whig Party after 1834.

1830

Mayoral membership in the Common Council was withdrawn to give the mayor power to veto council decisions.

The politicians of New York are not so fastidious as some gentle are, as to disclosing the principles on which they act. They boldly preach what they practice. . . . If they are defeated, they expect to retire from office. If they are successful, they claim, as a matter of right, the advantages of success. They see nothing wrong in the rule that to the victor belong the spoils of the enemy.

Senator William L. Marcy, defending Jackson's appointment of Martin Van Buren as minister to Great Britain in 1831

1834

The first direct mayoral elections were held in New York City. Democrat Cornelius Van Wyck Lawrence defeated Gulian C. Verplanck by 181 votes.

1838

Frederick Douglass, a Baltimore slave, escaped to NYC and became an abolitionist. He was a remarkably eloquent speaker who published an abolitionist newspaper called the *North Star*. He helped organize black regiments during the Civil War and devoted his entire life to civil rights and equality for blacks and women.

1844

President John Tyler married Julia Gardiner at the Church of the Ascension at 10th Street and Fifth Avenue. The wedding ceremony was held in secret for two reasons: Gardiner's father, David, was a close friend of Tyler's and had recently been killed when a cannon exploded onboard the warship *Princeton*. President Tyler had been inspecting the vessel along with Gardiner and narrowly escaped with his life. Because of this recent death in the family, the marriage wasn't publicized. Another reason for the secrecy was the fact that the president, a widower with seven children, was 54 years old and Julia Gardiner was 24. Tyler, however, fathered seven more children with Julia and lived to be 72 years old.

1849

The mayoral term was extended to two years. Most mayors in the nineteenth century were businessmen.

> *There is no foundation in reason or expediency, for the*
> *absolute and slavish subjection of the wife to the husband,*
> *which forms the foundation of the present legal relations. Were*
> *women, in point of fact, the abject thing which the law, in the-*
> *ory, considers her to be when married, she would not be worthy*
> *of the companionship of man.*
>
> LUCRETIA MOTT IN 1849

> *Men . . . show us great respect where form is concerned…but at*
> *the same time they are defrauding us of our just rights by*
> *crowding us out of every lucrative employment, and subjecting*
> *us to virtual slavery.*
>
> SUFFRAGIST AMELIA BLOOMER IN 1851

Q: What piece of clothing is Amelia Bloomer equated with?
A: She was a fashion innovator who wore pants under her dress. The pants were dubbed "bloomers" after her last name.

1852

The nickname for New York City's politicians in the notorious Common Council was "The Forty Thieves."

1854

Theodore Roosevelt's parents moved to 28 East 20th Street. They relocated to West 57th Street in 1873.

1862

During the Civil War a number of racial incidents plagued the city. In the summer of 1862 a group of Irishmen attempted to burn down a Brooklyn tobacco factory where black women and children were working.

A FINE IRISH TRADITION

The ward heelers of Tammany Hall used to create bonfires in the city streets to get out the vote. The bonfires were rallies, and the ritual was inherited from the Irish; the Irish used to mark special occasions with bonfires across the hills as a way to notify citizens to come out and celebrate or to riot

Tammany Hall was dominated by Irishmen after the 1840s. Election eves in every part of the city, from the Lower East Side to Harlem to Little Italy, were marked by several dozen bonfires in each neighborhood. Bar owners would provide politician-sponsored buffets on election eves, and the atmosphere in general was jubilant. The bonfire tradition faded in 1924.

1863

Irish longshoremen went on strike in June and federal troops were summoned to protect black strikebreakers.

Shortly thereafter, President Lincoln delivered the Emancipation Proclamation and city politicians fueled the fears of Irish workers concerned about job competition with black workers. The city's first draft lottery was then conducted on July

11 and the second was slated for July 13. However, on July 12 residents discussed the fact that there was a clause in the federal act that allowed exemption for those who could pay a $300 fee. Shortly after dawn on the thirteenth, workers attacked several police officers and smashed portions of a draft office. The draft riots swept through most quarters of the city and lasted for three days; they were the bloodiest riots in the history of the country. Leaders of the Republican Party were attacked along with their property, the Brooks Brothers store was ransacked, black residents and homes were attacked, and the Colored Orphan Asylum was set on fire. Five regiments of the Union Army were rushed north from Gettysburg, Pennsylvania, to quell the riots, and 105 people died. Boss Tweed and the Democrats of Tammany Hall conducted a draft later in August, which was carried out peacefully.

1863

William Marcy "Boss" Tweed was named chairman of the Democratic General Committee of New York County and was chosen to lead the general committee of Tammany Hall. He stood six feet tall and weighed nearly 300 pounds. Tweed then formed a smaller executive committee that wielded much more power than the general committee, and he appointed himself deputy street commissioner. He bought a controlling interest in the New York Printing Company, which became the city's official printer, and Tweed profited tremendously as a result. He also bought the Manufacturing Stationers' Company and sold supplies to the city at grossly inflated prices, and used his law practice to extort money disguised as legal fees for services rendered. By the late 1860s, Tweed was one of the city's largest landowners. Before finally being exposed, expelled, and put on trial in 1873, Tweed was elected to the state senate in 1867 and again in 1872. It's been estimated—but never proven—that Boss Tweed and his associates illegally siphoned between $30 and $200 million from the city.

As long as I count the votes what are you going to do about it? Say.

The way to have power is to take it.

You can't get anything without paying for it.
THREE FROM WILLIAM MARCY TWEED,
WHILE A NEW YORK STATE SENATOR

1863

Oswald Ottendorfer, owner of the German newspaper *Staats-Zeitung,* led the city's German Democrats in opposition to Tammany Hall. His German Democratic Union Party helped elect Mayor Charles Godfrey Gunther in 1863; he continued to fight Tammany Hall and Boss Tweed until 1874.

1865

Q: Which future president, then 6 years old, stood in the second-story window of his parents' home in Gramercy Park to watch Abraham Lincoln's funeral procession pass?
A: Theodore Roosevelt.

Q: What was Theodore Roosevelt's childhood nickname?
A: Teedie.

Q: How did Roosevelts end up in the New World?
A: Theodore Roosevelt's ancestor, Claus Van Rosenvelt, came to New York City from Holland in the 1640s.

Far better it is to dare mighty things, to win glorious triumphs, even though checkered by failure, than to take rank with those poor spirits who neither enjoy much nor suffer much, because they live in the gray twilight that knows not victory nor defeat.

The most successful politician is he who says what everybody is thinking most often and in the loudest voice.
TWO FROM THEODORE ROOSEVELT

1866

From 1866 to 1871 the corrupt Common Council ring controlled Tammany Hall, the municipal government, the county government, the judicial system, the governorship, and the Board of Audit, which supervised all city and county expenditures after its formation by the charter of 1870—a Boss Tweed-supported reform document that gave the city home rule.

1867

Prizefighter and Democratic politician John Morrissey opposed the Anti-Gambling Society in their efforts to raid gambling houses, underscoring the strong link between crime and local politics.

1868

The Democratic National Convention was held at the new Tammany Hall on 14th Street near Third Avenue. Governor Horatio Seymour was nominated for the presidency and lost to Ulysses S. Grant.

Grover Cleveland's lively 1884 presidential rally in Union Square was a portent of good things to come.

1870

The New York City Women's Suffrage Association was formed by physician Clemence Lozier, writer Lillie Devereux Blake, and Charlotte Wilbour.

1873

Boss Tweed is convicted after years of corrupt leadership in Tammany Hall.

1880

The city's first Irish Catholic mayor, businessman William R. Grace, was elected with the help of Tammany Hall.

1892

The Reverend Dr. Charles H. Parkhurst, preaching at his Madison Square Presbyterian Church, declared war on Tammany Hall's corrupt politicians. He accused the police department of corruption, and the *World* carried large portions of his sermon the next day.

> *There is not a form under which the Devil disguises himself that so perplexes us in our efforts, or so bewilders us in the devising of our schemes, as the polluted harpies that, under the pretense of governing this city, are feeding day and night on its quivering vitals. They are a lying, perjured, rum-soaked, and libidinous lot.*
>
> REV. CHARLES H. PARKHURST

Parkhurst needed solid evidence to back up his scathing sermon, and contacted David J. Whitney, one of the founders of the Society for the Prevention of Crime. Whitney put him in touch with Charles W. Gardner, a freelance private detective who offered to show Parkhurst the seamier side of the city for six dollars a night and expenses.

> *Take the doctor around, but be careful and not shock him too much, as it might sicken him for everything for all his life.*
>
> DAVID J. WHITNEY TO CHARLES W. GARDNER

Parkhurst had to roam the city undercover, as the newspapers had published sketches of him. He slicked back his hair and wore loud, cheap clothing. Gardner disguised Parkhurst, because Parkhurst's original disguise carried "the very aroma of the pulpit.

> *Dr. Parkhurst was a very hard man to satisfy. "Show me something worse!" was his constant cry. He really went at his slumming work as if his heart was in his tour.*
> CHARLES W. GARDNER, IN *THE DOCTOR AND THE DEVIL,*
> HIS 1894 BOOK DESCRIBING HIS UNDERCOVER
> ADVENTURES WITH DR. PARKHURST

Parkhurst's campaigns contributed to the election of William L. Strong as a reform mayor in 1894 and the appointment of Theodore Roosevelt as chairman of the Police Board in 1895.

Parkhurst wrote two books himself: *Our Fight with Tammany* in 1895 and *My Forty Years in New York* in 1923. He lived at 133 East 35th Street.

1892

Latin Americans first became active in political organizations such as the Caribe Democrat Club, the Hispanic-American Democrat Club, the Puerto Rican and Hispanic League, and the Federation of Puerto Rican Democratic Clubs.

1895

Political bosses such as Big Tim Sullivan and John Y. McKane sponsored boxing matches in the city and used their political influence to ensure police cooperation, since boxing was saddled with severe legal restraints in the 1890s.

1896

Tammany Hall politician Richard Crocker raced thoroughbred horses and other city politicians in the 1890s owned racetracks. Both wealthy horse owners and local politicians wanted to see the legalization of "on-track" betting and the banning of "off-track" betting, which they felt would lower attendance at the racetrack and sully the sport's image.

1898

The outer boroughs of Manhattan were consolidated into New York City.

1899

The Chinese Exclusion acts passed by the U.S. Congress barred Chinese immigrants from naturalization. The Chinese were the first ethnic group to be excluded from the U.S.

1900

Henry Goldfoggle, the first Jewish congressman to represent New York, was elected.

1902

Charles F. Murphy became the leader of Tammany Hall until his death in 1924. Democratic politics during these years was almost exclusively dominated by the Irish in the city.

1903

George Brinton McClellan Jr. was persuaded to accept the Democratic mayoral nomination by Charles F. Murphy, the new boss of Tammany Hall, who wanted to oust the incumbent, Seth Low. McClellan was elected by a wide majority.

Q: Who was McClellan's father?
A: Civil War General George McClellan.

1905

The mayoral term was extended to four years. George B. McClellan was reelected as mayor of the city after a vicious fight with political rival and newspaper magnate William Randolph Hearst. McClellan's government was efficient and honest; he expanded the city's water supply from the Catskills and attempted to expand the subway system. McClellan retired from politics after he quarreled with Murphy over patronage and Murphy's support of Hearst in the governor's race of 1906.

He then became a professor of economic history at Princeton and a fairly well-known writer.

1910

Chinese women were barred from joining their husbands in the U.S., which created an acute imbalance between the sexes. There were 40 Chinese boys to every 15 Chinese girls in New York City in 1910. By 1940 there were nine boys for every girl.

1913

The largest suffrage parades in the country were held in New York City on Fifth Avenue, complete with elegant banners, viewing stands for local politicians, and military-style organization.

> *Even the woman movement we have called feminism has not succeeded by and large in giving women any control over men. It has only changed the distribution of women...removing vast numbers of women from the class supported by men to the class working for them.*
> ELSIE CLEWS PARSONS IN 1916

1917

Edward Johnson, a Republican from Harlem's 19th District, became the first black elected to the state legislature.

1918

During World War I German language courses were canceled in NYC's public schools, as were German works at the Met.

Q: Hamburgers were renamed as a result of the war. To what?
A: Liberty Sandwiches.

Q; What was sauerkraut called during the war?
A: Liberty Cabbage.

1918

Q: What was the nickname for the all-black 369th Regiment in World War I?
A: The Harlem Hellfighters.

Q: What was their military distinction?
A: They were awarded the Croix de Guerre by the French.

1920

Prohibition—the Eighteenth Amendment—went into effect across the country, rendering the sale, consumption, transport, and manufacturing of all alcoholic beverages illegal. Fiorello La Guardia, a congressman at the time, denounced the amendment as unenforceable, discriminatory toward immigrants and workers, and likely to breed contempt for the law. New York City became a leading site for illegal alcohol, rumrunners or bootleggers, speakeasies, and blind pigs.

1920

Voting rights for women were ensured by the passage of the Nineteenth Amendment to the U.S. Constitution. Tammany Hall had backed local suffrage groups in New York City. The combination of Tammany Hall's political clout, the $150,000 spent in 1916 alone by suffragist organizations on the movement, and World War I led to the successful passage of the amendment.

1922

The Democratic Union of Women was created by women in Manhattan to oppose the gubernatorial candidacy of William Randolph Hearst, and to support Alfred E. Smith instead. The union's leaders included Eleanor Roosevelt, Belle Moscowitz, Emily Newell Blair, Francis Perkins, and Caroline O'Day. After the success of its first campaign, the organization created a series of workshops aimed at increasing political awareness among women. The organization was absorbed by the women's division of the Democratic National Committee in 1932.

1932

The city's black vote shifted from Republican to Democrat for the first time in a presidential election. The following year, the city's black voters shifted from Republican to Democrat for the first time in a mayoral race, and in 1934 the shift was again evident in the governor's race.

A politician will do anything to keep his job—even become a patriot.

WILLIAM RANDOLPH HEARST IN 1933

1933

Fiorello H. La Guardia, the son of a Jewish Austrian mother and an agnostic Italian father, was elected mayor of New York City. He set the standards for the modern mayoralty by remaining independent of political bosses and by actively seeking and controlling his own publicity. He served three terms as a Republican with strong backing from Italian and Jewish voters; this signaled a decline in the strength of the forcefully Democratic Irish.

La Guardia persuaded President Roosevelt to grant billions in funds to the city for the construction of bridges, schools, airports, hospitals, health centers, public housing, parks, highways, tunnels, reservoirs, and sewers. He unified the city's transit system and provided impassioned leadership. A newspaper wrote that his popularity was attributed to "lusty mugging and robust histrionics." The long-term effect of his policies, however, left the city plagued with debt and a rapidly expanding bureaucracy.

La Guardia fought against organized crime throughout the 1930s and was successful in banning Frank Costello's slot machines in the city.

Q: During a newspaper strike in 1942, La Guardia gave a dramatic reading of which comic strip over the radio?
A: Dick Tracy.

Every time the city built a school, a politician went into the real estate business.

Though I have been in politics for well over forty years, I loathe the professional politician. I have never been a regular. I have fought political machines and party politics at every opportunity.
TWO FROM FIORELLO LA GUARDIA IN 1948

1935

Supreme Court Justice Thurgood Marshall, originally from Baltimore, moved to New York City at the age of 27 to work for the NAACP (National Association for the Advancement of Colored People) at 69 Fifth Avenue. He and other NAACP leaders planned the lawsuit that led to the overturning of racial segregation in public schools (Brown v. Board of Education in 1954). He lived in New York City from 1935 to 1965.

Q: Which president nominated Marshall to the U.S. Court of Appeals for the Second Circuit?
A: President John F. Kennedy in 1961.

Q: Which president named Marshall as solicitor general?
A: President Lyndon B. Johnson in 1965.

1938

There were 38,000 Communist Party members in New York, and 80,000 members across the nation.

Q: What percentage of the 38,000 lived in New York City?
A: 50%.

Political power is merely the organized power of one class to oppress another.
KARL MARX AND FRIEDRICH ENGELS,
IN *THE COMMUNIST MANIFESTO* (1848)

Sooner or later all politicians die of swallowing their own lies.
CLARE BOOTHE LUCE IN 1940

1941

Adam Clayton Powell Jr. won a seat on the City Council. He won a seat in Congress as a Democrat three years later.

1944

Organized crime leaders such as Frank Costello (who used the wealth he accrued through a vast slot machine network in Louisiana to rig judicial appointments) and Joe Adonis (who controlled the drug trade and the Brooklyn docks), used their ill-gained wealth to dominate Tammany Hall and to enter political races themselves. For this reason, the 1940s marked the closest fusion of politics and crime.

1945

Mayor Fiorello La Guardia signed a law renaming Sixth Avenue "Avenue of the Americas" on October 2. At the hearing a citizen protested, claiming the name was "an awful mouthful." The name was chosen to persuade South American countries doing business in New York City at the time to relocate their headquarters and consular offices to the avenue. Several countries did agree to relocate as a result.

Q: In which decade were medallions with the names and flags of Latin-American countries posted on lampposts along the avenue?
A: The 1960s.

1945

Former Judge and Brooklyn District Attorney William O'Dwyer won the mayoral election. His administration was formed while Tammany Hall was influenced by organized-crime titan Frank Costello and it was marked by graft and corruption. O'Dwyer prosecuted the members of Murder Incorporated, an organized crime family run by gangster "Lucky" Luciano, but was forced to resign because of his links to organized crime. He resigned in the first year of his second term and became an ambassador.

Q: To which country did O'Dwyer become an ambassador?
A: Mexico.

1949

Carmine DeSapio became the first non-Irish leader of Tammany Hall since William "Boss" Tweed. La Guardia supporters initiated civil service reforms to diminish the Democrats' power of patronage. Since Tammany Hall was indifferent to New Deal policies, La Guardia was able to reap large shares of federal support.

1951

Vincent R. Impellitteri succeeded O'Dwyer as acting mayor, and in a special election held in 1951, he failed to win the support of the Democratic organization because he was perceived as incompetent.

1952

The long-standing ties between organized crime and the city's political machine were severed because district leaders, beginning in 1952, were chosen by direct election.

1953

Robert F. Wagner, the borough president of Manhattan, won the mayoral election, which strengthened the Democratic organization in the city.

1957

Wagner was reelected. During his terms he negotiated with municipal unions, worked with Robert Moses to initiate federally funded urban renewal and public housing programs, and recognized the significance of the black voter.

1960

Protest leader, politician, and frequent state senate candidate Al Sharpton was ordained. Born Alfred Charles Sharpton Jr. in Brooklyn in 1954, Sharpton toured at the age of four as a "wonder boy preacher." After being ordained, he preached at the World's Fair and toured with gospel singer Mahalia Jackson. In 1969 he was appointed youth director of Jesse Jackson's

"Operation Breadbasket," and spent two years leading boycotts and demonstrations to compel businesses to employ black workers. In 1971 he formed the National Youth Movement.

Q: Which soul singer did Sharpton work for as a manager from 1973 to 1981?
A: James Brown.

1961

Reforms to the city charter granted mayors the authority to prepare the capital budget, which had been previously prepared by the City Planning Commission. Mayors were also granted the authority to alter the operating budget and to reorganize municipal offices, authority that was formerly shared with the Board of Estimates.

1961

Robert F. Wagner was reelected to a third (and last) term as mayor of New York City.

1965

Q: Who was assassinated in New York City on February 21, 1965?
A: Malcolm X, at the Audubon Ballroom located at West 165th Street and Broadway.

Q: Why did he change his last name to "X" from Little?
A: To represent the lost African name of his ancestors.

Malcolm X's father, a minister, was killed by a group of white men when Malcolm X was six years old; he was then raised by white foster families. He moved to 23-11 97th Street in Queens' East Elmhurst district in 1954 at the age of 29 and lived there until his death. On Valentine's Day in 1965, Malcolm X's house was firebombed while he and his family were at home; a week later, he was shot while giving a speech. *The Autobiography of Malcolm X,* cowritten with Alex Haley, was published in 1965.

1965

Chinese families in the city were reunited after the Immigration Act of 1965 abolished restrictions on immigration according to race. New York City became a popular destination for Chinese immigrants. Garment factories supported much of Chinatown's economy.

1965

John Lindsay was elected mayor with 43.3 percent of the vote and the support of the Republicans, defeating Conservative Party candidate William F. Buckley Jr. and Democrat Abraham Beame. Buckley received 13 percent of the vote. There were 27,000 registered Conservatives in New York City, representing 0.8 percent of all registered voters.

Lindsay merged various city departments into ten streamlined umbrella agencies and grappled with an extended transit strike that fostered public resentment. He decentralized the school system and formed community school districts. His deficit financing is thought to be a primary cause of a fiscal crisis in 1975.

1968

Q: How did Shirley B. Chisholm of Brooklyn ensure a place in history?

A: In 1968 she was the first black woman to be elected to the U.S. Congress.

1969

Lindsay was narrowly reelected as mayor. The 1969 mayoral elections were significant in the city's history for various reasons: the election marked the decline of the political club and placed emphasis on the individual candidate instead, and television and political consultants entered the political process, playing a significant role in determining public opinion and perception.

1970

Herman Bandillo was elected the first Puerto Rican congressman.

1970

U.S. Congress passed the Racketeer Influenced and Corrupt Organizations laws (RICO) as part of the Organized Crime Control Act of 1970. The laws severely hampered organized crime in the city, as they made it easier for the government to prove criminal conspiracies and to prosecute organizations instead of individuals. Prosecutors were allowed to seize the assets of criminal organizations and could impose stiffer penalties on those convicted.

1972

After FBI Director J. Edgar Hoover's death in 1972, the FBI allied itself more closely with the Drug Enforcement Agency (DEA). Local police in turn devoted more resources to fighting organized crime in the city.

1973

Democrat Abraham Beame was elected as New York City's first Jewish mayor. The city faced a large deficit budget in the early 1970s that was worsened by increased borrowing.

1977

Edward Koch was elected mayor; he ran against Mario Cuomo and developed a conservative Democratic base by advocating fiscal discipline and responsibility, denouncing public unions, and favoring the death penalty. He was reelected in 1981 and 1985.

Q: What was Koch's signature phrase?
A: "How'm I doing?"

1981

Koch was reelected as mayor. He redefined the city's Democratic base as more conservative.

Q: What bestseller did Koch pen?
A: *Mayor,* which appeared on the bestseller list in 1984.

1982

Mario Cuomo ran against Ed Koch in the Democratic primary for the governorship and won. He defeated Republican businessman Lewis Lehrman in the general election. He was reelected as governor again in 1986 and 1990 and was noted for his eloquence, independent thinking, and effectiveness as a negotiator and budget planner.

1984

Geraldine Ferraro became the first woman nominated for national office by a major party when Democratic presidential nominee Walter Mondale chose her as his vice-presidential candidate.

1985

Koch was reelected yet again. Corruption in various city agencies was brought to light by the U.S. Attorney during Koch's third term, which hampered his bid as Democratic candidate for mayor in 1989.

Q: Who was the corruption-fighting U.S. Attorney?
A: Rudolph W. Giuliani.

I don't think there is anybody worse than a public official who sells his office and corrupts others—except maybe a murderer.
THEN U.S. ATTORNEY RUDOLPH GIULIANI, ALLUDING TO THE CORRUP-
TION IN MAYOR KOCH'S ADMINISTRATION IN 1987

1989

Democrat David Dinkins was elected mayor, narrowly defeating Rudolph Giuliani and making his mark in history as the city's first black mayor. His term was marred by racial and ethnic tensions across the city: black Flatbush residents in Brooklyn who boycotted a Korean grocer, an outbreak of violence between Hasidic and black residents in Brooklyn's Crown Heights, tensions between Dominicans and police in Manhattan's Washington Heights, and a well-publicized dispute between gay activists and the sponsors of the St. Patrick's Day Parade.

1989

There were 470 employees at the city's Bureau of Pest Control. After 1990 there were only 190.

1993

Rudolph Giuliani defeated David Dinkins to become the city's first Republican mayor in 28 years. The mayor of New York City oversaw a $32 billion enterprise.

Q: Where was Giuliani born?
A: Brooklyn.

Built in 1803, City Hall is the current home of "Hizzoner" Mayor Rudolph Giuliani.

1994

New York City Council members collectively ran up $66,572 in cellular phone calls. One City Council member from Brooklyn made 25 calls to Israel on a cell phone. The highest cell-phone call charges racked up by a single City Council member was $6,678.

Q: What is the average annual wage for a New York State government worker?
A: $38,200.

1994

The U.S. Senate average for taxpayer-funded mailings per constituent address is 1.7 cents. Senator Moynihan of New York spent 8.7 cents per constituent address in the first half of 1994.

1995

Seventy-five percent of state voters favored the death penalty.

1996

Councilman Charles Millard's toll-free number for residents of the Upper East Side received at least one complaint of excessive O.J Simpson media coverage. Councilman Millard received over 1,000 calls on his toll-free number in the mid-1990s.

MANHATTAN CONTRIBUTIONS

Q: Which zip code in Manhattan accounts for more federal and local campaign contributions than any other zip code in the United States?
A: 10021.

Q: Which part of Manhattan is covered by the 10021 zip code?
A: East 60s and 70s.

An average of $6.59 million is contributed by residents for campaign funds in federal elections.

1997

Q: What is the percentage voter of turnout in Chinatown?
A: 40%.

If my ancestors had known that Ellis Island was in New Jersey, they might have stayed in Italy.
MAYOR RUDOLPH GIULIANI, ON THE ONGOING
FEUD OVER WHICH STATE OWNS ELLIS ISLAND

Photo by Eric Capstick

Panhandling is illegal in NYC, but who's to say someone can't entertain the crowds for a donation?

CHAPTER 4

Crime & Punishment

New York City is the most exciting place in the world to live. There are so many ways to die there.

COMEDIAN DENIS LEARY

New York: Where everyone mutinies but no one deserts.

HARRY HERSHFIELD

Along with a diverse immigrant population and thriving business, media, education, arts, sports, literary, legal, medical, and architectural communities, New York City has also had a lion's share of racketeers, illegal drugs, prostitution, petty thievery, murder, con artists, organized crime figures, child gangs, child-labor abuse, hooligans, white-collar criminals, corrupt police and politicians, and general garden-variety depravity.

The growth of the city's population and ecomonic status was paralleled by the increase of crime in the city in the 1700s; when the economy faltered in the 1730s and 1760s and the population increased, the number of thefts and assaults rose. The city's busy ports attracted sailors and prostitutes, and riots were accepted as a natural form of political discontentment. Theft was especially difficult to control in the eighteenth century.

During the first half of the 1800s, immigrants were often targeted by con artists. Irish gang members favored saloons and were often charged with public drunkenness and more serious crimes. Economic inequities naturally led to ethnic and racial tension, and riots grew common and dangerous, resulting in vicious assaults and extensive property damage. During the second half of the century, political machines were able to rein in many of the potential rioters by improving social and economic policy; also, many residents had adapted by then to the unique stresses of the crowded city. Prostitution and gambling, however, were mainstays.

At the turn of the century, the organized criminal operations run by the Irish were replaced with Jewish and Italian gangs. Organized crime was centered around the distribution of liquor during the Prohibition, but organized crime began to branch out into gambling, narcotics, and waterfront racketeering as well.

New York City didn't experience a severe increase in violent crime until the 1960s. Along with other American cities at the time, New York City's crime rate—especially violent crime—continued to increase throughout the 1960s, 1970s, and well into the 1980s. Although other cities had proportionately more crime, New York became the poster city for urban violence because of its size and media visibility.

Mayor Giuliani was elected in 1993 largely as the result of his vocal crime-fighting platform. He greatly increased the police force, defined "quality of life" crimes (graffiti, loud radios, public urination, panhandling, low-level drug dealing, prostitution), and brought back the beat policeman, particularly in housing developments. By 1995, New York City was no longer on the list of the 25 cities with the highest homicide rates in the country. Along with the increased police force, however, came the increase in citizen complaints of police harassment and police brutality. By the 1990s, the organized crime torch seemed to have been passed to other ethnic groups in the city such as the Russians, Jamaicans, Dominicans, and the Chinese.

1609

Marauding pirates posed an occasional problem for Indians in the pre-European era.

1609

The first recorded homicide in New York City occurred on September 6, two days after Henry Hudson's crewmen from the *Half Moon* first stepped ashore. The victim was Englishman John Colman, Hudson's shipmate. Colman received a fatal arrow in the throat when a fight broke out between 26 Indian braves and four seamen from the *Half Moon,* including Colman. He was buried on Sandy Hook and the grave site was called Colman's Point.

1618

Residents in the city were self-policing, with bands of settlers joining forces to break up physical fights, retrieve stolen property, and guard homes.

1626

A city council imposed fines for wrongdoing but never administered corporal punishment. Any resident warranting corporal punishment was sent to Holland.

1632

Governor-General Van Twiller, noted for his monstrous thirst for alcohol, invited his staff to a drinking contest. After consuming a keg of brandy, a fight broke out between staff members. To break it up, the governor-general fired off a cannon in the middle of the compound. Unfortunately, a spark landed on a nearby thatched roof, and the besotted crew could only stand gaping as the structure burned to the ground.

1638

Governor General Kieft imposed severe penalties for "adulterous intercourse with heathens, blacks, or other persons [as well as] mutiny, theft, false testimony, slanderous language and other irregularities."

1640

Smuggling was the salient, chronic problem in the New World, and efforts to curb it were fruitless.

1641

New York City's first public hanging occured in Hanover Square. Some Dutch West India Company slaves had murdered another slave, Jan Premero, and authorities arrested nine suspects, threatening to torture the suspects unless they revealed who had been the killer. All nine suspects confessed, figuring that the company wouldn't want to lose nine valuable pieces of property. Governor Willem Kieft ordered them to draw straws to determine which one should be hanged, and an enormous man named Manuel Gerrit lost. The entire town and some rubbernecking Indians turned out to see the spectacle of the hanging. Two ropes were placed around Gerrit's neck and a ladder was pulled away; as Gerrit plunged to his death, the ropes broke and Gerrit writhed in pain on the ground. The scene had been too awful for the onlookers, and many people began to sob and begged Kieft to set Gerrit free. Gerrit was turned loose and told to stay out of trouble. Three years later, he was one of 11 black men emancipated in recognition of their service to the company. Gerrit became one of the earliest landowners in Greenwich Village.

1644

There was one sheriff in New Amsterdam.

1645

The period between 1645 and 1657 marked particularly strident Indian wars; the documentation of the era (the papers of the governor-general) was lost in a shipwreck.

1645

Visitors to the New World noticed Dutch and English "lasses" soliciting men in the Battery area.

GOING MOBILE IN THE WORLD'S OLDEST TRADE

A new trend in prostitution or "streetwalking" in New York City is for prostitutes to rent vans or limousines and ply their trade from the vehicle in a parking lot. The parking lot attendant receives $7 for the hourly rate in addition to $3 for looking the other way. This saves the cost of a hotel room, and for a "customer," it eliminates the risk of vehicle impoundment when arrested for visiting a prostitute. There used to be over 400 prostitutes walking down 11th Avenue each evening between 23rd and 44th Streets until Mayor Giuliani took aim at "quality of life" crimes in 1993. When a prostitute is arrested, the vehicle rental company has to pay the fine for the impounded van or car, which is usually not a problem for the company if it generates a lot of income from the tacit arrangement.

1646

Public order was maintained in New Amsterdam by a schout fiscal, or sheriff attorney, who administered the rules set by the Dutch West India Company. A burgher guard looked out for Indians during times of unrest, and when Indian raids were imminent, a paid nighttime foot patrol consisting of a captain and eight men armed only with rattles alerted residents of impending raids. The patrol also controlled rowdy sailors, drunkards, prostitutes, and watched for fires.

1648

Fires were a serious problem in the colony. Four fire wardens were appointed by Governor Stuyvesant to inspect the chimneys on thatched-roof homes. Anyone with a dirty chimney was fined three gilders.

1652

The city was proclaimed off-limits by law to hunters and to anyone desiring to fire a gun. The daily firing of guns had prompted an outpouring of complaints by residents, and punishment for breaking the law was forfeiture of the gun and a fine set at the discretion of a judge.

Law also required drivers of wagons, carts, and sleighs to walk within the city, leading their horses (with the exception of Broadway, where they could gallop, run, and ride their vehicles). Fines were "two pounds Flemish" the first time, double the second time, and arbitrarily set thereafter.

1659

Although it was a rare sight, the most ominous warning to wrongdoers in the colony was the tarred corpse occasionally left hanging in public, known to residents as the "field bishop."

1661

The Blue Dove Tavern was the favorite haunt of local "rattle watchers," unofficial police who rattled because they carried a wooden, hinged-clapper device for sounding an alarm. The patrol consisted of nine men who broke up brawls in taverns, arrested robbers, tended to disorderly (read: drunk) sailors, and maintained public order.

The dependable New York policeman of the late 1600s. His halberd probably wouldn't hold up to the semi-automatics of today.

1684

A night watch of 45 men patrolled the city from 1684 through 1689 and rendered the city the safest in the colonies.

NYPD BLUE

- 3.35% of New York City police reside in Manhattan.
- 9.21% reside in the Bronx.
- 17.41% reside in Queens.
- 14 of New York City's police officers speak Hindi.
- New York City spends $23,000 per cadet on police training.
- There are approximately 38,400 police officers in New York City, with 24,000 of them carrying semiautomatic 9 mm. guns.
- The current police force is the largest in the history of the city.
- There are 37 members on an NYPD team created specifically to persuade the homeless to move to shelters.
- There are 27 police in New York City's movie and television police unit.
- There are 2,255 uniformed officers on the Housing Police force.
- The police chief's salary in 1997 was $107,544. In 1985 it was $80,000.
- An average of 178,000 NYC police officers respond to 911 domestic abuse calls.
- There are 75 police precincts in New York City.
- New York City police recruits spend 8 days in firearms training at the academy. 3 additional days of training are required of New York City police when switching over to a 9 mm gun.

Q: How many times per year must a New York City police recruit qualify by scoring 80% on a target-shooting test?
A: Twice.

Q: Compared with a Los Angeles recruit?
A: 6.

Q: Per shooting incident, what is the average number of bullets fired by NYC police officers armed with 9 mm guns?
A: 4.08.

Q: Compared with police officers still armed with revolvers?
A: 2.04.

1695

City ordinance directed residents to sweep the streets in front of their homes or risk a fine.

1697

British patterns of social conduct often clashed with Dutch patterns, often creating friction and sparking altercations. Dr. Benjamin Bullivant, a Boston physician and former attorney general of Massachusetts, recounted his impression of New York in his journal, writing [sic]: "The Dutch seeme not very strict in Keepeing the Sabath, you should see some shelling peas at theyr doors children playing at theyr usuall games in the streetes & ye taverns filled."

1729

The unethical conduct of some lawyers and the unabashed greed of officers of the Court of Chancery led to the establishment of the first Committee on Grievances in the Practice of Law in New York. Many complaints were lodged, but the committee was mostly ineffective.

1734

After it was clear that a volunteer police force wasn't working due to a lack of service by residents, the volunteer force was replaced by a paid force of three to a dozen men who were standing guard over a city of 10,000.

1750

Prostitution was contained to certain key areas such as the Trinity Church area, the area next to St. Paul's Church, and City Hall Park. Prostitution was tied into the number of sailors brought to the city through maritime trade, and was often prosecuted under the guise of "keeping a disorderly house."

1755

Thefts and assaults rose as the city grew more crowded, and the legal system had particular difficulty controlling theft. Riots were simply perceived as expressions of political discontent.

1760

Crime rose with the economic fluctuations of the 1760s, particularly thefts and assaults due to overcrowding and an increase in maritime trade and the number of sailors in the city. Prostitution also rose in the years between 1760 to the early 1800s. Riots were commonplace and mostly tolerated as political expression.

CURBSIDE THIEVERY

An average of 110,000 people are arrested annually by the sanitation police for stealing newspapers and corrugated cardboard from curbs in the city.

1776

When the British army occupied New York City it policed the city's residents, but many residents continued to maintain their own voluntary police force throughout the British occupation.

1790

The first street gangs in the city were formed by single, young male apprentices and journeymen free of their boss's control outside of the workshop. They organized loosely by neighborhoods, streets, and trades, fought one another over territory, and often harassed terrified pedestrians.

1801

Much of the law enforcement work in the early nineteenth century was done or overseen by Jacob Hays, the high constable appointed by Mayor Edward Livingston in 1801. Hays governed a small force for almost 50 years and gained an international reputation for his efficient, autocratic organization. He made numerous arrests himself, and could disperse a rebellious crowd with a minimum of physical force.

1801

The crime rate remained low from 1801 to around 1820, as mass immigration and the growth of manufacturing and trade had not yet created the ethnic and class tensions evident in the 1820s.

1803

A police force of about 76 men were entrusted with lighting street lamps, watching for fires, subduing criminal activity, and guarding Potter's Field from grave-robbing medical students. Watchmen at the graveyards were paid so little that they worked by day as laborers and often slept through guard duty at night. One hundred and twenty watchmen were fined for sleeping on the job at Potter's Field in 1803; a year later 140 were caught snoozing. Watchmen wore no uniforms except for leather helmets, so they were usually referred to as "leatherheads."

CRIME ON THE HOOF

- There are 4,300 transit police in New York City and 10% to 15% are undercover. No other city in the country aside from New York City has a full-time police decoy unit. About 155 arrests are made each year by undercover subway police pretending to be drunk and asleep.
- Transit police decided that women who ride the subway topless would not be arrested or ticketed.
- The most felonious subway line is the No. 4 train.
- The average number of felonies committed each day on New York City subways is 32.
- There was a 50% decrease in subway crime between 1990 and 1997.
- There are approximately 320 reported felonies per year on the E train.
- An average of 3 felonies per day are committed on NYC buses.
- 15% of New York City's drivers have suspended licenses.
- There has been a 17% increase in police vehicles involved in accidents in the last decade.
- 57,000 stolen cars are towed annually to New York City pounds after being recovered by police.
- Approximately 35,000 cars are towed annually for parking violations.

1825

Immigration and the growth of manufacturing and trade fueled class and ethnic tensions. Immigrants were often swindled or falsely accused of petty crimes.

1825

There were 200 police officers in the city.

1827

Gangs attracted those least affected by industrialization, such as butchers and volunteer firemen. The Chichesters Gang was comprised of mainly apprentice butchers, maintaining a hierarchy of older leaders and young upstarts. Many gang members wore long sideburns called "soap locks." The Bowery is where most gang members lived and congregated, taking part in bawdy pursuits such as brawling, target-shooting, tattooing, and convivial drunken carousing.

1831

Reformers such as Joseph Fay convinced the public that in a credit-driven economy, poverty was a result of misfortune rather than moral failure, and that imprisoning nonfraudulent debtors was a mistake. In 1831 New York became the second state after Kentucky to outlaw imprisonment for poverty (or the "debtor's prison").

GANGS IN THE HOOD

- 6 gangs work the area of the Upper West Side that stretches from 105th to 110th Streets, Central Park West to Amsterdam Avenue.
- 65% to 70% of the drug customers for these gangs live in the same area as the gang.
- Over 100 different tongs/gang organizations are in Chinatown.
- There are an estimated 40,000 members in the Gee How Oak Tin Association in the New York area. The origin of current Asian gangs is the previous "soldiers" for the Tongs in the 1930s.
- Asian gangs noticeably increase extortion attempts on local businesses during the Chinese New Year.
- An estimated 3,000 teenagers pledge allegiance to a gang in NYC.

- There are 200 members in the Latin Kings and 200 in the Netas. The Netas differ from the Latin Kings in that the members are multicultural recruits. Federal officials investigated at least 12 murders that were possibly linked to the Netas.

Q: What is the main recruiting locale for gang members?
A: New York City jails.

Q: How many gangs are there in New York City?
A: 125.

1838

Neighborhoods in the city were increasingly separated along class lines and gang members began to congregate in saloons. Saloons became political institutions during elections, when saloonkeepers who were also politicians needed the allegiance of gang members. Gang members often stole ballot boxes, voted "early and often," and intimidated the supporters of rival candidates of their favorite saloonkeeper-politician.

1844

An influx of Irish immigrants combined with an economic depression fueled a power struggle between established and immigrant groups within Tammany Hall. Gangs fought violent battles with fists, clubs, and guns.

1845

Immigrants, factories, and tenements grew more numerous, tensions relating to class, ethnicity, and race increased, gambling flourished throughout the city, and it became clear that there was a breakdown of communal order in the city. A measure to reorganize the police force was signed into law by Mayor William Havemeyer, establishing a "day and night" force of as many as 800 men who would be identifiable as police by their star-shaped badges. The new force was nicknamed the "star police." Fixed police salaries led to the taking of bribes from those engaged in illegal business.

INSULTING HIS MAJESTY

CAUGHT IN THE ACT

A CASE IN HAND·

ON THE DEAD BEAT

1849

Three hundred police were on hand to stave off a riot at William Macready's performance at the Astor Place Opera House on May 10. English actors were the closest thing to English aristocrats for the gangs on the Bowery, mostly comprised of Irish and Germans; the Bowery's favorite actor, Ned Forrest, disliked Macready and felt competitive toward him. Forrest's jealousy melded nicely with anti-English sentiments at the time, and when Macready stepped on stage on opening night he was pelted with eggs, garbage, and a bottle of asafetida that broke at his feet. A riot erupted despite the 300 officers, and people were killed when police fired into the crowd.

1850

The first obvious red-light district was created, located north of Canal Street in Soho.

1850

New York City police began to wear uniforms. They didn't wear uniforms before this date because uniforms were perceived as "undemocratic."

1850

The Reverend Lewis Morris Pease opened the Five Points House of Industry for young orphans involved in the city's criminal underworld. Some of the child gangs in the Five Points slum (at the intersection of Baxter, Park, Worth, Mulberry, and what was called Dandy Lane) were the Little Dead Rabbits, the Forty Little Thieves, the Little Daybreak Boys, and the Little Plug Uglies. Since adult gang members were often in their teens, children in these gangs were most likely under the age of 10. Reverend Pease converted a little girl known as Wild Maggie Carson, who was the leader of the Forty Little Thieves and he oversaw her first bath at the age of nine and even gave her in marriage to someone from a good family.

1853

Formal training for police began and officers were armed with nightsticks.

1855

There were 1,200 police in the city and over 600,000 residents. In addition to fighting crime, police directed traffic, looked for lost children, settled domestic disputes, walked drunkards home, and found shelter for the homeless.

1857

Police officers were authorized to carry a service revolver.

1866

Between 1866 and 1870 the number of homicides per 100,000 residents was 4.

IN THE COOLER

- There are 69 prisons in New York State with approximately 66,000 inmates.
- The New York State prison population increased 112% between the mid-1980s and the mid-1990s.
- 100,000 passengers per year use Operation Prison Gap buses to visit a person in jail. Operation Prison Gap was founded in 1975 with one bus, and now at least 40 buses shuttle people to and from prison visits.
- The annual salary for the Commissioner of Correctional Services is $107,706.
- Throughout the 1990s, 76.4% of juveniles released from New York institutions were rearrested within 30 months. 81.5% were male. 80.9% were between 11 and 14 years of age.
- Taxpayers will pay $315.4 million between 1995 and 1999 for a new system of feeding 18,000 inmates in 16 prisons.
- New York City places an average of 24,000 inmates in work-release programs annually. One-sixth of the inmates simply walk away from their jobs. 1,000 are deemed "whereabouts unknown."

Q: In which month does the city's inmate population reach its seasonal peak?
A: September.

1869

Prostitution flourished for over 20 years in the Tenderloin, the area on the West Side between 10th and 42nd Streets. The Tenderloin became a national symbol for urban depravity and was often depicted in books and tabloids. More elegant bordellos were found in Gramercy Park and other upscale neighborhoods.

1870

Two opium dens were established in Manhattan: one on Baxter Street in a sailors' boarding house, another on Mott Street. A half-a-million pounds of opium flowed into the U.S. each year.

1871

Violent crime decreased as a result of the cohesiveness of political machines and stricter policies. Criminal operations at this time were run by the Irish.

1879

The southern end of Mulberry Street, then called Mulberry Bend, was the area with the highest crime rate in the city.

1879

The homicide rate per 100,000 residents was 4.8

1885

Chinese tongs controlled the diverse sales and consumption of opium in the city; there were about 12,000 Chinese residents in Manhattan. Small and sparse opium dens cropped up in basements, attics, and shabby back rooms throughout Chinatown and the Tenderloin section on the West Side between 10th and 42nd Streets. The press was eager to sensationalize the opium dens in Chinatown in lurid articles designed to attract as many horrified readers as possible.

1888

The homicide rate per 100,000 residents remained fairly steady at 4.5; there wouldn't be a surge in homicides in the city for another eighteen years.

1891

After a long campaign by the Women's Temperance Union, New York City became one of the last large cities in the country to employ police matrons.

1892

Vice crusades mushroomed and prostitution became more clandestine, with many prostitutes working out of tenement buildings, dance halls, massage parlors, and "call houses."

1894

The police were called "the buttons" by citizens because of their uniforms. The police department, which consisted of 4,000 men in 37 precincts, was finally investigated for corruption in 1894 by an Albany-based group called the Lexow Committee. Citizens had been demanding a state investigation for years. The public clamor was ignored as long as the state legislature was controlled by friends of the Tammany Hall Democrats, but when the Republicans captured the legislature in 1893, the New York City police were investigated the following year. Corruption plagued the police department for decades to come.

1895

New York City's most notorious little Fagin was Monk Eastman's sidekick Crazy Butch. Both boys had embraced their necessary life of vice at a young age. Butch trained his dog, Rabbi, to snatch purses, and then, as a sort of "crime consultant," he taught other preadolescents how to steal. Butch created his own criminal auxiliary called Squab Wheelmen, a group noted for one trick: a member would purposely crash a bicycle into a pedestrian, begin screaming at the victim, and attract a crowd of people with full pockets. The Squab Wheelmen would then move in for the picking.

1896

The dangerous, crime-ridden Five Points intersection at Baxter, Park, Worth, Mulberry, and Dandy Lane was renovated as a park.

1896

Reporter Stephen Crane estimated that there were 25,000 opium (or "hop") users in New York City in 1896.

PIPE DREAMS

Opium was popular with many of the city's residents. Wealthier opium smokers would bring their own gold, ivory, or silver paraphernalia to opium dens located throughout Manhattan, mainly in Chinatown. People sometimes stayed in opium dens for weeks on end, and were entertained in tonier dens by piano players.

Cocaine was readily available for next to nothing in drugstores throughout the city and was used by many of the opium smokers. It was considered to be a "poor man's high," and was injected with a needle until the turn of the century when snorting it became fashionable. Crystallized cocaine was called "burny." In the Tenderloin section at 40th Street and Seventh Avenue there was a hotel called The Lafayette, which featured a back room with a potted tree called the Burny Tree. The tree's branches were festooned with hundreds of lengths of the black rubber tubing used for snorting cocaine. Cocaine grew in popularity over the next few decades.

Cannabis indica extract was readily available in drugstores, too, but it didn't seem to interest much of the city's population. Drugs were a middle-class whim before the 1870s primarily because the poor didn't know about them or have doctors to recommend them for particular ailments. After the Civil War many in the city took morphine to relieve pains from wounds; Chinese residents who went to the West Coast as laborers on the construction of the transcontinental railroad brought opium use to the East Coast, and opium users in China had the British East India Company to credit for their addiction.

1901

Criminal operations shifted from the Irish to the Jews and Italians. Moral reformers put pressure on the government to control the vice at brothels, gambling dens, and drinking establishments, which Tammany Hall and other political organizations protected.

1901

The Five Points Gang of Paul Kelly (named after a crime-infested slum in what is now Soho) included Al Capone, "Lucky" Luciano, Frankie Yale, and Johnny Torrio. A rival group of Jewish gangsters was controlled by notorious mobster Monk Eastman.

1909

New York City police lieutenant Joseph Petrosino was murdered while pursuing an investigation of an individual in Palermo, Sicily. Many suspected the murder was linked to organized crime in the city.

1910

The number of murders in the city decreased, but there was a vastly differing murder rate between blacks and whites that reflected economic disparity: the rate per 100,000 residents for whites was 5.1, compared with a rate of 21.7 for blacks.

1911

The first black police officer, Samuel Battle, was hired in New York City.

1914

A bomb squad was created within the police department in response to a series of terrorist attacks.

1914

The Harrison Act was passed in Congress, which forbade the sale of narcotics without a prescription. Nevertheless, many New York City residents continued to use recreational drugs openly and gleefully in public until the 1930s, when the Bureau of Narcotics and Dangerous Drugs tackled drug problems in earnest.

1916

One-third of the city's habitual drug users were estimated to have been addicted to heroin. Heroin was originally the brand name for the diacetylmorphine solution synthesized in 1896 by the Bayer company, formed by German inventors and manufacturers of aspirin.

Q: How was heroin marketed in the city around 1900?
A: It was touted as a cough suppressant, and turned out to be quite popular by 1916.

1917

Motor patrol cars with radios were introduced to the police department.

1923

Murders reached a peak during Prohibition when criminal gangs were reorganized. Gangs adopted conventional business techniques for the importation and distribution of alcohol and their relationship with government grew more sophisticated.

Q: What were the last names of the leaders of the five "families" who controlled organized crime in the city in the 1920s?
A: Gambino, Genovese, Bonanno, Profaci, and Lucchese. The next generation of mob leaders included Meyer Lansky, "Lucky" Luciano, Frank Costello, and Joe Adonis.

1927

An Air Service Unit equipped with helicopters and small airplanes was added to the police department.

1933

Prohibition was repealed and organized crime focused on gambling, waterfront racketeering, loan-sharking, prostitution, and narcotics. Severe economic difficulties in black neighborhoods caused the murder rate among blacks to skyrocket to 35.1 per 100,000 residents compared with the citywide average of 4.3. Riots erupted in Harlem two years after Prohibition ended.

1937

Two-way communication between patrol cars and precincts began in New York City.

1945

There were 12,226 automobile thefts in the city, which would represent the smallest number of reported car thefts in the city for the next fifty-three years.

1955

There were 306 murders in the city; the rate would more than double to 681 by 1965.

1960

Nineteen percent of the homicides in NYC involved the use of handguns. By 1990, 73 percent of homicides involved handguns.

1964

The first black precinct commander, Lloyd Sealy, was appointed.

1964

Kitty Genovese was murdered in Kew Gardens on March 13. Her screams for help were ignored by 38 neighbors, all witnesses. Her murderer was found and convicted, but the case underscored the cold anonymity and lack of support often encountered in urban life. A movie, *The Kitty Genovese Story,* was made about the incident.

1965

New York City, along with most American cities at the time, experienced a dramatic increase in violent crime. Businesses began hiring security guards and using chain-link fences, residents began putting "No Radio" signs in their car windows and were more aware of crime.

1967

The City Council ended licensing requirements for massage parlors and they proliferated throughout the city, particularly in the Times Square area.

1968

Carlo Gambino was the leading organized crime figure in the city; he died of natural causes eight years later.

1969

Q: Why is a block of Christopher Street called Stonewall Place?
A: To honor the city's first gay rights rebellion at the
      Stonewall Inn.

GAY PRIDE

On June 27 a gay rights movement was launched in the city after police raided the Stonewall Inn on Christopher Street in Greenwich Village. Raids were typical at the time, often spurred on by a failure to pay off the police or a violation of liquor laws, and patrons were too skittish about having their names publicized to protest an arrest. The Stonewall Rebellion marked the first instance when a raid was met with violent resistance. Patrons and local denizens attacked police with bottles, rocks, and a firebomb. Similar rebellions occurred throughout the area for the next two evenings.

1972

Federal prosecutor Rudolph Giuliani garnered media attention and political clout by prosecuting organized crime figures. The mob was firmly entrenched in the city's heroin trade.

1972

There were 1,757 murders in the city—the city's highest murder rate until 1980.

1977

The mayoral victory of Edward Koch symbolized the city's frustration with crime: Koch was elected on a platform that emphasized law enforcement and condoned the death penalty.

1977

The murderer known as Son of Sam was arrested.

Q: What was his real name and occupation?
A: David Richard Berkowitz. He was a mail carrier.

Berkowitz shot five women and one man between July of 1976 and July of 1977; his targets were all women who were seated in a car with a man. Berkowitz was raised in the Bronx's Co-Op City. Police eventually found him at his Yonkers home.

Q: How did the police find him?
A: Through a parking ticket that had been issued to him on the night of the last shooting.

Q: The "Son of Sam Law" passed by the state legislature of New York was declared unconstitutional by the U.S. Supreme Court in 1991. What was the law?
A: Convicted criminals cannot profit from accounts of their crimes.

1980

There were 1,812 murders in the city; more than 100,000 cars were stolen as well.

1982

The Department of Consumer Affairs was granted the power to close down businesses for violating permits.

Q: How many days are failing businesses in NYC allotted by the Department of Consumer Affairs for closing sales?
A: 30.

Q: What is the fine, per day, for merchants who restock their merchandise after receiving a going-out-of-business license?
A: $100 a day.

HOME DISREPAIR

An average of 941 homeowners in New York City file complaints with the City Department of Consumer Affairs against home repair contractors each year. Home repair contractors are the most complained-about group in New York City.

The second group: . . . . .appliance/furniture stores
The third: . . . . .electronics stores
The fourth: . . . . .car dealers
The fifth: . . . . .tow companies and tow-truck drivers

1985

The leader of the Gambino family, Paul Castellano, was murdered while dining out. John Gotti replaced him as family leader.

Q: Which restaurant was Castellano eating at when he was murdered?
A: Spark's Steak House on West 46th Street in Manhattan.

Q: What was Gotti's nickname?
A: The Dapper Don. He was always well dressed.

1985

The approximate number of rental properties that reached the courts in foreclosure proceedings in 1985 was 100, compared to 4,000 a decade later.

1989

The place in New York City where most violent deaths occurred was Doyer Street near Pell Street in Chinatown. A portion of the street was dubbed "Bloody Angle."

1990

Q: What fraction of all robberies across the nation committed by people under the age of 15 occurred in New York?
A: One-fourth.

FELONIOUS PARK

The annual average number of felonies committed in the early 1990s in Central Park was 256. Mayor Guilliani has worked hard—and successfully—to lower that number.

1992

After evading numerous prosecutions, John Gotti was convicted on various felony charges (including the murder of Castellano) and sentenced to life in a federal prison.

1992

Real estate and hotel magnate Leona Helmsley was sentenced to an 18-month prison term for tax evasion. Her late husband, Harry B. Helmsley, had amassed a five-billion-dollar empire by 1992 and owned over 25 million square feet of office space, 20,000 apartments, and 7,500 hotel rooms.

1993

New York City police shot 111 pit bulls for attacking city residents or police officers.

1993

A bordello raid in April occurred two blocks from the mayor's home at Gracie Mansion.

1993

Three NYPD officers were assigned to break graffiti code as part of a special new graffiti unit; there were 200 arrests made within a year and a half of the unit's inception.

THE WRITING'S ON THE WALL

The NYC Public Housing Authority spent an average of $13 million annually throughout the 1990s to clean graffiti from buildings. The Federal Department of Housing and Urban Development slated $1.8 million in 1993 for a computer system in New York City to record photos of graffiti on disks.

1993

The Civilian Complaint Board, with 13 members and 66 civilian investigators, began operating independently of the police department in New York City in October. Within a half year, the board and the police department received 2,190 complaints—a 46-percent increase from the previous year in complaints of police brutality and other abuses.

Q: What percentage of cases were eventually substantiated?
A: 10%.

1994

Q: What percentage of total welfare cases in New York State involved fraud?
A: 3% or less.

1994

The average ratio of homicide deaths in the Bronx's Hunts Point-Mott Haven, as compared to Gramercy Park-Murray Hill in Manhattan, was 20 to 1.

1994

The largest theft at Tiffany's occurred in September when the store was robbed of $1.9 million in jewelry.

Q: How many carats are in the Tiffany Diamond?
A: 128.54.

Q: What cash amount is classified as petty larceny in New York?
A: Under $1,000.

1994

The Goods for Guns drive in 1994 took in 313 firearms, compared to 2,800 in 1993. New York City homicide detectives recover between 2,600 and 3,000 handguns per year.

Q: What is the average time that a person convicted on a weapons charge will spend in jail?
A: 2 years.

1995

A wave of plant and tree thefts plagued 102nd to 110th Streets near Riverside Drive. A four-foot evergreen was pilfered from Straus Park at Broadway and West End Avenue.

New York City's finest have their work cut out for them in a city this size, although crime rates have dropped in recent years.

1995

Thirty-three members of a cocaine organization called Young City Boys were indicted in a police crackdown. There were approximately 100 drug indictments in New York City between September 8 and 10, and 52 percent of the 33 indicted were arrested. Young City Boys handled $350,000 per week in the cocaine business, and operated on Columbus Avenue and 104th Street. Gang leaders once took 10 Young City Boys "employees" on a vacation to Hawaii.

1995

An airplane passenger from Los Angeles brought three gallons of the hallucinogen PCP, worth $2 million, into Kennedy Airport.

Q: How many mouthwash bottles was it stored in?
A: 13.

The maximum sentence for the smuggler was life in prison and a $4 million fine.

Q: What is the average amount of time that a person convicted on a drug charge spent in jail in New York?
A: 2 years, 2 months.

DRUGGED OUT

**Over 8,300 drug dealers move through the New York City crimi-
nal justice system annually.**

1995

Five hundred police officers fanned throughout Manhattan,
Queens, and Brooklyn to raid 69 locations in one evening and
crush a gambling empire that raked in $25 to $30 million annually.

1995

Three hundred Asian-American police in New York City band-
ed together to form a council and fight Asian-American organized crime.

1995

Q: How many Italian "families" or organized crime syndicates
maintain operations in the city despite successful federal
prosecutions throughout the 1980s and 1990s?
A: 5; the largest is the Gambino family, which is reputed to
have between 400 and 500 members and as many as 3,000
affiliates.

1996

A New York State prisoner convicted of rape won $157,000 in
a lawsuit because he was an outspoken Muslim and had been
transferred repeatedly as a result. This award was the highest ever
to be handed out in New York to an individual prisoner who
hadn't suffered serious personal injury.

ORDER IN THE COURT

- One of the purposes of Room 823 in the Manhattan Criminal Court Building is to provide storage space for miniature "Exhibit A" models that show the scene of a crime.
- The average annual number of sequestered juries in New York City each year is 1,400 at a $4 million cost to New Yorkers.

Q: How many states, aside from New York, require jury sequestration in felony cases?
A: None.

Q: What is the penalty for ignoring a notification to serve as a juror in New York City?
A: $1,000 fine and 30 days in jail.

Q: How much are jurors paid each day?
A: $15.

1996

The police corruption scandal in New York City's 30th Precinct in Harlem was the police department's biggest drug scandal in a generation, and also mushroomed into the most damaging perjury scandal in state history. Prosecutors were forced to toss out 125 cases against 98 defendants because their convictions were based on untruthful testimony by officers from the 30th Precinct. This number reflected more dismissals than any other police perjury case on record in the state of New York. At least 25 civil cases were filed against the police department, with $1.3 million paid in awards and settlements and an additional $10 million predicted to be paid in the future. About 70 of the 98 defendants cleared have admitted that they were committing crimes when arrested.

Q: How many officers were convicted?
A: 33.

1996

There were 25 men in the police scuba squad, and seven scuba police on duty at any given time.

Q: How many women were on the squad?
A: None.

A WATERY GRAVE

Half of the dead bodies found in New York City's waterways are found in April and May. The average number of bodies found in the rivers each year is 20, although 1984 was a gruesome year for the scuba squad: there were 92 bodies found in city rivers. The East River and the Harlem River are the most likely waterways for bodies to turn up in New York City.

1996

Q: How much did it cost the NYPD to buy a police robot?
A: $120,000.

1996

New York City bomb squads handle as many as 1,544 cases per year; an average of 59 cases include hand grenades.

1996

New York City police booted 2,493 people out of the subways for panhandling, arrested 900, and issued panhandling summonses to 2,500 people. Seventy announcements prohibiting begging appeared in populated subway stations.

Q: What is the maximum penalty for begging?
A: 10 days in jail.

THE STING

The police and the fire departments are the designated city agencies that deal with swarms of bees in New York City each spring. In May and June, a beekeeper can make over 20 emergency calls to Manhattan.

Q: What is the rate beekeepers charge the city for removal?
A: Nothing; the service is free because beekeepers use the bees for honey. One particular beekeeper harvests 1,000 pounds of

honey from New York City's bees, and another creates over 100 beeswax candles each year.

Q: What does it cost private homeowners to de-bee their property?
A: $35 and up.

Q: How many different bee species are there in New York City?
A: Over 100.

1997

New York City's crime rate dropped three times as much as the national average; at least 25 American cities had a higher crime rate than New York City.

> *This is a humbling time for all crime analysts. It (the reason for a sharp decrease in crime in major cities) is a puzzlement.*
> JOHN J. DIIULIO JR., PROFESSOR OF POLITICS AND PUBLIC AFFAIRS AT
> PRINCETON UNIVERSITY, TO FOX BUTTERFIELD OF THE
> *NEW YORK TIMES* AT THE START OF 1997

Part of the explanation for the decrease in crime is the 40,000-plus New York City police force—the largest police force in the city's history—and the increasing prison population.

1997

Four out of every five murder victims knew their killers.

1997

"Home invaders" was the term given to a new wave of violent robbers, primarily in Washington Heights and Harlem, who stormed into private residences and demanded money. The NYPD set up a special task force unit in 1997 comprised of a sergeant and six detectives to combat the crime; the city averaged two home invasions a day at the start of 1997, with as many as five reported in a single day.

1997

An elaborate police sting operation in the Bronx that entailed sending letters offering "unclaimed funds" of up to $6,000 duped 261 fugitives from the law. A total of 2,770 letters were mailed, and a phony office where police acted as receptionists was created. The office space was donated to the police, and the mass mailing cost the department $800. The fugitives who arrived to collect their money were surprised to discover they were under arrest. But first they were given a bogus check that featured a copy of the "Go Directly To Jail" Monopoly card in the left corner. One woman protested the arrest, claiming she was only pretending to be the fugitive in the letter in order to collect the money—she was then arrested for criminal impersonation. The police subsequently ran a warrant check on her after seeing her identification, and discovered that she, too, had a warrant out for her arrest.

A sting operation in the past offering 956 fugitives opening-day Yankees tickets bagged only three scofflaws.

1997

The nation's largest drug court, the Brooklyn Treatment Court, opened in January. For nonviolent offenders who test positive for drugs and plead guilty, entering a mandatory drug rehabilitation program in lieu of a prison term is now an option. If offenders don't comply with treatment, they're sent back to court and sentenced to jail time. The court is targeting women; 75 percent of all women felons in Brooklyn have been arrested for drug-related offenses. The program is funded with federal and city money and there was a 70 percent success rate for defendants who went through a similar court in Rochester, New York, one of five such courts statewide. If the Brooklyn court is successful, the drug court concept will be employed throughout the rest of New York City.

CHAPTER 5

Quality of Life: Health, Education, & Religion

New York is to the nation what the white church spire is to the village—the visible symbol of aspiration and faith, the white plume saying the way is up!

E. B. WHITE

Religious diversity has been a given in New York City since its founding, and cathedrals, mosques, temples, and Buddhist shrines are found within walking distance of one another. Although the city is still predominantly Catholic, its Jewish population has defined the character of the city for well over a century, rendering the bagel, pastrami sandwich, and deli as unofficial logos for New York City. New York has one of the largest Buddhist populations in the country, and the Baptist churches in Harlem and Fort Greene are famous throughout the world. There are few religions on earth that aren't practiced in New York, even Shango, Santaria, and Voodoo. The Presbyterians, Episcopalians, Lutherans, Muslims, and Seventh-Day Adventists have all erected fantastic churches and mosques across the city's boroughs.

The oldest school in New York City is Brooklyn's Erasmus Hall, which was erected for the children of Dutch farmers. The city's schools range from expensive private schools to parochial schools, specialized high schools and colleges, and the ivy-encrusted Columbia University and Barnard. There are more than 14 major universities, colleges, and art schools in New York City, dozens of dance and photography schools, and about half a dozen acting schools.

New York City has always been a place of innovation in public health and social policy pertaining to it, perhaps out of necessity. The number of people living together on marshlands with a limited water supply during the 1600s, 1700s, and 1800s created brutal outbreaks of disease; also, disease was introduced from abroad. Epidemics were manageable as long as living conditions remained clean and the population was sparse. In the mid-ninteenth century, many believed that disease could be staved off if the water supply and sanitary conditions remained clean, and others felt that quarantines were the answer, particularly with ships visiting from abroad.

After the British seized control in 1644, the city enforced codes governing waste disposal, food production and distribution, street cleanliness, and the clearing of swampland. During the grappling with population growth and waste burial issues, the Board of Health was formed in 1805.

New York City pioneered public health services such as vaccines, sewage facilities, refuse collection, ambulance service, air for the impoverished, chlorinated water, and medical record keeping, to name a few, and advocated the use of pasteurized milk.

1625

In religion, the Dutch West India Company permitted freedom of conscience in private matters but required public worship to be in keeping weigh the catechism of the Synod of Dordrecht in Holland. In practice, however, the Company's attitude toward religion was characterized by indifference.

1626

Settlers worshiped in individual homes until a room in a loft was created for worship services in 1626. There was one doctor in town, a surgeon.

1628

The city's first religious service was led by ordained Dutch Reformed minister Dominie Jonas Michaelius shortly after his arrival in the New World in April. The service was held for a French-speaking Walloon couple and their 50 guests in the loft of a mill at 20-22 South William Street. The clergyman delivered the service in uncertain, halting French.

1633

Colonists built their first church, a Dutch Reformed Church, which was a plain, rectangular structure at 33-39 Pearl Street near the East River.

1637

Dr. Jean Mousnier de la Montagne, Manhattan's first physician, arrived in the spring with his wife, Rachel, and four children, one of whom had been born recently at sea. He had studied at the (then famed) University of Leyden Medical School in Holland. One of his daughters eventually married Jacob Kip (of the family for whom Kip's Bay is named) and they lived on an estate at what is now 35th Street and Park Avenue.

Q: What was Dr. Jean Mousnier de la Montagne's contribution to the city?
A: He was one of the founders of Harlem.

1641

A law passed on April 11 forbid drinking on Sunday during church hours. New Amsterdam residents violated the law so flagrantly that a more strident ordinance was passed in October of 1656. The second law prohibited tennis, dancing, manual labor, sowing, mowing, fishing, hunting, gambling, card-playing, cricket, boating, building, frequenting taverns and tippling houses, having or attending parties, playing ninepin, and cart-riding. The fine for working on Sunday was "one pound Flemish" per person and the fine for drinking alcohol or enjoying "amusement" activities was "two pound Flemish." Stricter fines of six guilders per tavern and three guilders per customer served were enforced for tavernkeepers who served customers on Sunday. A guilder was approximately 50 cents.

1642

Director General Willem Kieft built the grand Dutch Reformed St. Nicholas Church to replace the colonists' modest church building. Since many colonists wanted a new church but few wanted to contribute to a building fund, Kieft waited to ask for contributions until after the fifth round of drinks at a wedding reception for the daughter of a prominent reverend. When sobered, many of the townspeople had second thoughts, but Kieft wouldn't let them renege.

The church was constructed of stone and heavy timber, stretched 70 feet long and 16 feet high, and boasted a tower and a bell. The building provided refuge during Indian raids that, ironically, were provoked by Director General Kieft himself. The church also blocked the wind supply to the surrounding windmills, creating flour shortages. It survived for 99 years.

1643

The town's first Roman Catholic priest, Father Isaac Jogues, arrived as a visitor and an honored guest. He narrowly escaped being burned at the stake by Iroquois Indians upstate, so he was smuggled down the Hudson River on a Dutch ship at Director General Kieft's request. He heard a confession from an Irish Catholic while visiting and was attacked and martyred by Mohawk Indians three years later.

1647

There were two perspectives on the cause and spread of infectious disease. "Sanitationists" believed disease was caused by vapors from stagnant water, open sewage, animal carcasses, rotting food, and filthy living conditions. Sanitationists were allied with Reformers, who sought to improve sanitation for moral reasons.

"Contagionists" believed that disease was usually carried aboard a ship and could be controlled by severe quarantines.

1648

In an effort to improve sanitary conditions, Governor Peter Stuyvesant prohibited goats and hogs from roaming the streets. The ordinance was poorly enforced and mostly futile.

1650

Peter Stuyvesant tried unsuccessfully to establish the exclusive rights of the Dutch church, which was poorly staffed and attended.

1654

Rosh Hashanah services were first held in America and the group consisted of: Abraham Israel de Piza, David Israel Faro, Moses Ambrosius, Asser Levy van Swellem, the wives and 13 children of these four men, and two single women named Judicq de Mereda and Rycke Nounes.

We have here Papists, Mennonites, and Lutherans among the Dutch [and] also many Puritans or Independents and many atheists and various other servants of Baal.
DOMINIE JOHANNES MEGAPOLENSIS, COMPLAINING TO OFFICIALS IN AMSTERDAM, WHILE RESIDING IN NEW AMSTERDAM IN 1655

1657

In an effort to improve sanitary conditions, Governor Peter Stuyvesant prohibited the disposal of refuse in the streets. As in 1648, the enforcement of his ordinance was mediocre and mostly barren of results.

1664

After the British gained control of the city, new laws pertaining to public health were introduced, covering stricter management of farm animals, food distribution and production, street cleaning, and waste disposal. Epidemics struck often and were perceived as divine judgment. Since most epidemics struck during hot weather, wealthy settlers fled the city during the summer. Moralists blamed the poor for choosing to live in filthy conditions and bringing disease upon themselves. Businessmen, religious groups, and leading physicians had an equal role in determining public health policy.

1680

The governor of New York noted that in the city there were "religions of all sorts, one church of England, several Presbyterians and Independents, Quakers and Anabaptists of several sects, and some Jews."

1685

The Dutch Reformed Church was led by Dominie Hendrik Selijns, who was popular among merchants and noted for his remarkable integrity.

1695

The 20 Jewish families in Manhattan had a synagogue as well as the city's first rabbi, Saul Brown (anglicized from the Spanish "Pardo"). The synagogue stood on what is now South William Street and was called Shearith Israel, or Remnant of Israel.

1697

King William III chartered the original Trinity Church on May 6 at Greenwich Street, Wall Street, and Broadway. The church faced Greenwich Street, which was directly on the shore of the Hudson River. Before the church was built, Church of England members had to worship at the Dutch Reformed Church. Practically everyone in town contributed to the building fund, including six Jewish families and nonconformist Protestants. A royal gift of land in 1705 rendered Trinity one of the richest parishes in the United States: the land ran from Broadway to the Hudson River and from Fulton Street to Christopher Street.

The church burned down in 1776 in a citywide rebellion

started by American patriots. A second Trinity church was erected in 1790 and torn down in 1839 after it was damaged by a
heavy snowfall. The present building was consecrated in 1846.

Q: Who designed the present Trinity Church?
A: Richard Upjohn, an English immigrant who became the
first president of the American Institute of Architects.

1702

As much as 10 percent of the city's population was killed in a
yellow fever epidemic.

*There are many couples [who] live together without ever being
married in any manner of way; many of whom, after they have
lived some years so, quarrel, and, thereupon separating, take
unto themselves...new companions. Even when couples marry,
the enjoyment precedes the marriage.*
ONE REVEREND MILLER IN A PUBLIC SERMON IN 1704

1707

The first Presbyterian clergyman to preach in New York was the
Reverend Francis Makemie, an Irishman who came to visit. He
was immediately arrested by the eccentric, transvestite governor
Lord Cornbury and charged with "disturbing the government."
His defense argued that Presbyterians had no established church
in New York and that the "province is made up chiefly of dis-
senters and persons not of English birth." The Reverend Makemie
won his acquittal but at great expense: the court's fee was 83
English pounds.

1731

A smallpox epidemic lasted three months in the late summer
and early autumn and killed 5 to 8 percent of the city's 10,000
inhabitants. A smallpox inoculation was first used in New York
City during this epidemic, the most devastating of the colonial
period, which sparked a debate between proponents and opponents of vaccination.

1746

Members of the local Hand-In-Hand Fire Company shouldered sacks for retrieving valuables during a local fire, while others formed a bucket brigade, drawing water from a public well to a hand-pumped engine that was then directed at the flames.

1748

There were nine places of worship in the colony: the Anglican Trinity church, two Dutch churches, a German Lutheran church, a German Reformed church, a Presbyterian church, a Jewish synagogue, a Quaker meeting house, and a Huguenot church.

1754

A subscription library opened in the city; members paid an annual fee of 10 shillings.

1736

Bellevue Hospital was opened as a six-bed municipal infirmary under the name of the Public Work House and Home of Correction on Lower Broadway where City Hall is now situated. The Bellevue establishment opened in 1816, comprised of a building the city purchased in 1794 at 26th Street and First Avenue to house victims of epidemics, and a site for an almshouse the city purchased in 1811 that ran from 23rd Street to 28th Street, and from Second Avenue to the East River. Bellevue Hospital took its current name in 1825 and was used mainly for victims of epidemics. Neglect, filthy conditions, and a high mortality rate plagued the hospital until the 1850s.

1754

Columbia University began as King's College, chartered on October 31, and opened with eight students in the vestry room of Trinity Church. The school moved uptown to 36 acres in Morningside Heights in 1760 and to its present location on the Upper West Side at 116th Street in 1897. Campus buildings were designed in the Italian Renaissance style by the firm of McKim, Mead, and White.

Notable eighteenth-century students included Alexandra Hamilton, John Jay, and Robert Livingston. A medical school was added in 1767, and the school served as a military hospital during the Revolutionary War (classes were suspended). In 1784 the school was rechartered as Columbia College; its name wasn't changed to Columbia University until 1896.

In 1939 more than 60 percent of the students at Columbia University pursued liberal arts and professional degrees simultaneously, a new option introduced by the school's president, Nicholas Murray Butler. John Dewey taught education, psychology, and philosophy at Columbia during the First World War, along with James McKeen Cattell (psychology), James Harvey Robinson (history), and Charles Beard (political science and history). During the war, Cattell defended the rights of conscientious objectors and was fired by Butler as a result. Beard then resigned in protest.

Q: After Beard resigned in protest, what did he establish along with Dewey and Robinson in 1919?
A: The New School for Social Research.

Those who attend Columbia University are in good company; Alexander Hamilton, John Jay, and both Roosevelt presidents all matriculated from its hallowed halls.

PHOTO BY ERIC CAPSTICK

Over 55 Nobel Prize laureates have studied or taught at Columbia.

Q: Which U.S. president was a president of Columbia University?
A: Dwight D. Eisenhower, from 1948 until he left for the White House in 1953.

Q: Approximately how many New York State inmates take college courses each year?
A: 3,000.

COLUMBIA, THE GEM OF NYC

Match the department at Columbia University with the year it was established:

1.1858	A. School of General Studies
2.1864	B. School of Engineering (formerly called School of Mines)
3.1881	C. School of Library Science
4.1887	D. Graduate facilities in Political Science
5.1892	E. School of Law
6.1889	F. School of Social Work
7.1880	G. School of Nursing
8.1890	H. School of Architecture, Planning, and Preservation
9.1892	I. Graduate facilities in Philosophy
10.1898	J. School of Business
11.1912	K. Graduate facilities in Pure Science
12.1916	L. Graduate School of Journalism
13.1917	M. The School of Dental & Oral Surgery
14.1920	N. School of Public Health
15.1921	O. Teacher's College

Answers: 1. E; 2. B; 3. H.; 4. C.; 5. G.; 6. O.; 7. D.; 8. I; 9. K; 10. F; 11. L; 12. J; 13. M; 14. A; 15. N

1774

There were sixteen churches in the city: three Presbyterian; three Anglican; churches for Anabaptists, Moravians, and Methodists; German Reformed, German Lutheran, Dutch churches; a Quaker meeting House; and the Huguenot church.

There was also a synagogue; services were read partly in Hebrew, partly in the Rabbinical dialect.

1786

St. Peter's, the first Roman Catholic church in the city, was erected at Barclay and Church Streets. It was rebuilt in 1838.

Q: What is distinctive about the church's wrought-iron fence?
A: It belonged to Trinity Church in 1790 and was donated to St. Peter's in 1846 when Trinity was rebuilt.

1787

Erasmus Hall High School was built in Brooklyn as a private school for the children of Dutch farmers. It's now distinguished as the first public school building in the U.S. to be designated as a landmark. The school is the second oldest public school in the country, and was deeded to the city of Brooklyn in 1896.

1798

Yellow fever killed 3 percent of the city's population. Residents in poor neighborhoods fared the worst, as their homes were usually located in swampy, mosquito-infested areas.

1800

The African Methodist Episcopal Zion Church, the city's first exclusively black church, was built at Church and Leonard Streets. The building of the church was organized by Peter Williams, a former slave of Tory tobacconist John Aymar. Williams wanted to remain in the country when Aymar left the country in 1783, so he persuaded the elders of the city's first Methodist Episcopal church, the John Street Methodist Church, to purchase him from Aymar and allow him to repay the purchase price. Williams, a church member, then became the church's sexton and undertaker. Williams paid back the church for his purchase price (40 British pounds) in about two years and went on to become a Liberty Street businessman and property owner. He and other successful blacks established their own church, the A.M.E. Zion Church. Williams's son Peter Jr. became the first black to be ordained in the Episcopal Church.

1805

A free smallpox vaccine became available for anyone who wanted one. Many physicians and public health officials argued for compulsory vaccination, but their efforts failed because settlers were either too suspicious or too apathetic.

1805

Lorenzo da Ponte, an Italian Jew, moved to the city from London to escape his mounting debts. He opened a grocery store in New York City, prospered, and eventually became the first professor of Italian language and literature at Columbia University.

Q: Which composer did he write librettos for?
A: Mozart

1809

Black Baptists organized the Abyssinian Baptist Church.

Q: Which reverend and congressman used the Abyssinian Baptist Church in Harlem as a base of political power for many years?
A: The Reverend Adam Clayton Powell Jr.

Q: How many terms did he serve in Congress?
A: 11.

1811

Social legislation was often influenced by public health concerns. Conditions in the debtor's prison were improved after an outbreak of disease.

1815

St. Patrick's Cathedral, originally located on Mott Street, opened as the city's first Catholic church.

1818

Black Episcopalians organized St. Philip's Protestant Episcopal Church.

1821

The first mental hospital in New York State opened in Morningside Heights. It was called Bloomingdale Insane Asylum was a branch of New York Hospital.

1823

Q: Physicians David Hosack and John Griscom were influential in the construction of an important public health improvement. What was it?

A: The city's first working sewage system.

1832

The number of new cholera cases reported by the Board of Health on July 18 was 138—72 deaths on that day alone.

"Contagionists" believed disease was carried aboard ship and could be controlled by severe quarantines, hence the Staten Island quarantine of 1833.

1833

The country's first school for blind children opened in the city.

Q: Why was there a pressing need for the school?
A: An outbreak of conjunctivitis in the almshouse left many children blind.

1844

There were 15 parishes in Manhattan to serve an estimated 80,000 to 90,000 Catholics in the city, most of them Irish.

1847

The College of the City University of New York (or City College) was formed by citywide referendum as the Free Academy and was located at 17 Lexington Avenue. The school had five faculty members and a president; its first baccalaureate degrees were awarded in 1853 and the school took its current name in 1866. Initially the student body consisted mostly of German Jews; in 1903 three-fourths of the school's student body was Jewish. City College enjoyed a reputation for academic excellence after the First World War. In 1961 the school became part of the City University of New York, and in 1970 the school instituted the policy of admitting anyone who had graduated from high school in New York City. Tuition fees were imposed for the first time in 1976. In 1997, 40 percent of the student body was black, 25 percent was Hispanic, and 16 percent was Asian. Currently, tuition is roughly $3,200 a year.

Q: How many courses are there in the Black Studies Department at City College each semester?
A: About 30.

Eight Nobel laureates graduated from City College in New York City, which is more than any other public college in the U.S.

NOTED ALUMNI OF CITY COLLEGE

- Ira Gershwin (1918)
- Bernard Baruch (1889)
- Upton Sinclair (1897)
- Lewis Mumford (1918)
- Senator Robert F. Wagner (1898)
- Edward G. Robinson (1914)
- Dr. Jonas Salk (1934)
- Edward Koch (1945)
- General Colin Powell (1958)

Other people who have attended CCNY: comedian Jerry Seinfeld, former Supreme Court Justice Felix Frankfurter (who helped found the American Civil Liberties Union), former Congressman and Deputy Mayor Herman Bandillo, actor Jimmy Smits, actor Judd Hirsch, and composer/conductor Marvin Hamlisch.

1850

Bellevue Hospital was separated from the almshouse and reorganized by a medical board; it averaged between 550 and 850 occupied beds each night.

1851

There were 15 synagogues in the city, and one-third of the Jewish population in America—50,000 people—lived in New York City. By 1859 there were 27 synagogues in the city.

1856

Bellevue Hospital was the first hospital in the United States to use hypodermic syringes.

1856

St. Vincents, a Roman Catholic hospital, opened on the corner of West 11th Street and Seventh Avenue where the St. Joseph's Half Orphan Asylum was located.

1858

An irate group of New Yorkers set fire to the city's quarantine station to protest the spread of contagious diseases.

1859

Cooper Union was founded as the country's first coeducational college, open to students of all races and creeds.

1860

A law was passed allowing communities to require vaccinations for schoolchildren.

APPLE POLISHERS

- 5% of New York City teachers earn over $53,805 annually.
- 5% earn $26,903 or less.
- The median annual salary for New York City teachers is $43,014.
- In Irvington, NY, $67,680.
- In Nassau County, $61,835.
- In Westchester, $62,316.
- In Bronxville, $70,500.
- A parochial school teacher earns 50% less than a public school teacher in New York City.
- On the average, 13 New York City teachers are assaulted each day, with 5 requiring medical attention.

Q: How many Catholic school teachers are unionized?
A: None.

1865

There were 15,244 completely submerged, lightless cellars inhabited by city residents. After the Metropolitan Board of Health was established in 1886, only 18 percent of these cellars passed inspection.

1866

Mount Sinai Hospital took its current name after incorporating in 1852 as the Jews Hospital in the City of New York. Originally located on West 28th Street between Seventh and Eighth

Avenues, it admitted only patients who were Jewish until a large number of Union soldiers during the Civil War required care. In 1872 the hospital moved to larger quarters on Lexington Avenue between 66th and 67th Streets.

1866

The Metropolitan Board of Health was established by the Metropolitan Health Act; it was the first agency of its kind in the country and became a model for cities across the country after preventing a cholera epidemic by removing thousands of tons of manure from lots in the city. After 1866 physicians replaced businessmen and reformers as makers of public health policy.

1867

The first tenement law passed in New York City. Provisions of the law included the presence of running water in house or yard, a fire escape, at least one window, and no inhabitants in cellars.

1869

Q: Which hospital in New York City was the first in the country to offer a hospital-based ambulance service?
A: Bellevue Hospital in 1869.

"SOMEBODY CALL AN AMBULANCE!"

- There is an average of 95 high-priority Emergency Medical Service (EMS) calls annually in Manhattan. The figure for Brooklyn is 30% higher.
- Citywide average 911 response time is 7.8 minutes.
- There are over 600,000 911 calls annually in New York City, with an average of 8 to 10 calls per EMS worker during an 8-hour shift.
- During a 2-week heat wave in 1995 the average number of calls per EMS worker rose to 13 calls per shift; over 700 people were transported to hospitals for heat-related health problems.

1873

Construction on St. John the Divine Cathedral began and John D. Rockefeller contributed $500,000 to its construction.

Q: How many people can the cathedral seat?
A: 10,000.

When completed, St. John the Divine will be the largest cathedral in the world—601 feet long and 177 feet high under the nave.

1878

Mount Sinai Hospital established the first pediatrics department connected to a general hospital in the city.

1879

Wards for alcoholics and a pavilion for the insane were added to Bellevue Hospital.

1880

A total of 1.4 million Jews emigrated to New York City between 1880 and 1910.

1887

The Jewish Theological Seminary was founded by Sabbato Morais on West 19th Street to train Conservative rabbis and to preserve traditional Judaism in the United States. Only eight students enrolled initially, one of whom later became the chief rabbi of the British Empire. After foundering and a reorganization, the seminary moved to West 123rd Street, set up a teacher's institute, and established the United Synagogue of America in 1913.

Q: In what year were women admitted to the school?
A: 1972.

1887

Doctors performed the first cesarean section in an American hospital at Bellevue's gynecology and obstetrics pavilion.

Bellevue was supported by various charities and correction boards until it came under the jurisdiction of municipal hospital boards in the early 1900s.

1889

Physicians were required to report cases of tuberculosis.

NEW YORK CITY INFANT MORTALITY RATE
(PER 1,000 LIVE BIRTHS)

1898	36.7
1920	88.2
1940	39.8
1970	21.6
1990	11.6
1997	11.4

1897

There were two Chinese temples, called "joss houses," in New York City.

1901

John D. Rockefeller Sr. established Rockefeller University as a center for medical education and research. Sixteen of the school's faculty members have won Nobel Prizes to date. Some of the Nobel prizes were awarded for the isolation of antibiotics, the first demonstration that DNA transmits hereditary factors, and finding a way to preserve whole blood, which rendered blood banks a reality.

1903

Bellevue Hospital opened a tuberculosis clinic. Balconies were an important part of a patient's hospital room, as fresh air was thought to speed recovery.

CONSUMPTION JUNCTION: NYC TUBERCULOSIS

- Manhattan is the borough with the highest rate of tuberculosis.
- The average rate of TB in Manhattan is 87 cases per 100,000 people; the citywide rate is 52 cases per 100,000 people.
- Central Harlem in Manhattan has the highest rate with 150 cases per 100,000 people.
- The age group with the highest incidence of tuberculosis is the 25- to 44-year-old group.
- The average job vacancy rate at New York City's Health Department is 20%; the area with the highest job vacancy is tuberculosis treatment.

1904

Mount Sinai Hospital moved to 100th Street and Fifth Avenue, into an area consisting of 10 buildings and 456 hospital beds.

Q: How many diseases, tests, instruments, and phenomena were named after doctors at the hospital who described them?

A: 21. Crohn's Disease, Tay-Sachs Disease, the Shwartzman Phenomenon, and the Rubin Test are a few examples. The first cardiac stress test was performed at the Mount Sinai Medical Center.

1905

Q: What percentage of New York City high school students went on to college in 1903?
A: 10%.

1905

Mary Mallon, or "Typhoid Mary," was recognized as a carrier of typhoid fever after an outbreak in an Oyster Bay household where she was employed as a cook. For the next three years she continued to work as a cook in New York City until she was finally traced to a residence on Park Avenue. She was institutionalized for three years, and released on the condition that she never again work as a cook and that she check in with the city's Board of Health on a regular basis. She promptly disappeared and spent the next five years working in hotels, restaurants, and resorts in New York City under an assumed name. When she was finally apprehended in 1915, she was implicated in over 50 cases of typhoid fever and three deaths. She spent the rest of her life in prison.

1911

Bellevue opened the nation's first ambulatory cardiac clinic.

1911

The city's water supply was chlorinated.

1912

Milk pasteurization was introduced in the city.

1913

The Salvation Army's largest, oldest shelter opened at 225 Bowery and held 235 occupants. The shelter's original purpose was to be a bed-and-breakfast hotel for railroad and merchant marine retirees; it became a haven for people with mental health problems in 1978 and closed in June of 1994.

1916

In October Margaret Sanger and her sister Ethel Byrne challenged state law by opening the nation's first birth control clinic. It was located in Brooklyn and was soon closed by the police.

Q: In the 1920s Sanger formed birth control organizations that eventually merged into which organization?
A: The Planned Parenthood Federation.

1916

Between 1916 and 1920, a total of 12,656 people in the city died from pneumonia, and an additional 4,480 died from influenza.

1917

There were 800 synagogues in New York City (compared to 250 in 1997).

1918

More than 12,000 people in the city died in an influenza pandemic that swept the country.

1920

Thirty percent of the population of New York City was Jewish, compared to 16 percent in 1997.

1925

There were 264,000 Jewish residents on Manhattan's Lower East Side, 285,000 Jewish residents in Brownsville/East New York and New Lots, and 104,000 in Williamsburg.

1928

The Department of Hospitals was formed and became the sole administrator of 26 municipal facilities. This system provided a more cohesive, organized approach to public health. The department was the largest of its kind in the nation.

1931

Statistics show that 1,369 people committed suicide between 1931 and 1935, probably because of the Great Depression. This is the city's highest suicide rate for a four-year period to date. The city's lowest suicide rate (in this century) was 600 suicides between 1986 and 1990.

1935

Many shipbuilders in the Brooklyn Navy Yard were exposed to asbestos at work. They were diagnosed with debilitating lung disease or cancer in the 1970s and 1980s, which led to the creation of asbestos laws.

Q: Where did the first statistical evidence that asbestos causes tumors originate?
A: Mount Sinai Medical Center.

1943

The Pap test for detecting cervical cancer was developed at New York Hospital.

Q: Who was the test named for?
A: George Papanicolaou, the man who developed it.

1944

Q: Where did Calvin Klein, Norma Kamali, Rebecca Moses, and Bob Abajan go to school?
A: The Fashion Institute of Technology at Seventh Avenue and 27th Street.

F.I.T., which opened in 1944, is currently the only school in the world with a toy design department.

1945

Penicillin was introduced and venereal disease was brought under control.

1947

New York University—Bellevue Medical Center opened and eventually became a center for limb reimplantation, treatment of traumatic and head and spinal cord injuries, and cardiac care.

1953

Bellevue Hospital had 2,700 beds, dwarfing all other hospitals in the city and Mount Sinai Hospital was named a major affiliate of Columbia University.

1954

Leona Baumgartner was the first woman to be appointed health commissioner in the city. During her tenure the health department began administering the Salk vaccine against polio. Ninety-four percent of all city schoolchildren had received the vaccine by 1962. She also oversaw the formation of the Poison Control Center in 1955 as well as the fluoridation of the city's water supply in 1965.

1959

The use of lead-based paints on or in buildings was outlawed.

LEAD POISONING

- By 1995 there were 21 lawyers in New York City who focused solely on representing lead-poisoned children. During the first half of 1995 there were over 440 lead-paint claims filed against the city, and by the start of 1997, there were 1,000 lead-paint suits pending.
- Low-income children are 4 times more likely to have excessive levels of lead in their blood than others.
- On the average, 2,000 children in the city become permanently

brain damaged annually from lead, and an estimated 80,000 city children suffer from varying degrees of lead poisoning.
• The Health Department only made 50% of its slated lead-poisoning inspections of homes and apartments by the mid-1990s.

1964

Methadone was first used as a substitute for heroin at Beth Israel Hospital.

1966

Medicaid and Medicare were established for the city's poor.

1968

Mount Sinai Medical School opened.

Q: What was its pioneering distinction as a medical school?
A: It was the first major medical school in New York City to be developed by a hospital rather than a university. With the founding of the school, the hospital complex became known as the Mount Sinai Medical Center.

1970

Control of Bellevue Hospital shifted from municipal hospital boards to the New York City Health and Hospitals Corporation, and Bellevue was still affiliated with the New York University School of Medicine.

1984

New York State passed a bill establishing free prenatal care and nutrition programs at 38 sites in New York City. Three years later, 98 sites for free prenatal health care were available, and 10 years later 360 sites were available. Thirty-three percent fewer low-weight babies are born to women who use the free prenatal services than to those who do not.

1985

None of the public schools in New York City had nutrition committees; by 1995 all of the city's public schools had them.

1986

The School of Visual Arts began offering a bachelor of fine arts degree in computer arts; it was the first accredited college in the country to offer this computer specialty degree.

1986

The Division of AIDS Services was established.

AIDS IN THE CITY

Average number of NYC residents who contract AIDS each year, per 100,000 . . . . .160.0
Average number of NYC residents with AIDS, per 100,000 581
Compared with New Haven, CT 37.4
Median age for NYC residents diagnosised with AIDS 39
Area of NYC with highest number of AIDS cases . . . . .Chelsea
Average number of Chelsea residents with AIDS, per 100,000 2,600
Area of NYC with lowest number of AIDS cases . . . .Bayside/Little Neck, Queens
Average number of Bayside/Little Neck residents with AIDS, per 100,000 108
Largest cause of new AIDS cases in NYC . . . .intravenous drug use

---

1990

There was a 30 percent increase in births in New York City over the course of a decade, and an 8.1 percent increase in the number of women of childbearing age. Women in the 40- to 44-year-old range bearing children increased an astounding 79 percent. Women in the 35- to 39-year-old range saw a 58-percent increase, women in the 30- to 34-year-old range a 35-percent increase, and teenage mothers a 22-percent increase.

Q: What was the average age of a first-time mother in New York City in 1997?

A: 27 years. The average age a decade ago was 25 years.

PRENATAL & CHILD CARE IN 1997

Infant mortality rate for black New Yorkers 15.8%
Compared with black Americans overall 16.8%
Infant mortality rate for white New Yorkers 7.1%
Compared with white Americans overall 6.9%
Overall infant mortality rate in NYC, per 1,000 live births ..11.4%
National rate 8.9%
Infant mortality rate in East Harlem, per 1,000 live births ..15.3%
In Lower Manhattan 3.2%

Q: What is the price in New York City to keep a child in foster care for one year?

A: $20,000.

1991

The city first began testing for cryptosporidium in its tap water.

1991

There were 1,000 cases of food poisoning in New York City schools reported in the three-year period between 1991 and 1994.

Q: What's the average percentage of school kitchens that have insect or rodent contamination?

A: 35% to 40%.

1991 SCHOOL MEAL SNAPSHOT

Price of a full-priced lunch $1.00
Price of a reduced lunch ....25 cents
Price of a full-priced breakfast ....35 cents
Price of a reduced school breakfast ....5 cents
Percentage of New York City school students who
receive free or reduced lunches 83.1%
Fraction of a child's daily nutritional needs that school
lunches in New York City are designed to provide ....one-third

Number of students nationwide who received free
lunches ....25 million

The number of public school students in New York City
receiving a free lunch increased 18.9% between 1991 and 1996.
Over 649,000 students now receive a free lunch.

1993

During the summer the New York Downtown Hospital gave
tourists coupons good for $25 off a visit to their ER

1993

Asbestos had been banned as a building material and was
removed from many public buildings. As a result of the decision
to remove asbestos from all of the city's 1,069 public schools, the
start of the 1993-94 school year was delayed.

1994

Fifty New York City high schools were targeted for airport-style
weapons scanners in a proposal by Chancellor Ramon Cortines.

The Innocents: a typical nineteenth-century New York City elementary school.

Q: How many schools already had metal detectors?
A: 59.

1994

Records show 101 cases of Lyme disease were reported in New York City, but only two were reported in 1995.

1994

Q: How many different countries are represented by the students in New York City's public school system?
A: 188.

Q: What is the average number of students in a kindergarten class in a New York City public school?
A: 26.57 children. The most children allowed in one kindergarten class is 35.

Forty-one of New York City's 100 most crowded schools were located in Queens, and five of the seven school districts in Queens surpassed available space. At least 17,000 new immigrants settled in Queens in the 1980s, representing 112 different countries.

1994

A total of 2,971 psychiatric patients walked away from state hospitals in New York City; 278 were listed as "escaped," indicating that they might be dangerous to themselves or to others (which denotes fewer than 1 in 10 patients).

1995

There are 63 special education schools in New York City; the city's 14 most violent schools (overall) were special education schools. There was a 400 percent increase in special education enrollment in the city from 1985, with approximately 130,000 special education students enrolled in city schools.

SPECIAL NEEDS

The percentage of special education students in New York City who attend regular classes is 7%, compared with 87% in Vermont.

1995

The New York City Health Department found 60 pigeons in one man's townhouse on 77th Street and Fifth Avenue, where he had allowed the birds to roam free in three of the five stories in his building. The Health Department found no violations there. The man spends approximately $20,000 a year caring for the pigeons and other pets in his home.

1995

There were 250 reported rat bites in the city, and 10,739 reported dog bites.

Q: How many reports were there of people being bitten by other humans?
A: 1,401.

Q: How many different diseases do rats carry?
A: 8. The ratio of rats to humans in New York City is 3 to 1.

Q: How many different species of cockroach exist in New York City?
A: 5 (and in 4 different color combinations). Roach droppings were linked to an unusually high number of asthma attacks in the South Bronx.

1995

Q: How many health inspectors are there for New York City's restaurants?
A: 74. The average length of time between inspections per restaurant is 18 months.

Q: What is the average percentage of city food stores that flunk state sanitary inspections?
A: 37%.

HOUSES OF THE HOLY IN 1995

- There were 2,200 Protestant and Orthodox churches and 351 Roman Catholic churches for 2.2 million Catholic members in the city.
- New York City's Jewish population is roughly 1.13 million, with 3 facilities for training American rabbis and about 250 synagogues.
- There were between 400,000 and 600,000 Muslims in the city, most adhering to the Suni tradition. Blacks account for 25% to 40% of the city's Muslims.
- There were 113 Presbyterian churches in the city; 2 were Chinese, 13 Korean, 15 Latin-American, and 27 black.
- There were 11 Buddhist temples in Manhattan Chinatown, as well as several others in the outer boroughs.

1995

The average number of weapons confiscated annually in New York City public high schools was 7,000. There was a 28 percent increase in crime within New York City schools between 1994 and 1995.

THE WAR ZONE

- Over 50,000 students attend parochial school in the New York Archdiocese each year. The dropout rate for these students is less than 1%, compared with the public school rate of 18%. 90% of the parochial school students go on to attend college.
- The ratio of administrators to students in New York City's public school system is 1 to 125. In the parochial school system, the ratio is 1 to 2,000.
- New York is ranked 41st in the nation for its graduation rate. New Jersey is ranked 7th. New York is ranked 40th as the state with students earning the highest S.A.T. scores. Tennessee is ranked 10th and Iowa is ranked 1st.
- Between 40,000 and 60,000 high school students in New York City have parents who are undocumented alien residents.
- 300 unanticipated freshman students arrived at George Washington High School on the first day of school in 1995.

Q: What is the average truancy rate at New York City's larger high schools each school day?
A: 23%

1996

Food for the Homeless distributed food and clothing on the E train subway for the homeless. The organization gave away:

- 70,000 sandwiches
- 4,400 pairs of socks
- 40,000 bananas, apples, and oranges
- 35,000 containers of fruit drink

1996

New York City began installing "water sampling stations" around Manhattan. The locked silver boxes contain spigots for workers to test drinking water more effectively. A worker unlocks the box, draws a bottle of water, and takes the sample back to a lab to test for disease-causing bacteria. Each box cost $5,000.

Q: How often each month does state law require the city to test its water supply?
A: At least 480 times.

Q: Water is piped into New York City from the Catskill-Delaware watershed in upstate New York. How much time does that journey take?
A: 1 month

WATERED DOWN

- New York City—and a few communities in Westchester who share the water supply—uses 1.5 billion gallons of water each day for 9 million people.
- New York City's water supply is at 100% capacity when there is a 1-year supply in store.
- The size of the watersheds supplying New York City is 2,000 square miles, or roughly the size of the state of Delaware.

1997

Heart disease was the leading cause of death in New York City, followed by cancer and then AIDS.

Q: Which borough has the highest death rate for both cancer and heart disease?
A: Staten Island.

The citywide average for cancer was 185 cases per 100,000 people; the rate in Staten Island was 221 cases per 100,000 people. The citywide average for heart disease is 357 deaths per 100,000 people, and the average in Staten Island is 444 deaths per 100,000.

1997 HOSPITAL SNAPSHOT

- East Harlem in Manhattan has the highest rate of hospitalizations in the city with 219 per 1,000 people; the average city rate is 129.
- 30% of homeless New Yorkers have a history of severe mental illness, and 35% have substance-abuse problems. Many suffer from both problems. A hospital bed in a psychiatric unit costs $113,000 per year in New York State; a prison cell costs $60,000 per year.
- An average of 6% of the people hospitalized in Manhattan are uninsured. An average of 5.3% are hospitalized because of mental disease, 4.6% with an HIV infection, and 7.5% because of substance abuse.
- The Marriott Corporation runs the food service at Columbia-Presbyterian Hospital.
- New York City medical centers pay $2 to $3 million annually for traditional advertising and marketing.

1997

Approximately 953,000 New Yorkers are over the age of sixty-five, with white residents by far the majority. Citymeals-On-Wheels delivers free nutritional meals each day to homebound elderly New Yorkers.

One of the most famous view in NYC: the Beaux-Arts facade of the New York Puclic Library on Fifth Avenue between 40th and 42nd Streets.

CHAPTER 6

Literary New York & the Media

Tradition Fades But The Written Word Remains Ever Fresh.

ULRICH B. PHILLIPS

All of everything is concentrated here, population, theater, art, writing, publishing, importing, business, murder, mugging, luxury, poverty. It's all of everything. It goes all night. It is tireless and its air is charged with energy.

JOHN STEINBECK

New York City is known as a mecca for writers and reporters; for many it's the end of the line and a career pinnacle. The list of writers who have lived in, worked in, and been inspired by New York City is a hefty book in itself, as is the list of newspapers that have been published in the city, and the thousands of seasoned reporters who worked for them.

New York City was already a literary center during colonial times, as it was featured in the national literature of the Knickerbocker group in the early 1800s. Washington Irving, the author of the *Legend of Sleepy Hollow,* was the country's first professional writer.

One of the greatest features of the media and literature from New York City is its stunning diversity. There is no one writing or reporting style that typifies New York City. The media and literature from New York are as varied as the population, which is as varied as any place on earth. New York City inspired Washington Irving and the Beat Poets, Walt Whitman and Edgar Allan Poe, John Steinbeck and the Round Table Writers, Tennessee Williams and Truman Capote, J. D. Salinger and the Harlem Renaissance writers, Jacob A. Riis and Theodore Dreiser, Norman Mailer and Edith Wharton, F. Scott Fitzgerald and Woody Allen, Harold Ross and Gore Vidal, each with a distinctive voice, each a mere fraction of the thousands of lauded writers from New York.

New York City, of course, is home to the *New York Times,* the *New York Post,* and the *Wall Street Journal,* as well as dozens of magazines, alternative newspapers, foreign newspapers, industry magazines and newsletters, business newspapers, and Internet channels. Major cable channels, radio and television stations, and wire services are located in the city, and many major publishing houses are traditionally located in New York as well. Technology has altered New York City's premier publishing, media, and literary status, as the spread of information, its accessibility, and the fracturing of a traditional newspaper, television, and literary audience have affected the media located in most American cities. But you still can't beat New York City for inspiration, grist for stories, and those all-important contacts.

1621

A Dutch scholar and physician named Nicolaes van Wassenaer published a news journal titled *Historisch Verhael* semiannually from 1621 to 1631. When writing about New Amsterdam in 1626, he relied upon information supplied by the crew and passengers of the ship *Arms of Amsterdam,* which returned to Holland in November of 1626. Apart from describing what New Amsterdam looked like, the journal included the passage, "When the fort, staked out at Manhates, will be completed, it is to be named Amsterdam.

1626

Early settlers were primarily businessmen, seafarers, traders, and their families. Henry Hudson wrote of an encounter with Indians in Manhattan, "The natives are very good people; for when they saw that I would not remain, they supposed that I was afraid of their bows, and taking the arrows, they broke them in pieces and threw them into the fire."

1694

Printer William Bradford's early publications reveal that New York was evolving into a literate society in which the written word would become significant. His early titles included *A New Primer, or Methodical Directions to Attain the True Spelling, Reading & Writing of English* and *The Secretary's Guide, Or, Young Man's Companion…Containing 1st. The Grounds of Spelling, Reading and Writing True English,* which had numerous printings.

WILLIAM BRADFORD—A PRINTER'S PRINTER

William Bradford, a Quaker born in England, had many claims to distinction; he owned the city's first bookstore and was involved in America's first freedom-of-the-press case. He was charged and tried in Philadelphia for having printed a seditious pamphlet—his defense was that a printer was obliged to print whatever a citizen wanted to communicate. Since a witness dropped and ruined the printer's form that constituted the evidence, Bradford was set free. He then moved to New York City.

Bradford's first job in New York City was to print the laws and acts of the General Assembly, and he received 38 government contracts during his first year. Bradford responded to constant complaints about typographical errors by pointing out the numerous rush orders and his dearth of proofreaders. The first book Bradford published was *A Paraphrastical Exposition* by John Philly. There is no record of how the book sold.

A young man from Boston applied for a job at Bradford's shop and he turned him down, suggesting he try Philadelphia instead. The young man's name was Benjamin Franklin.

Bradford lived to be 89 and was buried in the Trinity Church yard.

1695

Politician and entrepeneur Robert Livingston (1654-1728) was described as "a literate man in a society just verging on literacy."

1710

William Bradford printed *The Book of Common-Prayer, and Administration of the Sacraments,* the first American edition of the standard Anglican prayer book.

1713

The Reverend John Sharpe donated a collection of English and Latin books to the city "towards laying the Foundation of a Publick Library at New-York in America [sic]." The books eventually comprised the core of the New York Society Library.

1659

New Amsterdam's first poet was a man named Jacob Steendam who worked as a clerk for the Dutch West India Company. He sent the piece "The Complaint of New Amsterdam to Her Mother" to the Netherlands for publication. Two years later, he wrote "The Praise of New Amsterdam" as a fitting follow-up to his earlier work.

1725

New York City's first newspaper, a weekly called the *New York Gazette,* appeared on October 16. It was published by the city's first printer, William Bradford, whose business was located at 81 Pearl Street. The first newspaper was printed on gray, seemingly dirty paper and consisted of "borrowed" text or, on occasion, text that was clearly incorrect.

> *Being quite worn out with old age and labour he left this mortal state in the lively hopes of a blessed immortality. Reader, reflect how soon you'll quit this stage. You'll find that few attain to such an age. Life's full of pain. Lo, here's a place of rest. Prepare to meet your God then you are blessed.*
> EPITAPH ON THE TOMBSTONE OF WILLIAM BRADFORD

Q: Was New York City the first colony to have a newspaper?
A: It was the third, after Boston and Philadelphia.

1725

Over the course of the next century, more than 100 newspapers were published in the city.

1733

Bradford's former apprentice and partner, John Peter Zenger, began printing the *New York Weekly Journal* on November 5 to offset the royalist leanings of the *Gazette*. Zenger was supported by numerous wealthy merchants in the colony, but was arrested on charges of seditious libel for challenging the actions of Governor William Cosby. His wife, Anna Catherine, continued the newspaper while he was in jail. Zenger was acquitted.

1742

Zenger's wife, Anna Catherine, opened the second book shop in New York City. She specialized in pamphlets and stationery.

1750

Colonial bookstores also functioned as post offices, dry-goods stores, stationery stores, bulletin boards, and listening posts.

1766

The *New York Journal* was published by John Holt. The paper was one of several colonial papers to publish a series of anti-British articles called the "Journal of Occurrences," written by Samuel Adams and the Sons of Liberty.

1775

Political satirist and poet Philip Freneau returned to New York City from Princeton University to write poems such as "American Liberty" and "Libera Nos Domine."

1787

Essays written under the name Publius in the *New York Independent Journal* by Alexander Hamilton, John Jay, and James Madison were later compiled as the *Federalist Papers* and circulated throughout the States.

Q: How many essays did the statesmen write under the name Publius?
A: 85.

1791

Charlotte Temple, A Tale of Truth by Susanna Rowson went through 200 editions and was unmatched as a bestseller until 1852.

Q: Which book outsold Rowson's in 1852?
A: *Uncle Tom's Cabin* by Harriet Beecher Stowe.

1800

Q: How many daily papers were there in New York City?
A: 5.

The *New York Gazette* and *General Advertiser,* the *Commercial Advertiser,* the *Mercantile Advertiser, Porcupine's Gazette,* and *American Citizen* and *General Advertiser* were all published daily at the turn of the century. New York City was the leading commercial center for the States, a fact reflected in the city's newspapers.

1801

Alexander Hamilton began publishing the *New York Evening Post.*

1802

Booksellers and publishers in the city held their first Literary Fair and half a million books were sold in five days.

1804

Samuel Wood opened the first used-books store on Pearl Street.

1805

Alexander Hamilton defended Harry Croswell, editor of the Federalist newspaper *Wasp,* who was accused of reprinting material from the *Evening Post* and committing libel against President Jefferson. Hamilton maintained that in libel cases the truth of what a defendant wrote or published was relevant and admissible. This stance led to changes in New York State law in 1805 and later in federal law.

1807

Charles Wiley set up a bookshop at 6 Reade Street. His back room, known as the Den, was used as a meeting place by William Cullen Bryant, James Fenimore Cooper, and Samuel Morse.

Q: Which publisher began his career by working for Wiley?
A: George Palmer Putnam.

1808

The Public Library contained 10,000 volumes. There were more than twenty newspapers published in the city—half of which were daily papers—as well as several weekly and monthly magazines.

1809

The satiric *A History of New York* was published in the *New York Evening Post* in installments under the pseudonym Diedrich Knickerbocker.

Q: Who was the real author?
A: Washington Irving.

The collection of installments was eventually collected into a book about New Amsterdam that spanned "from the Beginning of the World to the End of the Dutch Dynasty." This was the first American work of fiction read abroad, and New Yorkers were given the nickname "Knickerbocker." Writers such as James Fenimore Cooper and William Cullen Bryant adopted the nickname in the 1820s.

"GOTHAM CITY"

Washington Irving was also the person who dubbed New York City as "Gotham City". Gotham was a town in England noted for its "wise fools," which led to the saying "More fools pass through Gotham than remain in it". The residents of Gotham in England wanted to discourage people from settling in their town, so they purposely acted insane whenever strangers would visit. Irving thought New Yorkers had adopted the same strategy.

1825

William Cullen Bryant began editing the *Evening Post*.

1825

The Cooper Club, also known as the Lunch, was formed by James Fenimore Cooper, William Cullen Bryant, Samuel Morse, Charles Wiley, James Kent, and others.

1827

The first black-owned and -edited newspaper in the world was *Freedom's Journal,* launched in New York City on March 16 by John B. Russwurm. He was also distinguished as the first black American to graduate from college (Bowdoin College in 1826). His partner was Presbyterian minister Samuel Cornish, who edited the *Weekly Advocate* after *Freedom's Journal* folded in 1829.

> *We are aware that there are many instances of vice among us, but we avow that it is because no one has taught its subjects to be virtuous; many instances of poverty, because no sufficient efforts accommodated to minds contracted to slavery and deprived of early education have been made, to teach them how to husband their hard earnings and to assure themselves comforts.*
> JOHN B. RUSSWURM, FROM HIS FIRST EDITORIAL
> IN *FREEDOM'S JOURNAL.*

> *We consider it a mere waste of words to talk of ever enjoying citizenship in this country.*
> JOHN B. RUSSWURM, IN HIS LAST EDITORIAL
> BEFORE MOVING TO LIBERIA

Q: What was the paper's slogan?
A: "Righteousness Exalteth a Nation."

1827

Samuel Rust invented the Washington hand press in New York City, which made printing more efficient. Steam-driven presses were introduced a few years later.

1828

The city's first French newspaper, *Le Courrier des Etats-Unis,* was founded.

1833

Benjamin H. Day first published the *Sun* on September 3. The paper was aimed at a wide audience and carried mostly features and human interest stories. Other similar papers become popular across the nation and were collectively known as the Penny Press.

1831

William C. Bryant, one of the editors of the *Evening Post,* and William L. Stone, editor of the *Commercial Advertiser,* engaged in a brawl on the street near Lower Broadway. Bryant commenced the attack by striking Stone over the head with a "cowskin"; after a few blows the fight ended and a whip was wrested from Bryant and carried off by Stone.

1835

The *New York Herald* was introduced. Though there were 35 Penny Press newspapers in the city throughout the 1830s, the *New York Herald* was the largest and most lauded. It contained foreign coverage, sports, financial news, and offered a Sunday edition.

1841

There were 10 daily newspapers in the city. The *New York Tribune* was introduced by Horace Greeley in 1841 and soon became the *Herald*'s main competition, offering global business and political perspectives and extensive local reporting. The *Journal of*

Commerce, originally published by Arthur Tappan, also covered the business realm.

Q: What was the *Herald's* distinction?
A: It was the first newspaper to be distributed nationally.

1844

Edgar Allan Poe came to NYC to edit the *Broadway Journal.* By the time he died, he had edited five magazines and contributed to over 30.

1846

Walt Whitman, who referred to himself as "Manhattanese," edited the *Brooklyn Eagle.* Since he couldn't interest a publisher in *Leaves of Grass* he published it himself in 1855.

> *Twenty months [in New York City] have presented me with a richer and more varied exercise for thought and life, than twenty years could in any other part of these United States.*
> WRITER MARGARET FULLER, UPON DEPARTING
> NEW YORK FOR EUROPE IN 1846

1847

Herman Melville wrote *Mardi, Redburn,* and *White-Jacket* in the city. He also started *Moby Dick,* but completed it in the Berkshires.

1848

The book-publishing industry burgeoned in New York City, with publishing houses such as D. Appleton; Dodd, Mead; E. P. Dutton; Harper & Brothers; Henry Holt; Doubleday, Page; Charles Scribner's Sons; and G. P. Putnam's Sons.

1850

There were more than 12 black literary and book-lending societies in Manhattan and Brooklyn.

1850

The literary magazine *Harper's New Monthly Magazine* was launched by the publishing firm of Harper & Brothers. The concept behind the magazine was to educate the reader while presenting books published by Harper. Artists such as John Singer Sargent, Winslow Homer, Frederic Remington, and Edwin Abbey contributed to the magazine, which reached its peak in 1900. The magazine was renamed *Harper's Monthly Magazine* in 1900, and took its current name, *Harper's,* in 1925.

Q: The magazine published *Confessions of Nat Turner* in the 1950s. Who wrote it?
A: William Styron.

1851

The *New York Times* was launched.

Q: Who launched the *New York Times*?
A: Henry J. Raymond.

The New York Times *building in the heyday of Newspaper Row. About fifteen daily papers called the Row (now Park Row) home in the late 1880s.*

NEWS TRAVELS FAST

Editors and reporters faced such stiff competition for stories that they used pigeons, railroads, steamboats, and the Pony Express for gathering news.

1853

An Austrian immigrant named August Brentano opened a newsstand on Lower Broadway that specialized in hard-to-find and foreign papers and books. He moved his operation, renamed Brentano's Literary Emporium, to Union Square. His store became a meeting place for Henry Ward Beecher and Edwin Booth.

1861

The *Herald* was able to print 135,000 copies of the newspaper a day.

1864

The *Journal of Commerce* and *New York World* published a forged document created by a stockbroker speculator—both papers were required to suspend publishing for two days.

1864

Q: How many of the 17 daily newspapers in the city endorsed Lincoln during the presidential election year?
A: 5: the *Times,* the *Tribune,* the *Sun,* the *Evening Post,* and the *Commercial Advertiser.*

1868

The weekly periodical *Revolution* was launched by Susan B. Anthony, emphasizing news of the reform movement. Its editors were Elizabeth Cady Stanton and Parker Pillsbury.

1871

The *New York Times* exposed the corrupt Tweed Ring. Cartoonist Thomas Nast was noted for ridiculing Tweed politicians in *Harper's Weekly.*

1876

Yudishe Gazeten was founded in New York City as the world's first Yiddish-language daily newspaper.

Q: How many Yiddish newspapers were there in New York City between 1876 and 1954?
A: 27.

1876

The humor magazine *Puck* was launched as a German language publication by cartoonist Joseph Keppler and publisher Adolph Schwarmann.

Q: What was it named after?
A: The character Puck in *A Midsummer Night's Dream.*

A year later an English version was launched by Henry Cuyler Bunner with the subtitle "Oh What Fools These Mortals Be!" It surpassed the German edition and became the first popular humor magazine in the country. The magazine's staff supported Democratic causes by supporting civil service, favoring lower tariffs, and striking out at big business monopolies. The magazine folded in 1918, partially because of the political importance of daily newspapers.

1881

Q: Which Henry James novel, published in 1881, is centered around life in the city's upper classes during the 1830s and 1840s?
A: *Washington Square.*

AUTHORS WHO HAVE LIVED IN NEW YORK CITY

- Saul Bellow
- Edna Ferber
- William Cullen Bryant
- Allen Ginsberg
- Herman Mellville
- Walt Whitman
- Isaac B. Singer
- Henry James
- Edith Wharton
- Theodore Dreiser
- Emma Lazarus
- Willa Cather
- Amiri Baraka
- James Weldon Johnson
- Anaïs Nin
- Norman Mailer
- Dorothy Parker
- Edna St. Vincent Millay
- e. e. cummings
- Hart Crane
- Robert Benchley
- Alexander Woollcott
- F. Scott Fitzgerald
- James Thurber
- Dashiell Hammett
- Zora Neale Hurston
- Ralph Ellison
- James Baldwin
- John P. Marquand
- Philip Roth
- William Styron
- Truman Capote
- W. H. Auden
- William Burroughs
- Ishmael Reed
- Terry Southern
- Tom Wolfe
- Arthur Miller
- Wendy Wasserstein
- Ishmael Reed
- Irwin Shaw
- Gay Talese
- Fanny Hurst
- Henry Roth
- Neil Simon
- Dylan Thomas
- Mark Twain
- William Dunlap
- Jack Kerouac
- O. Henry
- Edgar Allan Poe
- Joseph Heller
- J. D. Salinger
- Louisa May Alcott
- Washington Irving
- Stephen Crane
- Jacob A. Riis
- W. E. B. Du Bois
- Sinclair Lewis
- Dr. Theodore Rubin
- Henry Miller
- Nathanael West
- Eugene O'Neill
- John Dos Passos
- Sherwood Anderson
- Robert Sherwood
- George S. Kaufman
- Ring Lardner
- Lillian Hellman
- James Agee
- John O'Hara
- Rudolph Fisher
- Langston Hughes
- John Steinbeck
- Henry Roth
- Tennessee Williams
- Thomas Merton
- Carson McCullers
- Arthur Miller
- Susan Sontag
- Gay Talese
- E. L. Doctorow
- Malcolm X
- H. L. Mencken
- Djuna Barnes
- Terry Southern
- Peter Matthiessen
- Amy Tan
- Mark O'Donnell
- Paul Bowles
- Woody Allen
- Betty Smith

1883

Joseph Pulitzer bought the *World*. Within four years he owned morning, evening, and Sunday papers. The Sunday paper had a circulation of 250,000, which was the widest in the country.

1883

The city's first Chinese newspaper, *Mei Hua Shin Pao,* was founded.

1886

Q: On what structure was the sonnet "The New Colossus" by Emma Lazarus, whose father had formed the Knickerbocker Club, chosen to be inscribed on 1866?
A: On the pedestal of the Statue of Liberty.

1889

The *Wall Street Journal* was introduced by the Dow-Jones financial service.

1890

Jacob Riis, a Danish immigrant, published *How The Other Half Lives,* a book about poverty in New York City with startling, disturbing photographs (the photos also appeared in the *Sun* in 1888). The newspaper photos and book convinced many in the city that poverty was imposed rather than the result of loose moral standards. His photographs also led to the cleaning, fixing, or razing of many city slums. When Charles Dickens visited New York in 1842 and saw the Five Points slum, the area was so vile that even he was horrified.

1890

Printing plates invented during the Civil War were put to use in new types of presses, which allowed 48,000 12-page newspapers to be produced in an hour.

1892

The city's first Arabic newspaper, *Kawkab Amirka,* was founded.

1893

Color printing was first used by the *World,* paving the way for color comics in the Sunday paper. The most popular was "Hogan's Alley," which was dubbed "Yellow Kid" by readers because the central character was a toothless child in a tenement who wore a shirt stained with yellow blobs of ink.

1895

William Randolph Hearst moved to New York City and purchased the *New York Journal.*

Q: Where did he live before he moved to New York City?
A: San Francisco.

Q: How did Hearst contribute to the nickname "yellow journalism"?
A: Both the *Journal* and the *World* published the "Yellow Kid" cartoon strip. Both papers began overloading pages with enormous headlines and photographs. Critics dubbed this style "yellow journalism" and the style was adopted by newspapers across the country.

CREAM OF THE CROP

The *Sun, Herald, Journal,* and *World* attracted some of the country's best reporters—such as Nellie Bly, Lincoln Steffens, and Stephen Crane.

1895

Stephen Crane wrote *The Red Badge of Courage* in a studio in the Art Students League on East 23rd Street.

1896

Adolph S. Ochs took over the *New York Times,* which had been losing prestige throughout the 1880s and 1890s. Eight years later, Ochs moved operations to a building on Broadway known as the Times Tower.

1897

The Jewish *Daily Forward* was launched.

> *Of all the ambitions of the Great Unpublished, the one that is strongest, the most abiding, is the ambition to get to New York.*
> WRITER FRANK NORRIS, UPON HIS MOVE TO NEW YORK CITY
> FROM SAN FRANCISCO IN 1898

1900

The Harbor News Association was reorganized as the Associated Press.

1902

The Algonquin Hotel opened in 1902, providing a round table for Manhattan's wittiest—and frequently most impecunious—bon vivants. Alan Jay Lerner wrote *My Fair Lady* in Room 908 at the Algonquin Hotel.

WOMEN OF THE ALGONQUIN

From its opening near the turn of the century, the Algonquin's staff welcomed solo women travelers, which was practically unheard of in Edwardian times.

- Irish actress Lady Gregory created a memorable stir when she lit up a cigarette after dinner in the Algonquin lobby in the early 1900s.
- Ruth Hale, wife of Round Table participant Heywood Broun, and Jane Grant, wife of *New Yorker* founder Harold Ross, cofounded the Lucy Stone League before 1920 to encourage women to retain their maiden names. Hale threatened to boycott her own wedding unless the word obey was removed from the Episcopal service.
- Tallulah Bankhead arrived at the Algonquin from Alabama in 1919 at the age of 16 to study acting. Her father, William, was

the Speaker of the U.S. House of Representatives and her uncle John was a U.S. Senator. The high-spirited girl was sent to a convent school at the age of 10, where she scandalized the nuns by turning cartwheels during a mass, so her family hoped the Algonquin (the place where Commander Booth had resided) would infuse in her a sense of discipline. It didn't. She insulted the imperious Ethel Barrymore and was soundly slapped for her impertinence.

Either I can keep an eye on the Tallulah or run this hotel. No man does both!
ALGONQUIN HOTEL OWNER/MANAGER FRANK CASE, IN REPLY TO MR. AND MRS. BANKHEAD'S REQUEST THAT HE LOOK AFTER TALLULAH

- Algonquin owner Ben Bodne (1946-86) sold newspapers on the steps of the courthouse in Chattanooga, Tennessee, when he was 10 years old. Helen Keller and her teacher, Annie Sullivan, approached Ben and purchased a 2-cent paper with 10 cents, insisting he keep the 8 cents change for himself. In the late 1940s, when Ben Bodne saw Helen Keller and Annie Sullivan lunching in the Oak Room, he greeted them and reminded them of the incident. Miss Keller asked, "What did you do with the eight cents?" and he said, "I bought the Algonquin."
- Ella Fitzgerald used to go back to the Algonquin after late-night gigs and order Chinese food, which she would share with the bell staff.
- Angela Lansbury's first home in the U.S. after arriving with her mother from England was the Algonquin.

1902

O. Henry moved to New York City and wrote about the brothels and bars of the Tenderloin in his short stories. Within a year of his arrival he was writing the *Sunday World* a story a week for $100.

Q: What was his real name?
A: William Sydney Porter.

1903

Writer Willa Cather was named the managing editor of *McClure's* magazine.

Q: What was her profession before moving to New York City?
A: She was a schoolteacher in Pittsburgh.

1907

E. W. Scripps founded the United Press.

1909

The *Amsterdam News* was launched. The *Amsterdam News* is the nation's oldest continuously published black newspaper.

Q: How many computers were there at the Amsterdam News at the start of 1997?
A: 1.

1910

W. E. B. Du Bois moved to New York City to edit the *Crisis*. Published by the National Association for the Advancement of Colored People, it was the first magazine devoted exclusively to the work of black writers.

1911

The Serbian newspaper *Srpski Dnevnik* was founded.

1912

Edna Ferber, Sinclair Lewis, Sara Teasdale, Fanny Hurst, Dorothy Parker, J. D. Salinger, and Anaïs Nin all lived and wrote on the Upper West Side.

1913

The newspaper *La Prensa* was founded.

1914

H. L. Mencken and George Jean Nathan oversaw the magazine *Smart Set,* which was located in Greenwich Village. As a columnist and editor for the magazine, Mencken published pieces by Eugene O'Neill, James Joyce, and F. Scott Fitzgerald.

Photo by B. Kim Taylor

St. Luke's Garden in Greenwich Village has always been a haven for the literary cabal. Bret Hart's former home is right next door.

1915

Writers for the Provincetown Players included John Dos Passos, Eugene O'Neill, Theodore Dreiser, Edna St. Vincent Millay, and Walter Lippmann.

1916

Writers who moved to New York City in 1916 included e.e. cummings, Hart Crane, and Edmund Wilson.

FAMOUS ALGONQUIN HOTEL RESIDENTS
AND ROUND TABLE MEMBERS

- Alan Jay Lerner
- Dorothy Parker
- Robert E. Sherwood
- James Thurber
- Franklin Pierce Adams
- Ring Lardner

- Robert Benchley
- Edna Ferber
- John Barrymore
- Douglas Fairbanks
- George S. Kaufman
- Alexander Woollcott

- Heywood Broun
- Tallulah Bankhead
- Franklin P. Adams
- Harold Ross
- Angela Lansbury

George S. Kaufman was walking down Fifth Avenue one day with his wife, whose home town was Rochester. "All Rochester seems to be in New York this week!" she exclaimed. "What an excellent time to visit Rochester," mused Kaufman.

1918

Newspaper reporters began using the telephone more often for gathering news.

1919

The *Jewish Daily Forward* was edited by Abraham Cahan; the magazine published the work of Isaac Bashevis Singer, I. J. Singer, and Sholom Aleichem.

1920

The 1920s introduced yellow journalism's offshoot: tabloid journalism. Tabloid newspapers utilized the same large photographs and shocking headlines as the "Yellow Kid" papers, and one of the first in the city was the *Illustrated Daily News,* launched on June 26 in 1919, its name was soon shortened to the *Daily News.* The paper boasted a circulation of two million before World War II.

1920

The *Little Review* published James Joyce's *Ulysses* in installments and was fined $100 in an obscenity suit brought by John Sumner, the head of the New York Society for the Suppression of Vice.

1921

The city's first Hebrew newspaper, *Hadoar,* was founded.

1924

The Harlem Renaissance was in full bloom until the end of the 1930s and writers and artists traveled to Harlem from all over the country to be part of the artistic and literary movement. Charles

Johnson, editor of the National Urban League-published magazine *Opportunity,* held a meeting at the Civic Club in March to bring together prominent black writers and white publishers. The careers of many black writers were launched that day.

Q: Who were some of the writers?
A: Langston Hughes, Zora Neale Hurston, Countee Cullen, Claude McKay, and Rudolph Fisher.

Zora Neale Hurston was the daughter of a tenant farmer who moved to New York City and won a prize for a story she sent to *Opportunity.* She eventually became an anthropologist and wrote *Jonah's Gourd Vine* in 1934 and *Their Eyes Were Watching God* in 1937.

Rudolph Fisher moved to the city to study bacteriology and pathology at the Columbia College of Physicians and Surgeons. He became a radiologist, ran a hospital, and wrote *The Walls of Jericho* and *The Conjure Man Dies.*

Q: What was distinctive about *The Conjure Man Dies?*
A: It was the first mystery novel comprised solely of black characters.

1924

Hearst founded a tabloid newspaper called the *Mirror,* and the *Herald* and *Tribune* merged into the *Herald-Tribune.*

1924

The most influential publishers in the city were Boni and Liveright, founders of the Modern Library Series. The company published material by Sherwood Anderson, Freud, Faulkner, Hemingway, cummings, O'Neill, Hart, Crane, and Dreiser.

Q: Which female author worked at the company as a reader?
A: Lillian Hellman, author of *The Children's Hour* (1934) and *The Little Foxes* (1939).

Q: Which writer was married to Lillian Hellman?

A: Dashiell Hammett.

Another important publishing house at the time was Alfred A. Knopf, which published Willa Cather and H. L. Mencken.

1925

Q: Who wrote *Manhattan Transfer* in 1925?
A: John Dos Passos.

1925—A YEAR OF LITERARY PLENTY

Other books published in 1925 were *The Great Gatsby* by F. Scott Fitzgerald, *An American Tragedy* by Theodore Dreiser, and *Arrowsmith* by Sinclair Lewis.

1925

The *New Yorker* magazine was founded and published pieces by James Thurber and E. B. White.

Q: Who was the magazine's first editor?
A: Harold Ross.

1927

Many of the city's writers, actors, artists, journalists, critics, and playwrights resided in midtown's best hotels and met in restaurants, at parties, and in speakeasies.

FAMOUS NEW YORK CITY-BASED SUPERHEROES

Spider Man . . . . Forest Hills, Queens
The Fantastic Four . . . . The fictional Four Freedoms Plaza
in East Midtown
Daredevil . . . . Hell's Kitchen
The Avengers . . . . A mansion at 890 Fifth Avenue
(the site of the Frick Collection)
Doctor Strange . . . . 177a Bleecker Street

1928

The *Irish Echo* was founded.

1929

The Strand, a used bookstore and the largest bookstore in New York City, was opened by Ben Bass. The store moved to its current location on 12th Street and Broadway in 1956, where it occupies 32,000 square feet and four stories of a building. The Strand is currently run by the founder's son, Fred Bass. There are over two million books in the store.

Q: What is the Strand's slogan?
A: "8 Miles of Books."

1930

Q: Which mystery novel did Dashiell Hammett publish in 1930?
A: *The Maltese Falcon.*

1933

Esquire magazine was founded by Arnold Gingrich. The first issue featured Dos Passos, Hemingway, Dashiell Hammett, and Erskine Caldwell. The magazine published F. Scott Fitzgerald's *The Crack Up* in three installments in 1936.

1934

Henry Roth published *Call It Sleep.*

1935

Adolph Ochs died and the Sulzberger family took over the *New York Times,* which soon won more Pulitzer prizes and had more foreign correspondents than any of its competitors.

1935

Actress Bette Davis's attorney informed her a rumor was spreading throughout the city that she had died. Miss Davis retorted, "With the newspaper strike on, I wouldn't dream of it!"

1936

On his first day in Harlem, Ralph Ellison met Langston Hughes and arranged to meet Richard Wright later. Harlem in the late 1930s and early 1940s became the setting for Ellison's novel *Invisible Man* (1952). James Baldwin also set his novel *Go Tell It on the Mountain* (1953) in Harlem during the same era.

1943

Betty Smith's *A Tree Grows in Brooklyn* was published.

Q: What part of New York City is described in *A Tree Grows in Brooklyn*?
A: The Williamsburg-Greenpoint border.

Smith published *Tomorrow Will Be Better* in 1948, *Maggie—Now* in 1958, and *Joy in the Morning* in 1963. She also wrote more than 40 plays.

1945

The *New York Staats-Zeitung* was the city's largest foreign-language newspaper with a circulation of 250,000 at the height of its popularity.

1946

The *New Yorker* published John Hersey's *Hiroshima* in installments, as well as pieces by Truman Capote, A. J. Liebling, Joseph Mitchell, Rachel Carson, and Jonathan Schell.

Q: Who was the editor of the *New Yorker* then?
A: William Shawn.

1947

Arthur Miller, who lived in Brooklyn, published *All My Sons*. Two years later he wrote *Death of a Salesman,* which garnered a Pulitzer prize.

1948

Norman Mailer, who also lived in Brooklyn, published *The Naked and the Dead.*

MATCH THE AUTHOR WITH HIS OR HER PSEUDONYM

1. Hans Christian Andersen	A. Imamu Amiri Baraka
2. Isaac Asimov	B. O. Henry
3. Louis Auchincloss	C. Dr. Seuss
4. Robert Benchley	D. Mark Twain
5. William S. Burroughs	E. Constant Reader
6. Barbara Cartland	F. Joseph Conrad
7. Samuel Langhorne Clemens	G. Villiam Christian Walter
8. Theodore S. Geisel	H. Dr. A. Paul French
9. Dashiell Hammett	I. Andrew Lee
10. LeRoi Jones	J. Guy Fawkes
11. Teodore Jozef Korzeniowski	K. George Orwell
12. Edna St. Vincent Millay	L. William Lee
13. Dorothy Parker	M. Barbara Hamilton McCorquodale
14. Terry Southern	N. Peter Collinson
15. Gore Vidal	O. Nancy Boyd
16. Nathan Wallenstein Weinstein	P. Maxwell Kenton
17. William Sydney Porter	Q. Irving Tannenbaum
18. John B. Wilson	R. Edgar Box
19. Irving Stone	S. Nathanael West
20. Eric Arthur Blair	T. Anthony Burgess

Answers: 1. G; 2. H; 3. I; 4. J; 5. L; 6. M; 7. D; 8. C; 9. N; 10. A; 11. F; 12. O; 13. E; 14. P; 15. R; 16. S; 17. B; 18. T; 19. Q; 20. K

1949

John P. Marquand published *Point of No Return* and viewed the city as "an indefinable combination of triumph, discouragement, and memories."

1949

Maxwell Perkins, an editor at Scribner's, edited the work of John P. Marquand, Ernest Hemingway, F. Scott Fitzgerald, and Erskine Caldwell.

1953

Partisan Review published works by Mary McCarthy, F. W. Dupee, Meyer Shapiro, and Lionel Abel. Saul Bellow translated Isaac Beshavis Singer's "Gimpel the Fool" for the magazine and wrote *Seize the Day* (1956), *Herzog* (1964), *Mr. Sammler's Planet* (1969), and *Humboldt's Gift* (1975).

Q: Which country did Saul Bellow live in before moving to New York City?
A: Canada.

1953

Allen Ginsberg moved to East Seventh Street in the East Village. William Burroughs, Jack Kerouac, and Norman Mailer soon followed.

1955

The *Village Voice* was founded as a weekly alternative paper.

Q: Which literary figure was one of the paper's founders?
A: Norman Mailer.

LOST AND FOUND

Between 250 and 400 people each year in the 1990s place an ad on the back page of the *Village Voice* to find someone they met briefly in the city.

1955

Seventy-four percent of the children's books in America were published in New York City before 1955.

1957

Jack Kerouac's *On the Road* was published and the "beat generation" flourished. Kerouac published *The Subterraneans*, a novel about the Lower East Side, a year later.

1958

Truman Capote, who had been living in a basement apartment, wrote *Breakfast at Tiffany's.* He published *In Cold Blood* in 1966.

1960

A series of newspaper strikes in the city in the early 1960s crippled many papers and the number of dailies dropped from eight to three.

1961

Neil Simon's first full-length play, *Come Blow Your Horn,* was produced.

1961

Jane Jacobs wrote *The Death and Life of Great American Cities,* which criticized Robert Moses and centralized city planning.

1963

The *Mirror* declared bankruptcy in 1963.

1965

George Plimpton's apartment on East 72nd Street regularly drew together Gay Talese, Lillian Hellman, Norman Mailer, William Styron, Irwin Shaw, Philip Roth, Jack Gelber, Terry Southern, Blair Fuller, Peter Matthiessen, and John Marquand.

1965

Tom Wolfe published *The Kandy-Kolored Tangerine-Flake Streamline Baby* in 1965, and Neil Simon's *The Odd Couple* was produced.

1966

Three New York newspapers—the *Journal American,* the *World Telegram and Sun,* and the *Herald-Tribune*—merged to form the *New York World Journal Tribune,* quickly dubbed "Widget" by an amused public. The *Widget* folded in 1967.

New Yorkers wouldn't dream of missing their daily dose of news.

1967

The city's first Korean newspaper, *Hangkook Ilbo New York Pan*, was founded.

1968

Q: Which 1968 Norman Mailer novel won a Pulitzer prize?
A: *The Armies of the Night.*

1970

The newspaper *India Abroad* was launched in New York City and aimed at the widely spread expatriate Indian population.

1970

Jimmy Breslin wrote *The Gang That Couldn't Shoot Straight.*

1971

The *New York Times* won an important case in the U.S. Supreme Court involving an attempt by the federal government to prevent the release of the Pentagon Papers.

1974

Betty Friedan wrote *The Feminine Mystique.*

1975

E. L. Doctorow's *Ragtime* was published.

Q: How many of E. L. Doctorow's 9 novels are set in New
York City?
A: 7.

1979

Q: Which 1979 Norman Mailer novel won a Pulitzer prize?
A: *The Executioner's Song.*

1984

Jay McInerney wrote *Bright Lights, Big City,* which was based in
Manhattan.

Q: Which magazine did his main character work at, and what
   did he do?
A: He was a researcher at *The New Yorker.*

1986

Tama Janowitz wrote *Slaves of New York,* which chronicled life
in downtown Manhattan.

1987

Tom Wolfe explored racial tensions and economic disparities in
New York in *Bonfire of the Vanities.*

1988

The *New York Press* was launched as a free alternative weekly. *Our
Town* and *West Side Spirit,* owned by N.C.I. Communications,
were also offered free in the city.

1992

Starting in 1992, there was an increase within the city in name changes favoring Muslim names. The filing fee for a name change is $50, and a petitioner must wait eight weeks for a judge to sign off on the change. Stipulations of a name change are: the change must be published in a newspaper, and there can be no single names, numerals, or titles used as names.

Q: Which newspaper do most people choose to publish their name change?
A: The *New York Law Journal.*

Q: What is the average number of people each year who petition the New York Civil Court for a name change?
A: Approximately 300.

1994

A dead woman in a chair went unnoticed in a West Side Barnes & Noble bookstore for four hours because patrons thought she was napping. A group of mystery novelists had been visiting the store that particular day.

1994

Caleb Carr's *The Alienist* set in New York City at the turn of the century, was published.

Q: What was an alienist?
A: A psychiatrist.

1996

London and Paris's *Time Out* magazine was launched in New York City as competition to the *Village Voice, New York* magazine, and the *New York Press,* which was distributed free.

The *Village Voice* switched over to a free distribution on newsstands in April of 1996, partially in response to all of the competition.

1997

Caleb Carr published the sequel to *The Alienist,* titled *The Angel of Darkness,* which was also set in New York City.

1997

Mayor Giuliani's press officers receive, on average, 200 calls from the media each week.

1997

There are over six million volumes in the New York Public Library's main branch, with a total of 7,883,330 volumes in the overall library system, and the New York Public Library is the second largest public library in the nation. The number of annual reference inquiries handled by the Brooklyn Public Library is 5,842,590.

Q: How many library branches are located in Brooklyn?
A: 58; there are over 200 branches citywide.

Q: Where is America's leading library on African-American history located?
A: Malcolm X Boulevard and 135th Street in Harlem.

It is a time of phenomenal energy and growth for the foreign language media. The foreign language press is flourishing while the tabloids are floundering.
MITCHELL MOSS, DIRECTOR OF THE URBAN RESEARCH CENTER
AT NYU, TO CELIA W. DUGGER OF THE *NEW YORK TIMES*
AT THE START OF 1997

1997

Mayor Giuliani's immigrant affairs office does not communicate with all the ethnic media in New York City, but still communicates with 143 newspapers and magazines, 22 television stations, and 12 radio stations—in over 30 languages.

ETHNIC READERS

The number of newspapers in New York City that cater to:

Haitians 3
The Irish 2
Poles 2
The Chinese 6
Russians 25
Swedes 1
Lithuanians 1
Norwegians 1

- About 100 ethnic newspapers are published at Stellar Printing in New York City.
- Elmhurst, Queens, is home to people from more than 99 different countries. Newspapers in Polish, Arabic, English, Sanskrit, Gujarati, Spanish, Korean, Chinese, Greek, and Bengali can be found at Pronto Grocery in Elmhurst.

Q: Do English language newspapers outsell any of the others at Pronto?
A: No; Chinese and Korean sell the most.

Times Square—what more need be said?

CHAPTER 7

A Magnificently Unfinished Place

What is barely hinted at in other cities is condensed and enlarged in New York.

SAUL BELLOW

New York City will be a great place if they ever finish it.

O. HENRY

Although the city today is known for its complex architectural background, it claimed a lowly beginning back in the 1620s—wood and earth structures modeled on those built by the Indians. Small wonder, then, that the colonists soon adopted European building styles. Homes were built with stepped gables based upon the urban homes in Amsterdam, and farmhouses in Brooklyn and Queens were designed with low, swooping roofs similar to those found in the Dutch countryside. Likewise, the influence of English architecture was evident in the city's early Georgian mansions, New York Hospital, King's College (later Columbia University), and the city's churches.

The first people in the city to call themselves architects were Richard Upjohn, Alexander Jackson David, Ithiel Town, Minard Lafever, and Detlef Lienau. They were trained in Europe or England and first worked in the city in the early 1830s, especially after the great fire of 1835 destroyed much of Lower

Manhattan. Since there was no formal architectural training in America, they taught pupils in the city who were interested in becoming architects. In 1857 there were 24 architects in the city, and they founded the American Institute of Architects (AIA).

Those early architects were responsible for the various styles seen around the city today. The Greek Revival style popular in the city between 1833 and 1858 is typified by the Brooklyn Borough Hall and the Astor House Hotel, which was built in 1836 and was the city's first luxury hotel (inns and taverns were the norm). The Beaux-Arts style of architecture developed at the Ecole des Beaux Arts in Paris is evident in the architecture of the New York Public Library, Grand Central Terminal, the Metropolitan Museum of Art, and the Museum of Natural History. The best examples of Moorish architecture can be found at the Central Synagogue on Lexington Avenue and the Eldridge Street Synagogue. St. John the Divine Cathedral is a classic example of European Medieval architecture. And St. Patrick's Cathedral (designed by James Renwick Jr.) is the city's best known example of the German Gothic style.

Of course, as the years passed, newer styles developed. The International style favoring sleek, spare lines and the "glass curtain wall" dominated in the city from the 1950s through the early 1980s; this style is found in countless office buildings across the city. The Guggenheim Museum was designed by Frank Lloyd Wright in 1959, Grand Central Terminal was renovated throughout the 1980s and 1990s, and the last few years have seen many of the Hudson River pier areas below 25th in Lower Manhattan redesigned and renovated.

Space has always been scarce in New York City, which accounts for its density. By the 1800s taverns, homes, shops, workspaces, and places for worship were all closely knit in the compact city. Row houses or townhouses first appeared in the city between 1840 and 1850 and began to proliferate in the 1870s. Tenement housing for multiple dwellings was constructed between 1860 and 1900 to accommodate the city's population explosion—between 1865 and 1930 the city's population increased from one million to nearly seven million. Cast iron for fireproofing buildings and passenger elevators, introduced in the decade before the Civil War, altered the architecture of the city, rendering upper stories more accessible, and therefore more profitable, than before and paving the way for the steel-cage construction and skyscrapers that are today's answer to overpopulation.

New York continuously reinvents itself to adjust to the demands of commerce and immigration—two of the city's grand, flying buttresses. Unlike other American cities, it's impossible to imagine exactly how New York will look to future generations. One thing is certain, though: the city's famous skyline, with its Empire State Building, World Trade Center's twin towers, Chrysler Building, and Woolworth Building, will continue to delight admirers for many years to come. All of the above buildings, along with hundreds of other buildings and landmarks, are protected by the city's Landmarks Preservation Commission; which helped pass a Landmarks Preservation Law in 1965. That same year Columbia University introduced a graduate program in historic preservation—the first of its kind in the country.

Alas, from the city's earliest beginnings, less than 35 colonial buildings still remain today.

1626

A fortified trading post was the core of the future city; it stood at the southernmost tip of the island and was surrounded by 30 wooden houses for company employees. A stone "counting house" stood in the vicinity, thatched with reeds, and a horse-mill was under construction. The horsemill would later house a supply of flour and would have a room for public meetings and worship services.

1643

The gates and bastion of the stockades were faced with stone, the director's house was built of brick, worship services were held in a large stone church, a brewery and boatbuilding shed had both been erected, and a gabled inn served visitors.

1647

Many houses and barns full of wheat had been lost to fire during Indian raids. The fort was periodically in disrepair and equipment in the area was often broken.

1657

New Amsterdam had numerous roads and about 120 houses, but roads were without compact-designated names. (For example, one road was called "the path that Burger Jorisson made to go down to the strand.") It was during this time that streets were straightened, fences repaired, and lots improved. Slim frame dwellings extended along the East River at the tip of the island, and all the main thoroughfares were cobbled.

1658

Notaries began to mention streets by specific names. New Amsterdam soon became the first American city with formally designated streets.

One trail that led from the northern tip of Manhattan down through forests to the southern tip where the settlers lived was called "Beaver Path" because Indians used to it to bring their beaver skins in for trading. When the path was widened, it became "Breede Wegh" . . . which eventually became Broadway.

1661

There were 300 buildings in New Amsterdam, including a church, and gallows and a tall crane used to load and unload cargoes. A windmill, steeped gables, a main canal, and domestic gardens were reminders of Holland. The canal was malodorous and extended from Broad Street up through town to permit the entrance of boats at high water. Ferries passed back and forth to Staaten Eylandt (Staten Island), where a large plot of grass on the south shore served as a common bleaching ground.

The tallest roof in town belonged to Governor Stuyvesant's home, which the English later named Whitehall.

1662

A poorhouse, which was overseen by the deacons of the Dutch church, stood near the main canal. Broadway was lined with small homes, and a wall separated the city from the farms beyond it. Flower gardens and fruit farms were tended for the 75 employees of the Dutch West India Company. Settlers planted and sowed little, as trade was their main concern.

1664

The highest point in New Amsterdam was a two-story windmill, used as a meeting place and as a means to grind grain into flour.

1665

A burying ground was designated on the west side of town near the Hudson River and the windmill.

1670

Many settlers moved north into Manhattan above what is now Canal Street to less crowded territory.

1703

The British built a City Hall at 28 Wall Street, at the corner of Nassau Street. It was two stories high, made of red brick, and featured a cupola on the roof. The building contained offices, a library, courtrooms, a jail, and a cellar dungeon. The jail was used to house John Peter Zenger, the German immigrant publisher of the *New York Weekly Journal* who was arrested for criticizing Governor William Cosby in print in 1733 (see Chapter 6). In 1765 the building hosted representatives of nine out of the thirteen colonies, who met to protest the stamp tax. The building, then called Federal Hall, was remodeled by Major Pierre Charles L'Enfant for George Washington's inauguration after the American Revolution. On April 30 in 1789 Washington borrowed a Bible at the last minute from a nearby Masonic Lodge and was there sworn in as the first president of the United States.

1727

The New Dutch Church was erected between 1727 and 1731 at Nassau and Crown streets.

1785

Samuel Ellis bought Ellis Island, which had been called Oyster Island by the Dutch settlers.

THE HISTORY OF ELLIS ISLAND

In 1808 New York State purchased Ellis Island from Samuel Ellis's heirs and turned it over to the federal government. The federal Ellis Island immigration center began operation on January 1, 1892.

Q: How many immigrants were processed at Ellis Island on its first day of operation?
A: 2,250.

In 1897 a mysterious fire razed the wooden buildings used to house the immigration center, but by 1900 a replacement fire-proof building has been completed. The new building, constructed to accommodate a half-million immigrants annually, was soon deemed inadequate, though, because the number of annual immigrants turned out to be more than a million. The island was enlarged (using landfill) from three acres to 27.5 acres. New additions and a third floor were then added to the main building, and 33 more buildings were added to the immigration compound.

At the center of the compound was an enormous registry room, where health inspectors and officials denied entry to criminals, mental defectives, contract laborers, the impoverished, and those suffering from contagious illness (particularly conjunctivitis). Almost 99% of the hopeful immigrants were granted entry in less than eight hours. After being cleared, one-third of the immigrants usually took a ferry to the Battery and stayed in New York City. The rest boarded trains for destinations throughout the country.

Marriages were held on Ellis Island because women were not allowed to leave the island with any man who was not related to them, including fiancés. This practice continued until 1924, when Congress scaled back mass immigration and decided to screen immigrants in their country of origin.

After 1924 Ellis Island was used mainly to detain those being deported. Sixteen million immigrants had passed through the compound by 1924.

Q: How many immigrants returned to their homeland during the Great Depression?

A: 145,000.

Q: How many German sailors were interned at Ellis Island after being caught in Allied ports during World War II?
A: 2,000.

Q: Which president proclaimed Ellis Island a national monument to be run by the National Park Service in conjunction with the Statue of Liberty?
A: President Lyndon B. Johnson in 1965. 71% of immigrants to the U.S. had passed through Ellis Island before 1965.

Q: Which president created a private foundation to restore and repair Ellis Island and the Statue of Liberty with corporate and individual donations?
A: President Ronald Reagan. The budget was $160 million.

1793

Seventeen buildings that now comprise Schermerhorn Row at 18 Fulton Street, 91-93 South Street, and 195-97 Front Street, were created in the Georgian Federal and Greek Revival styles. This group of buildings is currently the oldest row of houses remaining in Manhattan. Peter Schermerhorn, a chandler, built the group of buildings as countinghouses to serve shipping merchants.

1799

St. Mark's Episcopal Church, in the Bowery at East 10th Street and Second Avenue, was built. It survives today as the second oldest church building in Manhattan. Peter Stuyvesant is buried in the churchyard; his great grandson sold the church to the Episcopal Church for one dollar.

1808

The homes on the Bowery and Broadway were considered the finest in the city, described as "lofty and well-built" in journals of the period. The City Hotel on Broadway resembled the London Tavern on Bishopsgate Street in both size and architecture.

1812

Federal Hall was torn down, and the Kirk and Eastburn Bookstore took its place on the spot until 1842.

1824

Castle Garden opened as the Madison Square Garden of its day. It had originally been built as a fort at the shoreline of the West Battery to protect New York Harbor from a British invasion. Castle Garden housed "fanciful gardens," live concerts, fireworks, balloon ascensions, and scientific demonstrations. The city reclaimed the fort in 1855 to use as an immigration station; in 1896 it was converted into the New York Aquarium, as which it remained until 1941. In 1950 the fort was designated a national monument. Castle Clinton was restored during the 1970s; it currently serves as a place for ticket booths for the Statue of Liberty ferries and Ellis Island.

1824

The Terhune brothers opened the Coney Island House near Shell Road in southwestern Brooklyn, which was soon visited by Daniel Webster and P. T Barnum. Coney Island developed further after the Civil War when five railroads were constructed that connected Coney Island with the rest of Brooklyn.

PHOTO BY B. KIM TAYLOR

Coney Island is now but a shadow of its original glory.

Q: How did Coney Island get its name?

A: There were so many wild rabbits in the area during the 1600s that the Dutch called it *konijn*, which is Dutch for "rabbit."

Q: How many times per year are operators required by law to test their rides for metal fatigue?

A: Zero. Operators are not required by law to test their rides for metal fatigue. 14 amusement-park ride accidents occurred in New York City between 1990 and 1997.

CONEY ISLAND SNAPSHOT

- The frankfurter was introduced to the public by Charles Feltman in 1870, not long after immigrant businessmen began operating concessions in the area.
- Roller coasters, public bathing, and carousels appeared in Coney Island in 1884.
- Horse races, boxing matches, dance halls, brothels, and gambling dens drew many to Coney Island in the 1880s and 1890s.
- Three major new hotels were constructed at Coney Island during the 1890s: the Hotel Brighton, the Oriental, and the Manhattan Beach Hotel.
- Three amusement parks opened along Surf Avenue between 1897 and 1904: Steeplechase Park in 1897, Luna Park in 1903, and Dreamland in 1904. Dreamland was destroyed by fire in 1911 and Luna Park was destroyed by fire in 1944. Steeplechase Park closed in 1964.
- By 1907, visitors on an average weekend would mail 250,000 postcards from Coney Island, providing free national advertising for the park.
- There was no year-round population in Coney Island until the early 1900s, when Italian and Jewish families moved into the area.
- The number of visitors to Coney Island declined dramatically after World War II. A small amusement district remained, which included the Wonder Wheel, the Hell Hole, the Cyclone roller coaster and the B & B Carousel.
- The first annual Mermaid Parade appeared at Coney Island in 1983, the first freak sideshow took place in 1985, and the first tattoo festival appeared in 1988. The freak show and tattoo show were discontinued in 1995.
- *Catch 22* author Joseph Heller was raised in Coney Island.
- A couple lived in a house below the Thunderbolt roller coaster at Coney Island for 40 years. The roller coaster ceased running in 1982, and in 1991 the house was gutted by a fire.

- The Polar Bear Club at Coney Island was founded in 1903 and still has 50 regular members who swim on the first day of each year regardless of water temperature. Annual dues are $20, and a candidate for club membership must have enjoyed 15 cold-water swims between November and May in order to join.

1827

New York City acquired the land that now compromises Washington Square Park for a public park. The land had previously been used as a site for public hangings and as a potter's field from 1797 through 1826, and the remains of 10,000 people are still buried there. Before 1797 it was a marsh fed by Minetta Brook near a Sappokanican Indian settlement. It was converted to a parade ground in the early 1900s.

Q: How long was Washington Square Park bisected by Fifth Avenue?

A: Until the 1960s, when the park's fountain became a public meeting place and the park was closed off to traffic.

Q: What was the Washington Square Monument first made of in 1889?

A: Wood. It was re-created with marble within a few years in response to public demand. The arch was designed by Stanford White.

1830

The Astor family built an exclusive neighborhood between 1830 and 1860 centered in what is now Times Square at Seventh Avenue and Broadway and the neighborhood remained exclusive until the 1890s. The area was called Long Acre Square, and before 1830 it had been a thriving commercial center and the site of William H. Vanderbilt's American Horse Exchange. Around the turn of the century, high-end prostitution houses dubbed "silk hat brothels" flourished discreetly in the area. When the *New York Times* erected a building nearby on 43rd Street in 1902, the area was renamed Times Square.

Q: How did Times Square become the site for a citywide New Year's Eve celebration?

A: *New York Times* publisher Adolph Ochs staged a New Year's Eve gala to celebrate the newspaper's new location in 1907. The event became a tradition.

AULD LANG SYNE

The Times Square ball was refurbished in 1948 and 1995. An estimated half-a-million to a million people attend the lowering of the ball each New Year's Eve, depending on the severity of the weather.

- 85% of the event's attendees are from outside of the city
- 35% are from abroad.
- 37% are between the ages of 19 and 25 years, although the number of young attendees is increasing with each year.
- 21% are between 26 and 35 years old.
- 4% are over 50 years old.
- 300 million view the celebration on television.
- 12,000 rhinestones cover the ball.
- The total cost of the 1996 festivities was $385,000.
- The amount of revenue for the city generated by the New Year's Eve celebration in 1996, based on an Ernst & Young study, was $48.5 million.

Q: How many pounds does the ball weigh?
A: 500.

Q: How many garbage trucks are currently used to clean Times Square after the ball has dropped on New Year's Eve?
A: 4.

1835

Just before Christmas, the Great Fire swept through Lower Manhattan, decimating over 600 buildings and forcing the business community to completely rebuild.

Everywhere they are building houses, repairing whole sections, constructing superb hotels, opening large squares, and as if to second this activity, laying out new streets and embankments.
RAMON DE LA SAGRA, A SPANISH BOTANIST, ECONOMIST, AND HISTORIAN IN 1835

Fires like this one were a chronic problem in New York City during the 1880s. The Great Fire of 1835 was by far the worst.

1837

Between 1837 and 1843 the city was plagued with a depression that temporarily halted bustling economic development.

1838

Green-Wood Cemetery in Brooklyn was commissioned from David Bates Douglass by a private group in Brooklyn. Richard Upjohn designed the ornate Gothic gatehouse in 1861. The cemetery covers 478 acres and currently has 550,000 interments.

FAMOUS PEOPLE BURIED AT GREEN-WOOD

- Boss Tweed
- Margaret Sanger
- Peter Cooper
- Leonard Bernstein

- Joey Gallo
- Samuel Morse
- Elias Howe
- Henry George

- Horace Greeley
- Duncan Phyfe
- Seth Low
- George Bellows

1842

The United States Custom House was built where Federal Hall and the Kirk & Eastburn Bookstore had been located at 28 Wall Street. It was made of stone and resembled the Parthenon. The Greek Revival style of architecture was preferred in the city from 1828 to 1845 partially because wars with England in 1776 and 1812 had distanced Americans from English architectural models. Part of the reason the Greek Revival style faded in the mid-1840s is because a building surrounded by columns couldn't easily be expanded. The building has served many purposes over the decades. In 1862 it became a branch of the independent treasury system, in 1920 it served as office space for numerous government organizations, and in 1940 it became a museum founded by the Federal Hall Memorial Association, complete with dioramas depicting Washington's inauguration.

Q: What color was the suit Washington wore when he took the oath of office?
A: Brown.

NOTABLE STATEN ISLAND RESIDENTS

- Aaron Burr (Port Richmond Hotel)
- Giuseppe Garibaldi (Rosebank)
- Frederick Olmsted (Eltingville)
- Cornelius Vanderbilt (Stapleton)
- William Vanderbilt (New Dorp)

1847

Bryant Park, at the corner of Sixth Avenue and 42nd Street, became a public park; it had been used as a potter's field since 1823. It was originally named Reservoir Square because it was adjacent to a reservoir.

Q: What is now located on the site of the reservoir?
A: The New York Public Library. The reservoir was drained in 1899 for the construction of the library, which was completed in 1911.

The Crystal Palace, an exposition hall made of glass and steel, occupied the park's area from 1853 until it was destroyed by fire in 1858. Bryant Park was given its current name in 1884.

Q: Who inspired the park's name?
A: William Cullen Bryant, the poet and newspaper editor who was an early advocate of public parks in the city.

The park was redesigned in 1934 with a sunken central lawn, side promenades encircled with a granite balustrade, and reshaped entrances off of Sixth Avenue. The park became a refuge throughout the 1970s and 1980s for the homeless and drug dealers, but another round of renovations in the late 1980s and 1990s added restaurant kiosks, outdoor patio seating, outdoor theater capabilities, a formal restaurant, improved landscaping and easier public access, and underground library storage space. The park is used for fashion shows and other large-scale media events.

Q: What are some of the monuments located in the park?
A: A bust of Goethe, a statue of Bryant, and a bronze statue of Gertrude Stein.

PIGEONS IN THE GRASS ALAS

Ornitrol is used as birth control for pigeons in Bryant Park, laced in corn kernels that the birds ingest—instead of eating the foliage and flowers in the park. Only 15 to 20 pigeons consider Bryant Park their home, as opposed to 150 in the pre-Ornitrol days. People for the Ethical Treatment of Animals (PETA) deemed Ornitrol a humane replacement for Avitrol, which gave pigeons the *delirium tremens* and made them keel over in front of park patrons.

Q: What was Ornitrol's original intended purpose?
A: To lower cholesterol in humans. It was discontinued because some people developed acute nervousness.

*The city is spreading north...out of all reason and measure."
There were three principle theaters in the city: the Park, the
Bowery, and the Olympic.*
GEORGE TEMPLETON STRONG IN 1848

1849

The first building with a full cast-iron facade, the Bogardus
Building, was constructed by James Bogardus at 258-62
Washington Street. It was considered a forerunner to the skyscraper because the walls bore no weight, which allowed for
enormous windows. When the building was razed in 1971,
thieves took two-thirds of the building's cast-iron panels. The
Landmarks Preservation Commission then stored the building's
remaining cast-iron panels in a locked warehouse, where they
were stolen anyway.

Q: When were many of the cast-iron structures in Soho built?
A: The 1850s. The cast-iron covering was popular for com-
    mercial buildings through the end of the century. The
    process consisted of making a mold of a single element
    found on a building—a leaf of the capitol or a column—
    and then pouring molten iron into the cast to duplicate that
    element. The process replaced expensive skilled, artistic
    stonecutters, and merchants could select elements for their
    building's facade from a catalog. The iron parts would be
    delivered within a matter of days or weeks and could be
    bolted onto the old brick facade.
    Manhattan's Soho currently has the largest area of cast-
    iron structures in the world.

1851

Fifth Avenue rivaled Broadway in the interest of the visiting
public. It was considered more fashionable to live on Fifth
Avenue than Broadway.

1852

The structures on Broadway were typically five or six stories
high and adorned with marble, cast-iron, and stone.

1853

The St. Nicholas Hotel between Broome and Spring streets was considered the finest building in the city, outstripping even the Astor House. It had 600 rooms, usually more than 1,000 guests, and 322 workers in the establishment.

1857

Central Park opened to the public.

THE GARDEN OF NYC

- Central Park's land was a swamp before it was fashioned into a park in 1857; one billion cubic feet of earth was moved to create the park, and by 1858 four to five million trees were planted.
- Three thousand Irish laborers worked on the building of Central Park, and 400 horses were required to clear the land.
- Cleopatra's Needle, a 3,000-year-old, 77-feet-high Egyptian obelisk, was presented by the Khedive Ismael Pasha in 1869.
- Strawberry Fields, a three-acre tribute to John Lennon, offers 161 different species of plants from 150 different nations.
- Central Park is two-and-a-half miles long and a half-mile wide and contains 36 stone arches and bridges. It covers 840 acres, with 185 acres set aside for lakes and ponds. The reservoir in the park holds one billion gallons of water and is 40 feet deep, and the Conservatory Gardens cover four acres.
- There are, on average, 42 bald eagles and 11,000 hawks spotted over Central Park annually. One golden eagle was spotted over the park, and 20 raccoons live in the park, mainly in the West 70s.
- Central Park first served as a camping ground for a significant number of destitute, homeless people in 1929. Now an average of 14 million people visit the park each year.

Q: What was the last year sheep grazed in the park?
A: 1933.

Q: How many hours is the park open each day?
A: 18.

Q: How much, per hour, is a horse-drawn carriage ride through the park?
A: Approximately $27.50. The cost to rent a boat at the Loeb Boathouse is $6.00 an hour.

Edible Plants with Medicinal Properties in Central Park

Tufted grasses (e.g., bluestems) ....tea for stomachaches
Chicory roots ....treat fevers and diarrhea
New England aster ....treat fevers and diarrhea

Milkweed . . . . .treat fevers and diarrhea
Beach roses . . . . .treat rheumatic pain and dysentery
Dogwood tree twigs . . . . .quinine substitute
Salicylic acid from willow bark . . . . .precursor to aspirin
Bark of witch hazel . . . . .astringent
Bark of redbud . . . . .astringent

Q: What is New York City's rank in the 5 largest U.S. cities, in terms of spending per capita on parks?

A: Last. New York City spends $17.38 per capita, compared to Los Angeles' $38.23 and Chicago's $72.31.

Q: Does the city remove plastic bags and other debris caught in trees?

A: No. A small group of volunteers does this on a regular basis. The Parks Department issued a maintenance permit in 1996 to a group of 4 who, in their spare time, use a carbon-graphite pole with a hook and blade at the end to remove debris from trees. They've patented the sectional pole, which extends 70 feet. This group of 4, self-dubbed the Bag Removal Guys, began removing debris from city trees in 1993. Only 2 of the 4 currently reside in New York City.

1862

Most of Manhattan was built up as far north as 42nd Street, which was referred to as "the suburbs."

1871

Grand Central Station was built as a monument to Cornelius Vanderbilt's railroad empire. Grand Central Terminal is 470 feet long, 160 feet wide, and 150 feet high. The current estimated renovation price of Grand Central Terminal is $113.8 million.

Q: What deity is visible atop Grand Central's triumphal arch?
A: Mercury.

Q: How many windows are in Grand Central's terminal?
A: 6. Each window contains 600 panes of glass.

Q: What is the average number of days required to clean them?
A: 30.

FYI: GRAND CENTRAL STATION

- An Otis freight elevator in Grand Central Station beneath the Waldorf-Astoria Hotel opens onto 49th Street between Lexington and Park Avenues just outside the door of the hotel's parking garage. The elevator is over 20 feet long and 8 feet wide and can carry up to 4 tons. President Franklin Delano Roosevelt, crippled by poliomyelitis, used the elevator to reach the lobby of the hotel.
- There is a "whispering gallery" outside the Oyster Bar in Grand Central Terminal, where people can stand at opposite ends of a hallway and hear one another's whispers. This is possible because the walls are curved and shaped so sounds follow the contour of the wall around a gallery, bouncing across the arcs of the surface and reaching a listener's ears at practically the same volume. Additionally, the surface of the area has no interfering projections and is extremely hard; it does not absorb sound. Domed or vaulted spaces, spaces with rotundas, or curved canyons and caves often feature this effect.

1880

Q: Which one of the Welsh poet Dylan Thomas's favorite New York City drinking spots features an oil painting of him on the wall?
A: The White Horse Tavern, which was built in 1880 at the corner of Hudson and West 11th Streets. The tavern was certified as a landmark by the city's Landmarks Preservation Commission because it's one of the few wood-framed buildings left in the city. It served as a speakeasy during the Prohibition, and then as a seamen's bar until the late 1940s.

NOTABLE GREENWICH VILLAGE RESIDENTS:

It is easier to count the noted Americans who have never lodged in New York City than those who have.

JOHN EASTMAN

- Yma Sumac (Perry St.)
- The "real" Serpico (Perry St.)
- Wystan Hugh Auden (7 Cornelia St.)

- John Barrymore (75 1/2 Bedford St.)
- Alexander Calder (249 W. 14th St.)
- Mark Twain (14 W. 10th St.)
- Willa Cather (82 Washington Pl.)
- Jimi Hendrix (55 W. 8th St.)
- e. e. cummings (4 Patchin Pl.)
- Hart Crane (54 W. 10th St.)
- John Dos Passos (14A Washington Mews)
- Winslow Homer (51 W. 10th St.)
- Edward Hopper (3 Washington Sq. N.)
- Fiorello La Guardia (39 Charles St.)
- Sinclair Lewis (69 Charles St.)
- Carson McCullers (321 W. 11th St.)
- Margaret Mead (72 Perry St.)
- Herman Melville (33 Bleecker St.)
- Thomas Merton (35 Perry St.)
- Edna St. Vincent Millay (75 1/2 Bedford St.)
- Eugene O'Neill (38 Washington Sq. S.)
- Thomas Paine (309 Bleecker St.)
- Edgar Allan Poe (85 W. 3rd St.)
- Katherine Anne Porter (17 Grove St.)
- Margaret Sanger (4 Perry St.)
- John Silas Reed (42 Washington Sq. S.)

1884

The Dakota, considered the city's first luxury apartment build-ing, was built at 72nd Street and Central Park West. At the time, the Dakota was surrounded by shanties for the homeless as well as roving pigs and goats. The Dakota derived its name from res-idents in Lower Manhattan who sniffed that the building was so far north that it might as well have been located in the Dakota territory. A lot of city residents thought Edward Clark, the man who built the Dakota, was crazy because no one would want to live in a luxury building 20 blocks from the edge of New York society. Clark liked the nickname "The Dakota" so much that he adopted it for the building, and soon other buildings in the area took names like "The Montana," "The Nevada," and "Yosemite."

Newcomers to the Dakota and its environs were upper mid-dle class businesspeople who represented new money and glee-fully shunned the stuffy, old money society that had excluded them. This set a nonconforming tradition on the Upper West Side that continues today. Clark died before the Dakota was completed, but he would have been happy to know that when the building opened in 1884, it was fully rented to families like the Steinways and the Schirmers (with friends like Mark Twain, Stephen Crane, and composer Peter Ilich Tchaikovsky, who thought Central Park belonged to the Dakota's tenants). More modern tenants include Leonard Bernstein, Lauren Bacall, and John Lennon and Yoko Ono, who purchased actor Robert Ryan's seventh-floor apartment in 1974 and claimed it was occupied by "the gentle ghost" of Ryan's deceased wife, Jessie. The Dakota switchboard received an average of 25 calls per day in the late 1970s from Lennon fans.

One of the prerequisites for buying an apartment in the Dakota is that you must be recommended by one of the building's residents.

Q: Who did John Lennon know in the building?
A: Edward O. D. Downes, a musicologist and opera critic.

1887

The Statue of Liberty was dedicated on October 28.

THERE STANDS A LADY

The Statue of Liberty was first proposed as a gift from France to the United States by the French statesman Edouard de Laboulaye to commemorate friendship between the two countries. Alsatian sculptor Frédéric Auguste Bartholdi began working on the sculpture in 1871 and was ready to begin construction four years later. The exterior, made of beaten copper, was placed on wrought-iron armature designed by engineer Gustave Eiffel to support the statue's weight and to provide bracing against strong harbor winds.

Construction of the statue's base was the responsibility of the United States, which was undertaken by French-trained architect Richard Morris Hunt. Joseph Pulitzer raised money for the base by requesting contributions in his newspaper, the *New York World*. The statue arrived in America in 1885 in hundreds of crates, and army engineer General Charles P. Stone supervised the statue's erection. Emma Lazarus's poem "The New Colossus" was inscribed on a tablet at the base of the pedestal in 1903, and the statue became a symbol of American immigration and freedom. Before the Revolutionary War, Liberty Island was used as a quarantine location during smallpox epidemics.

The average wait to climb to the statue's crown is two-and-a-half hours. The Statue of Liberty weighs 225 tons and the mouth is 35 feet wide.

Q: How long is the index finger?
A: 8 feet.

Q: What is Emma's Lazarus's inscription on the Statue of Liberty?
A: "Give me your tired, your poor, your huddled masses yearning to breathe free, the wretched refuse of your teeming shore, send these, the homeless, tempest-tost, to me: I lift my lamp beside the golden door."

Q: Which woman is the Statue of Liberty modeled after?
A: Frédéric-Auguste Bartholdi's mother.

1899

The Bronx Zoo opened; it was founded in 1895 as the New York Zoological Society, and its first naturalistic habitats didn't appear until 1941. The zoo devoted 265 wooded acres to naturalistic habitats. The Bronx Zoo is the largest metropolitan wildlife park in the country, and the New York Zoological Society supervises 150 wildlife conservation projects in 40 nations.

Q: How many animals live at the Bronx Zoo?
A: More than 4,000.

Q: How many people, including toddlers, enroll in the zoo's wildlife conservation education courses?
A: More than 35,000.

NOTABLE BRONX RESIDENTS

- Bela Bartok (Riverdale)
- Mark Twain (Riverdale)
- Lou Gehrig (Fieldston)
- Anne Hutchinson (Eastchester)
- John F. Kennedy (Riverdale)
- Robert F. Kennedy (Riverdale)
- Fiorello La Guardia (Riverdale)
- George Meany (Port Morris)
- Lee Harvey Oswald (Crotona Park)
- Edgar Allan Poe (Fordham)
- Theodore Roosevelt (Riverdale)
- Leon Trotsky (Claremont)

- Elizabeth and Ann Seton (Edenwald)
- Arturo Toscanini (Riverdale)

Q: Why is "the" used before the Bronx, and not before Brooklyn, Queens, Manhattan, or Staten Island?
A: People used to speak of going to the Broncks estate, the home of Jonas Bronck, for country excursions, and "the" survived over the centuries.

1902

Q: The 20-story Fuller Building at the intersection of Broadway and Fifth Avenue was completed. What do most people in the city call the building?
A: The Flatiron Building, because it's shaped like an enormous flatiron.

Q: What percentage of the Flatiron district is protected by the city's Landmarks Preservation Commission?
A: 90%.

1903

John D. Rockefeller instigated the concept of sidewalk peepholes in streetside retaining walls to monitor construction sites himself and to spark public interest and curiosity about a project or new building.

THE ROCKEFELLERS AND NEW YORK CITY

- John D. Rockefeller (1839-1937): organizer of the Standard Oil Trust and longtime Baptist Sunday school superintendent.
- William Rockefeller (1841-1922): brother of John D., oilman, Wall Street promoter, and utility and railroad magnate.
- John D. Rockefeller Jr. (1876-60): son of John D., founder of Rockefeller University and the Cloisters in New York City, builder of Riverside Church and Rockefeller Center, and contributor of the land on which the United Nations headquarters stand. A teetotaler who fathered five sons: Winthrop, David, Laurance, John D. III, and Nelson.
- Abby Aldrich Rockefeller (1874-1948): wife of John D. Jr. and founder/benefactor of the Museum of Modern Art.
- John D. Rockefeller III (1906-78): founder of Lincoln Center for

the Performing Arts and the Asia Society in New York City.
- **Blanchette Hooker Rockefeller (1909-):** wife of John D. III and president and chairman of the Museum of Modern Art.
- **Nelson Aldrich Rockefeller (1908-79):** four-term Republican governor of New York and vice president of the United States.
- **David Rockefeller (1915-):** chairman of Chase Manhattan Bank.

1904

Developer W. E. D. Stokes built the Ansonia between 73rd and 74th Streets. The building's interior walls were designed to be so thick that neighbors could do as they pleased. Stokes enjoyed his own rooftop menagerie, which included a bear, goats, ducks, and chickens. (The building's tenants could buy fresh eggs from Stokes at half price.) The building's residents over the years have included Babe Ruth, Enrico Caruso, Theodore Dreiser, Igor Stravinsky, Florenz Ziegfeld, Arturo Toscanini, and Ezio Pinza.

1905

The Chelsea Hotel opened. It had previously been a 12-story apartment building with 40 units. The hotel offers 250 units ranging from one to five-and-a-half rooms.

Q: What percentage of the hotel is permanently occupied?
A: 75%.

FAMOUS CHELSEA HOTEL DENIZENS AND GUESTS

- Patti Smith
- R. Mapplethorpe
- Mark Twain
- O. Henry
- Lillian Hellman
- Thomas Wolfe
- John Sloane
- James T. Farrell
- Arthur Miller
- Sarah Bernhardt
- Bette Davis
- Jasper Johns
- Bob Dylan
- Dylan Thomas
- Sid Vicious
- Andy Warhol
- Virgil Thompson
- Edgar Lee Masters

1907

The Pierpont Morgan Library at 29 East 36th Street was completed to house J. P. Morgan's collection of books and manuscripts. Architect Charles McKim based his design on the attic of the Nymphaeum, which was built in 1555 in Rome for Pope Julius III.

1910

The Brooklyn Botanic Garden was built next to the Brooklyn Museum along Washington and Flatbush Avenues. The garden was built over rough meadowland previously used by the Parks Department as an ash dump. The garden's Steinhardt Conservatory blooms year-round, featuring tropical and desert climates from southern Africa to the Mediterranean to Australia, and the evolution of primitive life to sophisticated flowering plants can be traced on the garden's Trail of Evolution. The garden is comprised of 52 acres with over 12,000 kinds of plants.

"A Day in Brooklyn" trolley picks up passengers every hour on the hour and takes them to the garden. Trolley stops include: the Wollman Skating Rink in Central Park, the carousel in Prospect Park, the Grand Army Plaza, the main branch of the Public Library, the Brooklyn Museum, and the Brooklyn Botanic Garden.

NOTABLE BROOKLYN RESIDENTS

- Wystan Hugh Auden (Brooklyn Heights)
- Henry Ward Beecher (Brooklyn Heights)
- Clara Bow (Bay Ridge)
- Al Capone (Manhattan Bridge area)
- Jennie Churchill (Cobble Hill)
- Anthony Comstock (Williamsburg)
- Hart Crane (Brooklyn Heights)
- John Dos Passos (Brooklyn Heights)
- Theodore Dreiser (Bed-Stuy)
- W. E. B. Du Bois (Brooklyn Heights)
- George Gershwin (East New York)
- Woody Guthrie (Williamsburg, Coney Island, and Gravesand)
- Howard Lovecraft (Flatbush)
- Carson McCullers (Brooklyn Heights)
- Henry Miller (Williamsburg and Brooklyn Heights)

- Marianne Moore (Fort Greene)
- Jackie Robinson (Flatbush)
- John D. Rockefeller (Prospect Park)
- Walt Whitman (Fort Green)
- Thomas Wolfe (Brooklyn Heights)
- Richard Wright (Bed-Stuy)

That "New Yawk" Accent

The famous Brooklyn accent that transforms "th" to "d" and "er" to "oi" is disappearing so quickly that a project of the Long Island Historical Society is to record and preserve the unique New York accent.

1911

Pennsylvania Station was completed for passengers using the Long Island Railroad, for those traveling south along the East Coast, and for passengers to New England. The Pennsylvania Railroad had wanted to build a station in New York City to compete with Grand Central Terminal of the New York Central Railroad much sooner, but there was no bridge or tunnel across the Hudson River from its terminal in Hoboken, New Jersey, until the 1890s. The original, austere and gorgeous Pennsylvania Station was demolished in 1965 to create a new station that would house offices and Madison Square Garden.

A result of the demolition was the creation of the Landmarks Preservation Commission in New York City in 1965, as well as a national trend to preserve historic buildings. The second Pennsylvania Station was completed in 1968, and it's the busiest train station in North America.

Q: How many tracks does the station have?
A: 21. About 600,000 passengers use the station every day, sometimes at a mind-bending rate of 1,000 passengers every 2 minutes.

1912

The Audubon Theater and Ballroom was constructed at West 165th Street and Broadway. The building was one of the first theaters in William Fox's chain. It contained a movie theater that sat 2,368 and a ballroom on the second story. The Audubon

Ballroom was the site of the rally where Malcolm X was assassinated in February of 1965.

1913

J. P. Morgan & Company, now called the Morgan Guaranty Trust Company, was built at 23 Wall Street near Broad Street. At the time, skyscrapers were being erected in Lower Manhattan, but the Morgan Bank preferred an unmarked, small headquarters building made of white marble on one of the city's most valuable pieces of land. The absence of a name on the exterior served to underscore the fact that those wealthy enough to bank there didn't need an introduction.

Q: Why does the building's Wall Street side contain pockmarks in the stone?

A: On September 16, 1920, a driver parked his horse-drawn cart next to the bank during a weekday lunch hour and then disappeared. The cart was filled with dynamite and it exploded, killing 33 people and the horse, injuring 400, and scarring the side of the building. The driver was never found and J. P. Morgan was in Scotland at the time. Only one person in the bank was injured.

NOTABLE LOWER MANHATTAN RESIDENTS

Everyone ought to have a Lower East Side in their life.

IRVING BERLIN

- Benedict Arnold (3 Broadway)
- John Jacob Astor (362 Pearl St.)
- P. T. Barnum (52 Frankfort St.)
- Dr. Elizabeth Blackwell (126 Second Ave.)
- William "Billy the Kid" Bonney (Rivington St.)
- Diamond Jim Brady (corner of Cedar & West Sts.)
- Matthew Brady (Broadway & Fulton St.)
- William Cullen Bryant (Fulton St.)
- Aaron Burr (28 Wall St.)
- Gov. De Witt Clinton (3 Cherry St.)
- Gov. George Clinton (80 Pine St.)
- James Fenimore Cooper (6 St. Mark's Pl.)
- Stephen Foster (97 Greene St.)
- Robert Fulton (1 State St.)

- Samuel Gompers (Houston & Attorney Sts., or "Little Germany")
- Alexander Hamilton (58 Wall St.)
- Washington Irving (131 William St.)
- John Jay (133 Broadway)
- Thomas Jefferson (57 Maiden Ln.)
- James Madison (19 Maiden Ln.)
- Herman Melville (6 Pearl St.)
- Eugene O'Neill (252 Fulton St.)
- John Trumbull (128 Broadway)
- William Tweed (1 Cherry St.)
- Louis Comfort Tiffany (57 Warren St.)
- George Washington (3 Cherry St.)
- Walt Whitman (12 Centre St.)

1922

The 21 Club, a restaurant located in three connecting brownstones, was founded in Greenwich Village by Jack Kriendler and Charlie Berns. It moved to 52nd Street on New Year's Eve in 1929 and was raided once during the Prohibition in 1930, the result being the construction of a secret wine cellar still used today and an elaborate system of collapsing shelves in the bar. The 21 Club was bought by London-based Orient Express Hotels in 1995.

Q: How many other speakeasies were there on West 52nd Street during the Prohibition?

A: 38.

1927

Samuel Rothafel, a showman who called himself "Roxy," opened a baroque 6,000-seat theater called The Roxy at 50th Street and Seventh Avenue. It was the most expensive theater ever constructed. Rothafel pioneered the idea of presenting stage shows along with movies. Within five years, six other New York City theaters featured stage shows with first-run movies. The stage-show-and-movie concept endured at Radio City Music Hall until 1979.

We don't produce the pictures. Some are good and some are not so good. But we can build the show around the picture on the theory that if the appetizer is good and the dessert is good, the entrée will be acceptable even if only fair.

SAMUEL ROTHAFEL

NOTABLE MIDTOWN RESIDENTS

One belongs to New York instantly. One belongs to it as much in five minutes as in five years.

THOMAS WOLFE

- Horatio Alger (26 W. 34th St.)
- John Andre (455 E. 51st St.)
- Caroline Astor (350 Fifth Ave.)
- P. T. Barnum (438 Fifth Ave.)
- David Belasco (111 W. 44th St.)
- Alva Vanderbilt Belmont (5 E. 44th St., 660 Fifth Ave. at 52nd St.)
- Robert Benchley (The Royalton Hotel)
- Enrico Caruso (Hotel Knickerbocker at Broadway & 42nd St.)
- Jennie Churchill (Madison Ave. & 26th St.)
- Noel Coward (450 E. 52nd St.)
- Theodore Dreiser (200 W. 57th St.)
- David Glasgow Farragut (113 E. 36th St.)
- Edna Ferber (Hotel Lombardy at 111 E. 56th St.)
- Jay Gould (579 Fifth Ave. at 47th St.)
- Admiral "Bull" William Halsey (530 Park Ave.)
- Scott Joplin (252 W. 47th St.)
- Marilyn Monroe (444 E. 57th St., Apt. 13E)
- John Pierpont Morgan (219 Madison Ave. at 36th St.)
- John O'Hara (Pickwick Arms Hotel at 230 E. 51st St.)
- Westbrook Pegler (Park Lane Hotel at 299 Park Ave.)
- Cole Porter (Waldorf Towers, Suite 33A)
- Lillian Russell (57 E. 54th St.)
- Francis Spellman (452 Madison Ave. at 50th St.)
- John Steinbeck (330 E. 51st St.)
- Igor Stravinsky (Essex House Hotel at Central Park S.)
- William Vanderbilt (Fifth Ave. between 51st and 52nd St.)
- Edmund Wilson (314 E. 53rd St.)
- Victoria Woodhull (Madison Ave. & E. 38th St.)

Strange Bedfellows at the Waldorf Towers

The Waldorf Towers at 100 East 50th Street has been home to Marilyn Monroe, President Herbert Hoover, Cole Porter, Henry Robinson Luce, General Douglas MacArthur, and Adlai Stevenson.

1929

The Chanin Building was constructed and named for Irwin S. Chanin, who was once a subway construction worker. Chanin started to amass his fortune as a young man by building two houses in Bensonhurst for $7,000. Chanin also received a $500 first prize in the "America's finest bathroom" contest in 1929.

Q: What other New York City landmark did Chanin construct?
A: The Roxy, which is the largest movie theater in the world.

1930

The art deco Chrysler Building was completed at 405 Lexington Avenue. The skyscraper originated as a business venture by William Reynolds, the developer of Dreamland at Coney Island, and in 1927 the plans for the building were bought by automotive titan Walter Chrysler. Chrysler added decorative stainless-steel eagle heads, the pointed helmetlike tip, and Chrysler radiator caps. The building was the tallest in the world when it was completed in 1930, but the distinction was short-lived, as the Empire State Building—still under construction—surpassed its height within a few months. The top vertex of the building wasn't lit until 1981, although the original plans included illumination at night.

NOTABLE UPPER WEST SIDE RESIDENTS

Once you have lived in New York and it has become your home, no place else is good enough.
                                                    JOHN STEINBECK

- John Dos Passos (214 Riverside Dr.)
- Bette Midler (W. 57th St.)
- J. D. Salinger (Riverside & 111th St.)
- Charles Scribner (258 Riverside St.)
- Adolph Ochs (308 W. 75th St.)
- Billie Holiday (26 W. 87th St.)
- Harry Belafonte (300 West End Ave.)
- Hannah Arendt (317 W. 95th St.)
- Theda Bara (500 West End Av.)
- Bernard Baruch (51 W. 70th St.)
- Bix Beiderbecke (119 W. 71st St.)

- Humphrey Bogart (245 W. 103rd St.)
- Diamond Jim Brady (7 W. 86th St.)
- John Coltrane (203 W. 103rd St.)
- James Dean (19 W. 68th St.)
- John Dewey (2880 Broadway)
- Theodore Dreiser (The Ansonia)
- F. Scott Fitzgerald (200 Claremont Ave.)
- George Gershwin (316 W. 103rd St.)
- Meyer Guggenheim (36 W. 77th St.)
- William Randolph Hearst (137 Riverside Dr.)
- Ben Hecht (39 W. 67th St.)
- Victor Herbert (300-321 W. 108th St.)
- Harry Houdini (278 W. 113th St.)
- Charles Hughes (325 West End Ave.)
- John Lennon and Yoko Ono (The Dakota)
- Groucho Marx (Riverside Dr. and W. 161st St.)
- Thelonious Sphere Monk (243 W. 63rd St.)
- Henry Morgenthau Jr. (211 Central Park W.)
- Robert Oppenheimer (155 Riverside Dr.)
- Dorothy Parker (57 W. 57th St.)
- Sergei Rachmaninoff (33 Riverside Dr.)
- Grantland Rice (450 Riverside Drive)
- Norman Rockwell (Amsterdam Ave. at W. 103rd St.)
- Richard Rogers (161 W. 86th St.)
- Babe Ruth (110 Riverside Dr.)
- William Tecumseh Sherman (75 W. 71st St.)
- P. G. Wodehouse (375 Central Park W.)
- Leonard Bernstein (The Dakota)
- Lauren Bacall (The Dakota)

"Hello, Jerry"

Jerry Seinfeld's television character lives on the Upper West Side at 129 West 81st Street, #5A. The character George lives in Queens, Kramer lives across the hall from Seinfeld, and Elaine lives "downtown."

1931

Builders began digging a hole on Fifth Avenue between 49th and 50th Streets in July to build Rockefeller Center. When the plans were shown to the public in the spring of 1931, the *New York Times* called it "a collection of architectural aberrations and monstrosities." That part of town was informally known as the speakeasy district. John D. Rockefeller Jr. had agreed to finance the land acquisition for the Metropolitan Opera Company, which wanted to move out of the garment district on Broadway and 39th Street. Rockefeller negotiated a lease and then offered to sell it to the Metropolitan Opera Company at cost through a long-term mortgage, which he would finance. The proposal was made in the summer of 1929 and in the fall of that year the stock market crashed. Rockefeller was left with a long-term lease on land with decreasing value, so he decided to make something out of the project anyway and chose RCA (Radio Corporation of America) as his star tenant in the plaza's main building. RCA was granted the right to name the entertainment complex.

Q: What name did RCA choose?
A: "Radio City."

Q: How many buildings comprise Rockefeller Center?
A: 21.

O' CHRISTMAS TREE

The first Christmas tree was plugged in at Rockefeller Plaza in 1933. The tallest Rockefeller Plaza Christmas tree was 90 feet, used in 1948. Sixty-five trees have been on display through 1997, with an average weight of seven and a half tons. Five miles of Christmas lights are used on each tree.

Q: What date is the tree taken down?
A: January 8. Then the tree is ground into 3 tons of mulch for ground cover at a Boy Scout camp in New Jersey.

Some of the color schemes used to light the tree over the decades:

- Monochromatic blue (1938)
- White floodlighting (1934 and 1939)
- Black light (1945 and 1946)
- Clear electric bulbs (1950s and 1960s)

1931

The Empire State Building's opening ceremonies were held on May 1. The skyscraper spans two acres and is 1,250 feet high. Construction costs were originally estimated at $50 million, but the building was completed a month and a half ahead of schedule and $5 million under budget. Contracts to build the Empire

State Building were signed only weeks before the stock market crash in 1929. Leasing was slow as a consequence of the depression and the building was only half rented until after World War II, prompting the nickname "Empty State Building."

The Empire State Building is made of granite and limestone, and trimmed with stainless steel. It was the tallest building in the world at 1,250 feet until the World Trade Center surpassed it.

Q: What was located on the site at Fifth Avenue between 33rd and 34th Streets before the Empire State Building was constructed?
A: The Waldorf-Astoria.

WILL YOU MARRY ME?

There's no charge to marry in the Empire State Building's 80th-floor chapel on Valentine's Day. Some of the benefits of marrying there are: free admission to the Empire State Building every Valentine's Day, a shopping bag full of gifts from local merchants, and "surprise" Broadway stars who will sign wedding licenses.

A 51-percent increase in visits to the Empire State Building during the month of December was noted in 1995, reflecting the highest December attendance in the building's history—perhaps because of a renewed interest in the film *An Affair to Remember.*

Q: How many elevators are in the Empire State Building?
A: 72. The elevators rise 1,200 feet per minute.

EMPIRE STATE BUILDING DISASTERS

- On August 27, 1936, 23-year-old Robert Francis Erskine yelled, "So long!" to horrified onlookers and jumped to his death.
- On July 28, 1945, a B-52 bomber pilot named Col. Bill Smith got lost in a dense fog after incorrectly changing his landing plans and crashed into the 79th floor of the Empire State Building, killing 14 people and injuring 21.
- In December of 1983, 25-year-old David Sutter asked a photographer on the observation deck for a Charlie Chaplin costume.

He paid the photographer $10, tipped his bowler hat, went outside, and jumped from the building.
- In 1988, arsonists set 2 fires in 4 days, disrupting radio broadcasts from the antenna and forcing the observatory deck to close.
- In 1990, 38 people were injured in a fire on the 51st floor.
- On November 22, 1995, two transformers in a basement electrical room exploded, injuring 22 people.
- In February of 1997, a gunman on the 86th-floor observatory deck fired 7 shots with a Beretta at the people standing around him, killing 1 and injuring several others. The gunman then shot himself.

Q: When did the practice of floodlighting the upper stories of the building start?

A: 1964. The white lighting in place most of the year is turned off during migration seasons to prevent birds from crashing into the building.

Q: How late do the exterior lights stay on?

A: 3:00 A.M.; the Chrysler, Helmsley, and Woolworth Buildings are lit until 1:00 A.M.

SOME EMPIRE STATE BUILDING HOLIDAY COLORS

Twenty different events or holidays prompt an Empire State Building lightbulb color change each year. There are 13 different color combinations. The red, white, and blue combination was first used on Independence Day in 1976. The colored bulbs were changed by hand in 1976; now they are changed with colored gels that are operated by remote control.

Red, white, and blue . . . . .Lincoln's birthday, Fourth of July, Washington's birthday, Memorial Day, Labor Day, and Veteran's Day.
Purple . . . . .Gay Pride Parade
Green and red . . . . . .Martin Luther King Jr.'s birthday, Christmas
Yellow and white . . . . .Easter
Red and white . . . . .Valentine's Day
Green . . . . .St. Patrick's Day
Red and yellow . . . . .Halloween

1932

Radio City Music Hall opened with over 400 floodlights and 6,200 seats.

Q: What was Radio City Music Hall patterned after?
A: The Grosses Schauspielhaus in Berlin.

Q: How many Rockettes are in the Radio City Music Hall Christmas Spectacular?
A: 57.

Q: What's the record for the highest attendance in Radio City Music Hall's history?
A: 35,000 people at the Christmas Show, December 10, 1994.

1933

The Palazzo d'Italia and the Deutches Haus were slated to open across from St. Patrick's Cathedral as an extension of Rockefeller Center, but since war was imminent in Europe, the Deutches Haus was renamed; the building opened as International Building North. Lee Lawrie's oft-photographed statue of Atlas graces the front of the 40-story International Building on Fifth Avenue.

Q: Which statue looks down on winter skaters and summer diners in Rockefeller Center's sunken plaza?
A: Paul Manship's "Prometheus."

1934

A two-story Georgian house with eight rooms was built during the Great Depression for $8,000 at Park Avenue and 39th Street. The house was intended to be a "national demonstration of what the dollar will buy in the construction field." Dubbed "America's Little House," Mayor Fiorello La Guardia broke ground for the house, Eleanor Roosevelt laid the hearthstone, and CBS used it to broadcast three radio programs a week. Over 16,000 people paid 10 cents to visit the home before it was demolished a year later in 1935. The home was built on one of the most expensive sites for housing in Manhattan, located near costly Park Avenue apartments. In June of 1936 another temporary home was built on the same spot: the all-steel House of the Modern Age, designed by Chrysler Building architect William Van Alen. The house stood for five months.

NOTABLE GRAMERCY PARK RESIDENTS

- President Chester Alan Arthur (123 Lexington Ave.)
- Theda Bara (132 E. 19th St.)
- John Barrymore (36 Gramercy Park E.)
- Edwin Thomas Booth (The Players Club at 16 Gramercy Park S.)
- Stephen Crane (Art Students League Building at 143 E. 23rd St.)
- Antonin Dvorak (328 E. 17th St.)
- Horace Greeley (35 E. 19th St.)
- Edith Hamilton (24 Gramercy Park S.)
- William Randolph Hearst (123 Lexington Ave.)
- Winslow Homer (128 E. 16th St.)
- Charles Edward Ives (120 E. 22nd St.)
- Herman Melville (104 E. 26th St.)
- Sidney Joseph Perelman (52 Gramercy Park N.)
- O. Henry (55 Irving Pl.)
- Franklin Delano Roosevelt (28 E. 20th St.)
- Theodore Roosevelt (28 E. 20th St.)
- Elihu Root (20 Irving Pl.)
- Norman Mattoon Thomas (206 E. 18th St.)
- Samuel Tilden (15 Gramercy Park S.)
- Stanford White (Lexington Ave. & Gramercy Park N.)

1938

The Cloisters, a branch of the Metropolitan Museum of Art, opened on land given to the city by John D. Rockefeller Jr. at Fort Tryon Park at the northern tip of Manhattan. The building, parks, and view are the result of Rockefeller's philanthropies. Rockefeller also purchased the land in New Jersey directly across the river from the Cloisters park and gave it to the state to guarantee that the view from the Cloisters would remain beautiful.

1941

The Diamond Dealers Club, which handles disputes between dealers, moved to 47th Street in 1941. The club handles 80 percent of all diamonds entering the country.

At least three quarters of all diamonds that currently enter the United States each year pass through Manhattan's diamond district on West 47th Street between Fifth Avenue and the Avenue of the Americas. The block evolved into a retail and wholesale diamond district after the 1920s, when diamond dealers began moving north to 47th Street from Canal Street near the Bowery and from Nassau Street near Fulton.

The first Diamond Dealers Club was formed in 1931 on Nassau Street, but the diamond trade in the city grew more significant after Hitler invaded the Low Countries and thousands of Jews came to New York City from Belgium's diamond district in Antwerp and from Amsterdam. The diamond trade is dominated by Orthodox Jews, and each transaction in the district is sealed with a handshake and the Yiddish words *mazel und brucha*.

Q: What does *mazel und brucha* mean in Yiddish?
A: "Luck and blessing."

Q: How many diamond-related businesses are located on this narrow city block?
A: 2,600. The dollar amount of the diamonds that pass through the district annually is about $4 billion.

NOTABLE UPPER EAST SIDE RESIDENTS

All I need is enough space to lay a hat—and a few friends.
DOROTHY ROTHSCHILD PARKER

- Dorothy Parker (Volney Hotel at 23 E. 74th St.)
- John Jacob Astor (E. 87th St. near York Ave.)
- Wystan Hugh Auden (237 E. 81st St.)
- Bernard Baruch (4 E. 66th St.)
- Stephen Vincent Benet (220 E. 69th St. & 215 E. 68th St.)
- Andrew Carnegie (2 E. 91st St.)
- Willa Cather (570 Park Ave.)
- George Michael Cohan (993 Fifth Ave.)
- Katharine Cornell (23 Beekman Pl.)
- John Foster Dulles (72 E. 91st St.)
- Hamlin Garland (71 E. 92nd St.)
- Lou Gehrig (1994 Second Ave.)
- George Gershwin (132 E. 72nd St.)
- John Paul Getty (One Sutton Pl.)
- Samuel Gompers (E. 91st St.)

- Ulysses Simpson Grant (3 E. 66th St.)
- Marguerite Guggenheim and Max Ernst (Fifth Ave. & 72nd St.)
- Dag Hammarskjold (778 Park Ave. & E. 73rd St.)
- Oscar Hammerstein II (1067 Fifth Ave.)
- James Jerome Hill (8 E. 65th St.)
- Charles E. Ives (164 E. 74th St.)
- George Simon Kaufman (410 Park Ave. & 158 E. 63rd St.)
- Jerome David Kern (128 E. 74th St.)
- Fiorello La Guardia (East End Ave. & 88th St./23 E. 109th St.)
- Gypsy Rose Lee (153 E. 63rd St.)
- Herbert Lehman (5 E. 62nd St.)
- Sinclair Lewis (21 E. 90th St.)
- Walter Lippmann (121 E. 79th St.)
- John Marquand (161 E. 75th St.)
- John Dewey (125 E. 62nd St.)
- Harpo, Groucho, and Chico Marx (179 E. 93rd St.)
- Henry Miller (450 E. 85th St.)
- Edward Murrow (580 Park Ave.)
- Ogden Nash (27 E. 79th St. and 55 E. 85th St.)
- Eugene O'Neill (35 E. 84th St.)
- Emily Post (39 E. 79th St.)
- Joseph Pulitzer (9 E. 73rd St.)
- Richard Rogers (50 E. 77th St.)
- John D. Rockefeller (1220 Fifth Ave. at E. 103rd St.)
- Henry Kissinger (The River House on E. 51st St.)
- Eleanor Roosevelt (47-49 E. 65th St., 55 E. 74th St. & 211 E. 62nd St.)
- Mark Rothko (118 E. 95th St.)
- David Sarnoff (44 E. 71st St.)
- Robert Sherwood (25 Sutton Pl. S.)
- John Steinbeck (206 E. 72nd St.)
- Leopold Stokowski (10 Gracie Sq.)
- Louis Tiffany (19 E. 72nd St.)
- Edith Wharton (884 Park Ave.)
- Bennett Cerf (132 E. 62nd St.)
- Wendell Wilkie (1010 Fifth Ave.)
- P. G. Wodehouse (1000 Park Ave.)
- Thomas Wolfe (865 First Ave.)

1946

John D. Rockefeller Jr. donated 17 acres of land in Turtle Bay (East 42nd to 46th Streets, extending to the East River) to the United Nations. Rockefeller bought the land for $8.5 million from William Zeckendorf, and the city agreed to contribute $5 million toward clearing the land of cattle, slaughterhouses, shanties, and tenement houses. The city also agreed to resettle 270 residents and to grant street and waterfront rights to the

United Nations. More than 158 member states have U.N. missions in the city, contributing to the millions of dollars that United Nations affiliates spend in the city each year (perhaps offsetting enormous accrued parking ticket debts). The grounds of the organization are not considered part of the United States, so national, state, and city laws don't apply to the organization. The U.N. even has its own police force, fire department, and postal service, and employs about 6,000 people.

Q: What is the sales tax on items bought in the United Nations Gift Center?
A: None. There is no tax on items purchased there.

There is one annual session conducted by the General Assembly.

Q: How long does the session last?
A: 3 months.

Q: How many original member states are in the United Nations?
A: 51.

Q: How many different languages can the United Nations tours be conducted in?
A: 17.

U.N. BOYCOTT

When deciding where in the United States to place the United Nations, the Soviet Union threatened to boycott the organization if it was located on the West Coast.

1959

Construction began in May on the country's largest performing arts complex: the Lincoln Center for the Performing Arts at 62nd Street and Columbus Avenue (stretching up to 67th Street and over to Amsterdam Avenue). Over the course of a decade the center's buildings were completed with financial backing from John D. Rockefeller Jr., John D. Rockefeller III, and others. The first performance at the Philharmonic Hall took place in September of 1962, and the New York City Ballet began performances in 1964. The Metropolitan Opera House opened on September 16, 1966, with a performance of *Antony and Cleopatra* (Leontyne Price sang the role of Cleopatra). The Julliard School was completed in 1969, which included Alice Tully Hall.

Lincoln Center was developed to stave off the decay of the West Side and to greatly enrich the city's cultural life; an estimated 1,647 families and 383 businesses in 188 buildings were displaced. The center was designed by Wallace K. Harrison.

Q: What other New York City landmarks did Harrison help to design?
A: Rockefeller Center and the United Nations Building.

Q: The Philharmonic Hall was renamed in 1973. What was the new name?
A: The Avery Fisher Hall.

CONTRIBUTING TO THE ARTS

People who toss coins into the reflecting pool at Lincoln Center's Vivian Beaumont Theater are actually contributing to the pool's upkeep. The pool is swept and cleaned every two months, and the total value of the coins, which are usually pennies, averages $50 to $100. The money is used to maintain the plaza.

1959

The Guggenheim Museum opened in October at 88th Street and Fifth Avenue.

Q: Who designed the museum?
A: Frank Lloyd Wright. The museum was his only important commission in New York City. Shaped like a white spiral that is narrowest at its base—and built entirely of hand-plastered concrete over steel both inside and out—exhibitions can be mounted in a continuous line.

PHOTO BY B. KIM TAYLOR

A poignant tableau graces Columbus Circle on 59th Street near Central Park

1965

The Landmarks Preservation Commission was established by law to identify and protect landmarks, buildings, historic districts, and historic public interiors in New York City. The outcry over the loss of the original Pennsylvania Station in 1965 underscored the need for architectural protection and spurred the creation of the commission. The commission includes three architects, one historian, one city planner or landscape architect, one real estate agent or developer, and one resident from each of the five boroughs. There are over 19,000 properties protected by the commission in the city, as well as 89 interiors.

Q: How many areas in the city have been deemed historic districts by the commission?
A: 65.

NOTABLE HARLEM RESIDENTS

New York City is the most fatally fascinating thing in America. She sits like a witch at the gate of the country.
JAMES WELDON JOHNSON

- Duke Ellington (381 Edgecomb Ave.)
- George Gershwin (520 W. 144th St.)
- W. C. Handy (400 Convent Ave.)
- Jimi Hendrix (Room 406 of the Theresa Hotel at 2090 Seventh Ave. & W. 125th St.)
- Billie Holiday (286 W. 142nd St.)
- James Weldon Johnson (2311 Seventh Ave.)
- Scott Joplin (133 W. 138th St.)
- Jack Kerouac (Amsterdam Ave. & W. 118th St.)
- Allen Ginsberg (Amsterdam Ave. & W. 118th St.)
- William Burroughs (Amsterdam Ave. & W. 118th St.)
- Fiorello La Guardia (1274 Fifth Ave.)
- Henry Robinson Luce (514 W. 122nd St.)
- Thomas Nast (125th St. near Fifth Ave.)
- Charlie Parker (411 Manhattan Ave.)
- Paul Robeson (555 Edgecomb Ave.)
- Norman Rockwell (St. Nicholas Ave. & W. 147th St.)
- Igor Ivan Sikorsky (506 W. 135th St.)
- Joe Louis (Theresa Hotel)
- Malcolm X (Suite 128 of the Theresa Hotel)
- Oscar Hammerstein II (509 W. 121st St.)
- Asa Philip Randolph (2453 Seventh Ave.)

Q: Which 3 famous men lived (at separate times) at 409 Edgecomb Ave. in Harlem?
A: Thurgood Marshall, Roy Wilkins, and W. E. B. Du Bois.

Q; What do rap entrepreneur Russell Simmons and the actress Cher have in common?
A: They both lived above Tower Records on Lower Broadway. Simmons moved into Cher's apartment when she relocated to the Police Building in Soho in the early 1990s.

1966

A large, black, 15-foot-high rotating cube that weighs 3,000 pounds was placed at its current location at Astor Place. An identical cube is located in Ann Arbor, Michigan, behind the Student Union Building.

Q: What is its title?
A: "The Alamo."

1967

The Westbeth housing complex opened on Bethune, Washington, and Bank Streets in Greenwich Village, offering subsidized housing to artists. There are 383 apartments in Westbeth, ranging in price from $370 to $660, which the J. M. Kaplan Fund underwrote.

Q: What was housed in the location before Westbeth?
A: Bell Laboratories.

Q: What does the word Greenwich mean in Saxon?
A: "Green Village."

1970

The World Trade Center's first buildings opened at Church and Liberty Streets as part of a massive urban renewal project by the New York Port Authority.

Q: How many buildings comprise the World Trade Center?
A: 7, but the 110-story twin-tower skyscrapers clearly dominate the other 5 buildings. The towers are the tallest buildings in New York City.

Q: How many New York City buildings are on the top-ten list of the tallest buildings in the world?
A: 3: the Empire State Building and the twin World Trade Center towers.

NOTABLE QUEENS RESIDENTS

- Louis Armstrong (Corona)
- Bela Bartok (Forest Hills)
- Bix Beiderbecke (Sunnyside)
- Dale Carnegie (Forest Hills)
- De Witt Clinton (Maspeth)
- John Coltrane (St. Albans)
- Woody Guthrie (Howard Beach)

- Helen Keller (Forest Hills)
- Jack Kerouac (Richmond Hill)
- Malcolm X (East Elmhurst)
- Glenn Miller (Astoria)
- Jacob Riis (Richmond Hill)
- Fats Waller (St. Albans)
- Tony Bennett (Astoria)

1983

An eleven-block waterfront historic district called the South Street Seaport was created around Fulton and Water Streets, an area that was once the heart of the Port of New York in the 1700s and 1800s, featuring craft shops, antique stores, and upscale dining.

1986

The Jacob K. Javits Convention Center on 38th Street and 11th Avenue, designed by the I. M. Pei firm, replaced the Coliseum on Columbus Circle as the city's largest convention center. The center can accommodate six simultaneous events and 85,000 people. The center accounted for almost 2 percent of the city's economy in the mid-1990s.

Q: How is Jacob Javits Center ranked nationally in terms of most square feet of exhibit space?
A: Sixth. Chicago has the largest exhibit hall in the country, followed by Cleveland and Las Vegas.

Q: How many city blocks does the Jacob Javits Center cover?
A: 4.

Q: How many entries are usually submitted for the Fancy Food Show's Product Awards Competition at the Jacob Javits Center?
A: About 1,000.

Q: How many people attend the annual Fancy Food Show?
A: Approximately 5,000.

In 1997 more than 50,000 people attended an art expo at the convention center that featured work from about 2,000 artists— including Matisse, Miro, Picasso, and Chagall.

1996

There were 19,000 buildings in New York City under a degree of architectural protection by the Landmarks Preservation Commission. NYC ranks first in the nation as the city with the highest architectural survival rate.

Q: How many neighborhoods are designated as "historic neighborhoods" retaining many original buildings and elements)?
A: 55.

NOTABLE CHELSEA RESIDENTS

No one should come to New York to live unless he is willing to be lucky.

E. B. WHITE

- Sherwood Anderson (427 W. 22nd St.)
- Stephen Crane (165 W. 23rd St.)
- George McClellan (22 W. 31st St.)
- Samuel Morse (5 W. 22nd St.)
- Ogden Nash (470 W. 24th St.)
- O. Henry (28 W. 26th St.)
- Jack Kerouac (149 W. 21st St.)
- Edith Wharton (14 W. 23rd St.)
- Edwin A. Robinson (450 W. 23rd St.)
- Richard Wright (235 W. 26th St.)

1997

10,000 buildings in New York City exceeded six stories, and the city had 76 building inspectors.

1997

The Chelsea Piers opened at Pier 63 on the Hudson River at 23rd Street, featuring a brewery, two restaurants, film studios, a gymnasium, a netted golf range, a cigar bar, rollerblading facilities, a cafe, and an outdoor concert area.

CHAPTER 8

Arts, Entertainment, Pets, & Lifestyles

The only credential New York City asked was the boldness to dream. For those who did, it unlocked its gates and its treasures, not caring who they were or where they came from.

MOSS HART

New York City's reputation as a theater town can be summed up in one word: Broadway, or two: Off-Broadway, or four: Shakespeare in the Park. Theater in New York City originated with the amateur offerings of the early colonists and has steadily mushroomed into one of the city's most recognizable, lucrative, and significant institutions.

Colonial theater began on Nassau Street in the 1690s, and spread to Beekman Street, Park Row, and John Street in Lower Manhattan by the mid-1700s. In 1824, a theater opened between Pearl and Duane Streets at Chatham Gardens, and then theaters began to concentrate on the Bowery and Lower Broadway. The theatrical "star system" started around 1810, and beginning in 1820, the value system of the patriotic laborer was incorporated into "Yankee" plays. Theaters began moving north from the

Bowery to Union Square during the last quarter of the nineteenth century. Theater flourished in Times Square after 1900.

There are more than 300 theaters operating in New York City, ranging from massive auditoriums to neighborhood lofts, employing not only acting talent but administrative assistants, designers, directors, hair and makeup artists, backdrop painters, carpenters, lighting people, advertising firms, writers, lyricists, composers, choreographers, and public relations firms.

Almost every major acting talent has cut his or her teeth in the theater in New York City; it's considered a rite of passage and is so common that it's almost a given. Theater, like the media and literature from the city, is as diverse as the city's population. Audiences can choose from dozens, if not hundreds, of theater offerings on a given night that range from a performance art piece that entails smearing glue over a body part to *The Life* or *Les Miserables* on Broadway and everything conceivable in between. The city's political, economic, and social climates have always been reflected in its theater offerings, and that remains true today. While Broadway moves increasingly toward higher ticket rates, special effects, spectacle, and massive budgets of $8 million or more, alternative theater continues to thrive and to offer something different, as it always has, in Off-Broadway theaters and in neighborhood playhouses across the city.

New York's reputation as a theater town is matched by it's status as a siren for artists of all types: painters, photographers, modern dancers, spoken-word poets, illustrators, clothing designers, furniture designers, grand chefs, graffiti artists, opera singers, ballet dancers, stand-up comedians, and the broad spectrum under the umbrella of musicians. Most of America's substantial musicians, painters, and dancers started—or finished—their careers in New York City.

Television has reflected the country's love of New York stories practically since it began broadcasting, as evidenced by *The Honeymooners; The Thin Man; Naked City; That Girl; The Patty Duke Show; The Dick Van Dyke Show; The Odd Couple; All in the Family; Rhoda; Kojak; Barney Miller; The Jeffersons; Welcome Back, Kotter; Taxi; Cosby; Seinfeld; NYPD Blue; Law & Order; Friends; Mad About You; Caroline in the City; Saturday Night Live;* and dozens of other sitcoms, police dramas, soap operas, and television dramas that draw inspiration from life in the city.

To pinpoint a particular lifestyle that sums up the experience of living in New York is impossible; to say that there are as many lifestyles as there are people is closer to the truth. It does seem accurate, however, to say New Yorkers love their pets, are annoyed by car alarms, and dislike waiting for anything.

1600

Indians in the New York City region used stone, bone, copper, and, antler artifacts such as fishhooks, knives, drills, needles, whistles, flint points, choppers, scrapers, awls, and pestles—as well as pieces of pottery.

1613

Local Indians dined on maize, osters, beans, maple syrup, duck, partridge, strawberries, apples, both salt and freshwater fish, squash, deer, elk, bear, marten, turkey, and beaver and otter. In April and May of each year the women planted crops while the men rebuilt their dwellings. A Strawberry Festival and Corn Planting Ceremony were the high points of spring.

Summer was a time for politics and the renewal of alliances and friendships, while autumn brought the harvest and the Green Corn Festival and performance of the Thanksgiving Dance. It was also a time for naming children born since the last midwinter. Late fall and winter was the time for hunting, fighting, and foraging for animal meat and furs.

1630

Eighteen percent of the immigrants to New Amsterdam between 1630 and 1644 arrived as members of a family with three or more children. The largest family to immigrate to New Amsterdam before 1644 contained nine children, one of whom was still an infant.

1644

New Amsterdam had four official tailors, one baker, one surgeon, one minister, two wheelwrights, four shoemakers, one skipper, one brewer, ten carpenters, thirty-eight farmers, nineteen servants, two millers, one hog dealer, one blacksmith, one cooper, one clerk, one weaver, and one magistrate.

Q: Which occupation garnered the most money?
A: The minister at 1,000 florins, compared to a shoemaker's 65 florins. A carpenter's boy earned the least at 25 florins.

They all drink here, from the moment they are able to lick a spoon. The women of the neighborhood entertain each other with a pipe and brazier; young and old, they all smoke. The country suits me exceedingly well. I shall not try to leave it as long as I live.
NICASIUS DE SILLE, WRITING TO A FRIEND IN HOLLAND UPON HIS ARRIVAL IN NEW AMSTERDAM IN 1653. HE SPOKE ALSO OF OYSTERS SO LARGE THEY HAD TO BE CUT INTO PORTIONS.

1670

Settlers enjoyed beef, pork, wheat, butter, and tobacco from Long Island; beaver, otter, musk, and skins from the Indians; and malt, fish, cider apples, iron, and tar from Virginia.

1679

The taverns provided excellent food and drink, as did country resorts in the area like Clapp's. "Good cyder & mead" was often promised, along with bean-and-bacon soup, roasted lamb and salad, young peas, a dish of tarts, a dish of curds and cream, mulberries, and currants.

1699

Richard Hunter filed a petition with Governor John Nanfan requesting a license to stage plays. His petition was granted, but there is no record of where he staged productions nor what plays he presented. For the first half of the seventeenth century, theatrical productions were presented in makeshift quarters around town.

1732

Rip Van Dam, president of the Common Council in the town, opened the New Theatre (also known as the "Theatre in Nassau Street" in a house he owned.

1736

The first public concert on record took place at Todd's Tavern when a harpsicordist, violinist, and German flutist entertained the crowd.

1737

Residents enjoyed "turtle feasts," barbeques, dance balls, sleighing expeditions, and riverside formal parties.

1750

An advertisement for a play appeared in the *Weekly Post-Boy* on February 26, announcing a performance at 64 Nassau Street. The ad read, "By his Excellency's Permission, At the Theatre in Nassau Street . . . will be presented the Historical Tragedy of King Richard 3rd! Wrote originally by Shakespeare and altered by Colley Cibber, Esquire. In this play are contained the Death of King Henry 6th; the artful acquisition of the crown by King Richard, the murder of the Princes in the Tower; the landing of the Earl of Richmond, and the Battle of Bosworth Field." The cast members, director, and producer were not mentioned in the advertisement, and tickets cost either three or five shillings.

The tragedy of 'Cato' was played at the theatre in this city, before a very numerous audience, the greater part of whom were of the opinion that it was pretty well performed. As it was the fullest assembly that has ever appeared in that house, it may serve to prove that the taste of this place is not so vitiated or lost to a sense of liberty, but that they can prefer a representation of Virtue to one of loose character.

A THEATER REVIEW PUBLISHED BY THE
WEEKLY POST-BOY ON SEPTEMBER 24, 1750

1754

The Theatre in Nassau Street, the only official theater in town, ceased operation.

1767

There were three theaters in town, all constructed under the leadership of David Douglass, the head of a British troupe called The London Company of Comedians.

1784

The martini was popular at drinking establishments in the city; the British provided gin and Frenchmen provided vermouth.

The cafe set in nineteenth-century New York.

1797

The Park Theater on Park Row was built. Because of the American Revolution, all theatrical productions ceased except for amateur offerings for the benefit of the British troops. The American Company theatrical troupe left the city and went into exile in the West Indies during the war.

1800

The Park Theatre was the most popular place for live entertainment in the city and attracted patrons of all classes.

1821

A theater for blacks only was established as the African Grove Theater at Bleecker and Mercer Streets. *Richard III* and *Othello* were performed there, and drinks were served during intermissions in a garden connected to the theater.

Q: Who was Ira Aldridge?
A: He was America's most lauded black actor from 1820 through his death in 1867. He made his first stage appearance at the African Grove Theater in the early 1820s while still a teen and was raised in the neighborhood near the theater. He enjoyed fame, wealth, honor, and a multitude of royal decorations for his Shakespearean roles in England, Ireland, Saxony, Prussia, Austria, Poland, Switzerland, and Russia. He eventually took British citizenship, and died in Poland.

Q: Where is a chair named in his honor?
A: At the Shakespeare Memorial Theater in Stratford-upon-Avon.

1824

Theaters began to open on two of New York City's major streets—Broadway and the Bowery—and stage actors from England came to the city hoping to meet with fame.

1825

The first grand opera presented in full in its original language in New York City and America was *The Barber of Seville* on November 29 at the Park Theater on Park Row.

Q: Who was the composer?
A: Rossini.

The audience was captivated by the beautiful music, elegant setting, and dramatic set designs. The *New York Evening Post* proclaimed that the city would never again be without a magnificent opera.

1827

American actors and acting families entertained an increasingly "democratic" audience comprised of laborers and patriots. The Booths, the Barrymores, the Drews, and the Jeffersons were four of the acting family dynasties in the 1800s.

1831

Theater prices and fare were tailored more to the needs of the working class.

1832

The English actress Fanny Kemble was considered a hit in a play that opened at the Park Theater. She eventually married a South Carolina planter named Pierce Butler.

1836

Thomas "Jim Crow" Rice and other entertainers set the stage for the mass popularity of minstrel shows in the 1840s by presenting variety-show-style songs and dances.

1842

The New York Philharmonic Orchestra was formed as the Philharmonic Society. The first concert, beginning with cofounder Urelli Corelli Hill conducting Beethoven's Symphony No. 5, took place on December 7 with 63 musicians performing for an audience of 600. The concert took place in Carnegie Hall, where the orchestra was based until 1962, when it moved to Lincoln Center's Avery Fisher Hall.

Q: How many permanent musicians does the Philharmonic currently employ?

A: 106. The orchestra performs about 190 concerts a season.

FEARLESS LEADERS

- Gustav Mahler was principal conductor of the New York Philharmonic Orchestra from 1909 to 1911, at which time the season expanded from 18 to 54 concerts a year (some of which were performed on tour in New England).
- The orchestra made its first commercial recording in 1917 with Josef Stransky conducting American and European pieces.
- Stravinsky and Arturo Toscanini first conducted for the orchestra in 1921. The orchestra also absorbed three smaller orchestras in the 1920s.
- Nationwide radio broadcasts of the orchestra began in 1930.
- Leonard Bernstein began conducting the orchestra in 1957; two television series began in 1958. In the fall of 1969 Leonard Bernstein was honored with the lifetime position of laureate conductor, which was the first in the history of the orchestra.
- Zubin Mehta held the post of music director from 1978 through 1991, longer than anyone else in the twentieth century. He conducted the orchestra's ten-thousandth concert on March 7, 1982.

1843

Vaudeville attracted male audiences and was performed in saloons and concert halls. Circuses opened on large vacant lots in the city and buildings were built for the purpose of displaying enormous, painted panoramas on canvas.

1853

Uncle Tom's Cabin opened at the National Theater and ran for more than 300 performances. This indicated a public desire for long-running shows that continues today.

1866

The Black Crow, a play based on material written by Charles Barras, required an investment of $24,000 and grossed $1.1 million after 475 performances. This was an important step in the evolution of theater because it introduced the long-running musical. Actors began to require agents, and theaters began to require publicity and compete for patrons. The theatrical printer and the theatrical poster became necessities. Restaurants and hotels cropped up to cater to theatergoers, and by 1870 the first theater district had been created in Manhattan around Union Square at 14th Street on the East Side. Tony Pastor's New Fourteenth Street Theater was considered to be the birthplace of vaudeville in the city.

1870

The Metropolitan Museum of Art was founded by the members of the Union League Club, which included William Cullen Bryant, John Jay, lawyer Joseph Choate, railroad executive John Taylor Johnston, and painters John Frederick Kensett and Worthington Whittredge. Its first gift was a Roman sarcophagus, and the museum currently owns three million works or objects.

MUSEUM-QUALITY CITY

- There are over 80 museums in New York City and at least 8 different museums are involved in expansion efforts.
- The price of a Lichtenstein-designed scarf at the Guggenheim Museum gift shop is between $85 and $95. A Danish stapler at the MoMA design store costs $60.
- The American Museum of the Moving Image in Astoria, Queens, is 7,200 square feet, offers more than 500 programs in its theater each year, and has 70,000 objects for viewing.
- The Anthropology Museum of the People of New York was founded by Margaret Mead and others in Flushing, Queens, in 1977. The museum presents events at the Queens College campus too.
- There are 1,000 items on display at the Chung-Cheng Art Gallery/Center of Asian Studies in Jamaica, Queens. 50% of the items there are Japanese and 50% are Chinese.
- There are 2,200 full-time employees at the Metropolitan Museum of Art.

1881

Carnegie Hall opened with a five-day inaugural festival. Over 50,000 events took place and 1,300 compositions received their world or American premiere at Carnegie Hall during its first century. New York City bought Carnegie Hall in 1960, and it was registered as a National Historic Landmark in 1964. The main hall seats 2,804 people.

ILLUSTRIOUS OCCUPANTS OF THE STUDIOS ABOVE CARNEGIE HALL

- Isadora Duncan, dancer (1897)
- Martha Graham, dancer (1933)
- Marlon Brando, actor (1953)
- Leonard Bernstein, composer and conductor (1944)
- Fanny Hurst, author (1930s)
- Evangeline Adams, astrologer (1900s-40s)
- Gerry Mulligan, musician (1950s)
- Dorothy Maynor, singer (1950s)
- Joe Raposo, composer (1980s)
- Charles Dana Gibson, artist (1909)

Q: When did the Beatles make their first American appearance at Carnegie Hall?
A: February 12, 1964.

1882

The first Labor Day Parade was held in New York City.

THE MET

In 1883 the Metropolitan Opera Company was formed to coincide with the opening of the Metropolitan Opera House on Broadway and 39th Street. It was designed by J. C. Cady in a conservative Renaissance style and was promptly criticized by James Mapleson, an impresario at the Academy of Music, as "a yellow brick brewery." The company had acquired a well-deserved reputation as an exclusive enclave of wealth and snobbery, but the company's widening audience began to alter this perception after 1918. The influx of immigrants who wanted to hear opera from their homelands led to radio broadcasts and corporate sponsorships by 1931. The City Opera was founded in 1944 by Mayor La Guardia to provide "opera for the masses."

In 1950, when Rudolf Bing became the manager of the Metropolitan Opera Company, emphasis was shifted away from the hundreds of famous singers that had lured patrons over the decades to famous conductors such as Leonard Bernstein and Zubin Mehta. The first black soloist, the contralto Marian Anderson, was engaged by the company in 1955, followed by Leontyne Price and others. The company has been increasing its visibility through regular television broadcasts throughout the 1990s.

- The Metropolitan Opera pays major opera stars up to $13,000 for a performance.
- The price of a season subscription at the Met is $132 to $1,440.
- Opera fans start lining up for standing-room tickets at 6:00 A.M.

Q: How many standing-room spots are available for each opera performance at the Met?
A: 175.

- There are currently 40 opera companies are in New York City.
- An average of 150 admirers wait outside Luciano Pavarotti's dressing room after each of his shows at the Metropolitan Opera
- Belle Silverman, born in Brooklyn, first sang for the New York City Opera in 1955 as Rosalinde in Strauss's *Die Fledermaus*.

Q: What was her stage name?
A: Beverly Sills.

Q: What is one of her lesser known accomplishments?
A: She performed the first radio announcement that included singing.

1890

The play *The Old Homestead* was launched at Tony Pastor's New Fourteenth Street Theater and ran for three years.

1890

Amateur night was held at Miner's Bowery Theater every other Friday. Vaudeville was gaining in popularity, and it originated on the Bowery. Anyone willing to take the stage and perform at Miner's during amateur night was paid $1, regardless of quality of talent, and audience reaction became part of the show's entertainment. The phrase "give 'im the hook!" was born at Miner's, as the worst acts were forcibly removed, mid-act, with a shepherd's crook attached to a pole.

1890

The ferret was first brought to the United States; 100 years later, the animal was banned as a pet in New York City.

The New York City Friends of Ferrets are planning a federal lawsuit against New York City to overturn the prohibition. The curator for the Bronx Zoo receives the most calls in the city from ferret owners who want to part with their pet.

Q: How much does it cost to buy a ferret at a pet shop?
A: $100 to $150.

ANIMAL KINGDOM

- There were 120,000 licensed dogs in New York City in 1997.
- The number of pet stores in the city that offer pet grooming has increased fivefold since 1960.
- The price for a painted pet portrait runs between $500 and $15,000. The price for a pet funeral, including monument, starts at $1,000. Pet massage therapy runs $60 per hour. Hammocks designed for dogs range from $65 to $98.
- The price per hour for an animal psychiatrist to tend to Gus, the Central Park Zoo's polar bear, was $50.
- An average of 5,000 people attend St. John the Divine's Feast of St. Francis annual celebration of pet ownership.
- Labor Day and Memorial Day are when most animals are abandoned in New York City.
- Approximately 35,000 animals are euthanized annually by the ASPCA in New York City.
- There are 2,000 members in the New York Turtle and Tortoise Society.
- New York City has the highest concentration of peregrine falcons in the world. 70% of New York State's breeding population is located in New York City.
- The average number of cats taken to the Animal Medical Center each summer after surviving falls from tall buildings is 150 to 200. An average of 10 cats that fall from windows are tended to each week in the summer at the Bergh Memorial Animal Hospital.

Q: What is the New York City record for the number of stories a cat fell and survived?
A: 46 stories.

Q: How many turtles that survived a fall have been taken to the Bergh Memorial Animal Hospital?
A: 1.

Q: What is the average amount of kitty litter that is disposed of annually by each multi-cat apartment in New York City?
A: 390 pounds.

1895

The first nude sculpture in America was located in New York City atop Madison Square Garden. Augustus Saint–Gaudens was the sculptor. The reason the statue of a young woman wasn't removed in spite of the fact that it shocked Manhattanites was because J. P. Morgan, Madison Square Garden's major stock-holder, liked it.

1896

Jacob Sandler composed the song "Eili, Eili"; it was first sung in 1896 at the Windsor Theater on the Bowery. The song remains cherished over a century later.

1897

New York City's most lavish nineteenth-century party, the Bradley-Martin Ball, was held at the Waldorf Astoria.

Q: How much did it cost?
A: $9,000.

1900

By the turn of the century the theaters at Times Square (then called Long Acre Square) replaced the Union Square area as the city's theater district. The Union Square area was known for having "dime museums," places where you could view odd, interesting objects and exhibits. Film studios and movie theaters moved into the Union Square area as theaters moved uptown. Second Avenue just below 14th Street became a district of Yiddish theaters. Producers with business acumen instead of theater experience replaced the actor-manager, and booking practices were standardized by a consortium of businessmen who had created a company called the Theater Syndicate.

1904

The Jewish Museum was founded by a gift of ceremonial objects and books given to the Jewish Theological Seminary by Judge Meyer Sulzberger. It is located at 1109 Fifth Avenue, and is the largest, most comprehensive museum of its kind in the world.

Q: How many years of Jewish life and culture are documented at the museum?

A: 4,000. The museum has 27,000 materials in its permanent collection.

1913

Q: For whom is the Frick Collection named?
A: Henry Clay Frick.

Frick was a steel and railroad industrialist. In 1913, he chose New York City for his collection over his home town of Pittsburgh because New York City had less air pollution. A museum houses his collections in his former mansion at 1 East 70th Street, which was designed by Thomas Hastings. A reference library there contains 750,000 photographs and 174,000 books and catalogs.

1915

Irving Berlin's *Stop, Look, and Listen* featured the first shadow dance, in which a woman does a striptease behind a backlit sheet.

1919

Actors found that theater rehearsals were unpaid and seemingly endless. When traveling out of the city in a road show, actors sometimes earned so little that they were stranded out of town without the means to return home. On August 6, just minutes before official curtain time, actors throughout the city went on strike. A contract was negotiated between theater managers and the Actor's Equity union.

1920

Art collector Louisine Waldron Havemeyer, whose collection is now the pride of the New York Metropolitan Museum, was once cornered by a wealthy, bejeweled dowager who scornfully asked, "Why do you spend so much money on dabs of paint on canvas and paper?" Mrs. Havemeyer examined the woman's pearl necklace and said, "I prefer to have something made by a man than to have something made by an oyster."

PHOTO BY B. KIM TAYLOR

Soho is well known for its eclectic and artistic atmosphere. This mural brightens the view east of Sixth Avenue.

1921

Audiences were expressing a desire to see drama with more psychological realism. Chekov, Ibsen, Shaw, and Pirandello were featured on Broadway and in smaller Greenwich Village theaters. Theater offerings from France, China, Spain, Israel, and Italy came to Broadway and American playwrights such as Marc Connelly, George S. Kaufman, Eugene O'Neill, Paul Green, and Robert Sherwood came to prominence.

PLAYS BY EUGENE O'NEILL PRODUCED IN THE 1920S

- *Beyond the Horizon* (1920, Pulitzer prize)
- *Anna Christie* (1921, Pulitzer prize)
- *The Emperor Jones* (1921)
- *The Hairy Ape* (1922)
- *Mourning Becomes Electra* (1925)
- *Desire Under the Elms* (1925)
- *Strange Interlude* (1927, Pulitzer prize)

1925

Ed Smalls opened the jazz club Small's Paradise in Harlem at 2294 1/2 Seventh Avenue. The club seated 1,500 and was advertised as "Harlem's House of Mirth and Music." Musicians such as Billie Holiday, Willie "The Lion" Smith, Fletcher Henderson, and James P. Johnson regularly performed, and the club featured floor shows, Chinese food, singing waiters, and patrons like Harlem Renaissance figures Countee Cullen and Carl Van Vechten.

1926

The Savoy Ballroom dance hall, accommodate up to 5,000 people, opened in Harlem at 596 Lenox Avenue between 140th and 141st Streets and was touted as "the world's most beautiful ballroom". It was dubbed "the track" by some because it sometimes featured dog races. Throughout the 1930s and 1940s the Savoy promoted band battles and dance contests that inspired innovative dance steps such as the Lindy Hop. The Savoy Ballroom closed in 1958 after hosting more than 250 big band orchestras, including those of Duke Ellington, Benny Goodman, and Chick Webb.

1927

A total of 750,000 pounds of ticker tape and paper were used to greet Charles Lindbergh on June 13, 1927.

1927

Showboat opened on Broadway, ushering in the concept of the nonromantic musical.

Q: Who composed *Showboat*?
A: Jerome Kern and Oscar Hammerstein II.

A REAL MUST SEE

The New York theater season of 1927-28 still remains as the most successful in the city's history; 264 shows opened in 76 Broadway theaters. "Talking" movies, introduced in 1927, quickly curtailed the short-lived theater audience peak, though, as did the depression. By 1930 only 187 shows opened in 64 Broadway theaters.

1928

Sir Thomas Beecham was guest conductor at the New York Philharmonic from 1928 to 1932. Once, while riding with a friend in a New York cab, Beecham repeatedly whistled a passage from Mozart. This annoyed his friend, who eventually complained, "Must you do that?" Beecham replied, "You may be able to hear only my whistling, but I can hear the full orchestra."

When we sing "All we, like sheep, have gone astray," might we please have a little more regret and a little less satisfaction?
SIR THOMAS BEECHAM TO THE PHILHARMONIC CHOIR
WHEN REHEARSING HANDEL'S *MESSIAH*

1930

Pianist Oscar Levant complained to composer/songwriter George Gershwin that when they traveled together on trains, he always had to take the upper berth while Gershwin had the lower. "That's the difference between talent and genius," said Gershwin.

1930

The Whitney Museum of American Art was founded in 1930. The extent of Edward Hopper's artistic estate was bequeathed to the Whitney in 1970. It included: 2,000 oils, watercolors, drawings, and prints. This was the largest donation in the museum's history.

MATCH THE MUSEUM WITH ITS NEIGHBORHOOD

1. IBM Gallery of Science and Art	A. Queens
2. Old Merchant's House	B. Upper East Side
3. Pierpont Morgan Library	C. Upper West Side
4. Asia Society Galleries	D. Greenwich Village/Soho
5. Dyckman House	E. Staten Island
6. Lefferts Homestead	F. Murray Hill
7. Isamu Noguchi Garden Museum	G. Midtown
8. Jacques Marchais Center of Tibetan Art	H. Brooklyn

Answers: 1. G; 2. D; 3. F; 4. B; 5. C; 6. H; 7. A; 8. E.

1930

Five thousand actors in New York City were unemployed because of the depression. The government became a theatrical producer through the national Federal Theatre Project and New York City was the site of its largest branch.

1933

Russel Markert, the man who created the first precision dance team called "the Rockets" in St. Louis, was hired along with the dancing Rockets by Samuel "Roxy" Rothafel to be part of his show at the Roxy Theater. The Rockets were renamed the Roxyettes and moved with Rothafel to Radio City Music Hall. In 1933, when Rothafel retired, the Roxyettes were renamed the Radio City Rockettes.

LIVE AT THE APOLLO

The Apollo Theater, although built in 1914, wasn't used for stage shows until 1934. Billie Holiday, Bessie Smith, Ethel Waters, Duke Ellington's orchestra, and Charlie Barnet's orchestra performed at the Apollo throughout the 1930s and 1940s. The Apollo offered revues from the Cotton Club and the Ubangi Club and showgirls backed up the performers. The Apollo was also used for political speeches and for appearances by major sports figures.

Q: Whose careers were launched at the Apollo's Wednesday "Amateur Nights"?
A: James Brown, Sarah Vaughn, and Ella Fitzgerald.

In the 1950s and 1960s performers or actors such as Nat "King" Cole, Charlie Parker, Sidney Poitier, Ossie Davis, the Jackson Five, Marvin Gaye, Diana Ross, Bo Diddley, and Stevie Wonder appeared at the Apollo. The Apollo was used as a movie theater from 1975 until 1983 when the building was bought by Percy E. Sutton's Inner City Broadcasting firm . The television series *Show Time at the Apollo* began broadcasting live from the theater in the 1990s.

1935

Porgy and Bess opened on Broadway.

Q: Who composed *Porgy and Bess*?

A: George Gershwin.

1936

The owner of Bloomingdale's department store once backed an out-of-town theatrical production by writer George S. Kaufman. The morning after the show opened, Bloomingdale called Kaufman and asked how the play had been received. "Close the play and keep the store open nights," Kaufman responded.

1939

Abby Aldrich Rockefeller, Mrs. Cornelius J. Sullivan, and Lillie P. Bliss collected modern works of art for a new museum made of tile and glass that opened on West 53rd Street: the Museum of Modern Art, designed by Edward Durrell Stone and Philip L. Goodwin. Featured artists included Picasso, Mondrian, Matisse, and Van Gogh.

1943

Oklahoma! presented a great fusion of libretto, dance, and score.

Q: Who wrote *Oklahoma!*?
A: Rogers and Hammerstein.

1945

Violinist Fritz Kreisler told socialite Mrs. Vanderbilt that his fee for playing at her party would be $18,000. "That's agreeable," she said, "but I hope you understand that you should not mingle with my guests." "Oh!" he replied. "Well, in that case, my fee is only $500."

SALARIES AT NEW YORK CITY'S LARGER JAZZ CLUBS:

For top jazz musicians . . . .$40,000 to $100,000 a week
For mid-draw performers . . . .$25,000 to $40,000
For promising starters . . . . .less than $10,000 to $25,000

1947

A Streetcar Named Desire was produced.

Q: Who wrote it?
A: Tennessee Williams.

Tennessee also wrote *The Glass Menagerie,* produced in 1945, *Summer and Smoke* (1948), *The Rose Tattoo* (1951), *Camino Real* (1953), *Cat on a Hot Tin Roof* (1955), *Orpheus Descending* (1957), and *Sweet Bird of Youth* (1959).

1949

Arthur Miller's *Death of a Salesman* was produced.

1950

Supper clubs and floorshows in New York City became all the rage. The Copacabana, the Latin Quarter, and the Stork Club were the most lauded.

1952

Allen Stewart Konigsberg took the name Woody Allen.

Q: Where was he raised?
A: Flatbush in Brooklyn.

During his freshman year in Midwood High School Allen wrote material for columnist Earl Wilson. He briefly attended New York University and City University of New York before appearing as a stand-up comedian at the Bitter End in Manhattan. He appeared on *The Ed Sullivan Show* and appeared on and hosted *The Tonight Show.* His first play, *What's New, Pussycat?,* opened in 1965 and his second, *Don't Drink the Water,* opened in 1966 and ran for 18 months.

1952

Q: How much was Andy Warhol paid to illustrate a Spanish-wedge shoe in 1952?

A: $15.

1954

Sotheby's auction house, based in London, opened a branch in New York City on East 72nd Street. It merged with the Parke-Bernet Galleries to form Sotheby Parke Bernet. In 1983 the firm and its branches again took the name Sotheby's.

Q: What were the 2 best years for auction sales at Sotheby's?
A: 1988 and 1989.

Q: What were the 2 worst years?
A: 1991 and 1992.

PHOTO BY ERIC CAPSTICK

The mighty Lincoln Center—home to the New York City Opera, the New York City Ballet, the New York Philharmonic Orchestra, and the Julliard School of Music. President Eisenhower laid the first stone in 1959.

1956

Eugene O'Neill's *Long Day's Journey into Night* was produced. The play was so autobiographically painful for O'Neill that he didn't want it produced until after his death.

1960

The Fantastiks opened Off-Broadway and was performed 14,582 times over the course of 35 years.
Neil Simon's play *Barefoot in the Park* was produced.

The truest expression of a people is in its dances and its music. Bodies never lie.

AGNES DE MILLE IN 1969

1967

Leo Castelli, who had moved to the United States from Italy in his thirties, opened the Leo Castelli Gallery at 4 East 77th Street. The gallery moved to Soho in 1971 and helped establish the area as an art gallery district. His gallery has displayed the works of some of the century's leading artists, including Roy Lichtenstein, Andy Warhol, Jasper Johns, Frank Stella, Robert Rauschenberg, John Chamberlain, Ellsworth Kelly, and Cy Twombly.

Q: Of the 500 art galleries in Manhattan, what percentage are in Soho?
A: 50%. 25% are on 57th Street.

THE DANCE THEATRE OF HARLEM

Arthur Mitchell was in a cab on his way to Kennedy Airport when he learned that Martin Luther King Jr. had been shot. Mitchell was a principal dancer with the New York City Ballet and the first black man to dance with George Balanchine's company. He asked the cab driver to return to Manhattan, and out of his resolve that day he created the Dance Theatre of Harlem at 466 West 152nd Street, including a school as well as a dance company.

1969

Q: Woody Allen directed his first complete feature film. What was it?
A: *Take the Money and Run.*

1969

The Museo del Barrio opened at 1230 Fifth Avenue between 104th and 105th Streets. It was founded in a classroom in East Harlem in order to preserve and document the art of Puerto Rico and Latin America.

Q: How many other museums in America are devoted exclusively to Puerto Rico and Latin America?
A: None.

1970

The Metropolitan Museum of Art began charging admission. The museum currently buys 1.6 million metal admission buttons at a time, and places orders for buttons 3 times a year.

Q: How many different colored buttons does the museum use?
A: 16.

Q: One wing at the Metropolitan Museum of Art is named for Lila Cheson Wallace. What did she do for a living?
A: She was the founder of *Reader's Digest.*

1977

Studio 54, a disco at 254 West 54th Street, opened on April 26.

Q: Who owned the club?
A: Ian Schrager and Stephen Rubell.

The club, constantly mentioned in the press, became a symbol for nightlife in Manhattan and drew celebrities such as Halston and Mick Jagger. The owners were convicted of tax evasion in 1979 and the club was reopened by a new owner in 1981, and closed permanently in 1988.

Q: Which club predated Studio 54 at its location?
A: The Casino de Paree. The club's owner was promoter/columnist/producer Billy Rose, who was married 5 times. One of his wives was comedian and Broadway performer Fannie Brice.

Q: Which movies were based on Fannie Brice's life?
A: Barbra Streisand portrayed her in *Funny Girl* and *Funny Lady*. Brice was the first female Yiddish comedian to work in commercial, mainstream musical comedy and radio.

1977

Christie's auction house, based in London, opened a branch in New York City at 520 Park Avenue. Two years later Christie's East was opened at 219 East 67th Street. The auction house set several records in New York City.

Q: What is the highest bidding record at Christie's for a collection bought by a single owner?
A: $25,824,700 in 1988 for the Tremaine Collection of Contemporary Art.

Q: What was the largest sum paid for a single item at auction at Christie's?
A: $82.5 million for Vincent Van Gogh's *Portrait of Dr. Gachet*.

1977

Annie opened on Broadway and won a Tony Award for Best Musical.

1979

Q: Which Woody Allen film was released in 1979?
A: *Manhattan*.

1985

Tourists were first allowed entry to the services at the Memorial Baptist Church in Harlem on Sundays. Between 170 and 200 tourists currently attend services, and each tourist pays $5 to attend. Visitors from every country around the world have attended the church service and heard the choir. The Sunday service lasts for 2 hours.

1987

Q: Which Woody Allen film was released in 1987?
A: *Radio Days.*

1989

Wendy Wasserstein's play *The Heidi Chronicles* was produced and won a both Pulitzer prize and a Tony Award for Best Play.

Like Woody Allen, Wasserstein was raised in Brooklyn's Flatbush area. She then moved to the Upper East Side, attended the Calhoun School on the Upper West Side, graduated from Mount Holyoke College, and attended the Yale School of Drama.

1990

Neil Simon's play *Lost in Yonkers* opened and won a Tony Award.

1991

The cost of producing a Broadway show had reached $8 million and a run of 65 successful weeks was required to recoup the initial investment (or "the nut"). Ticket prices could run as high as $100 a seat. Spectacle, special effects, and revivals epitomized Broadway theater in the 1990s. Broadway theaters drew an audience of 7.36 million people in the 1990-91 season.

TREADING THE BOARDS

- About 1,200 people in the Actor's Equity make more than $35,000 annually in New York City, and there are 100,000 people in the Actor's Equity union.
- An Off-Broadway actor earns approximately $500 per week.

- $2.5 million was required to bring *On the Waterfront* to Broadway. It ran only 8 performances and required 2 directors.
- 15 brokers were cited for illegally pricing tickets to a Barney (the purple dinosaur character for children) show at Radio City Music Hall.
- The Shubert Organization owns 17 Broadway theaters in New York City. There are approximately 45 Broadway theaters in the city altogether.

Q: What is the average number of actors who work during any given week in New York City?
A: 800.

1992

Q: Which Woody Allen film was released in 1992?
A: *Hannah and Her Sisters.*

1992

Neil Simon's play *Prisoner of Second Avenue* was produced.

1993

Approximately 100,000 people attended the West Indian Labor Day Festival parade in Brooklyn. The average annual overtime bill for police for parades is $5 million, and for sanitation workers it is $500,000.

1994

The first pro-Mainland Chinese parade was held in New York City.

1995

New York City's Fourth of July fireworks display became completely computerized, and Jones Beach first featured a fireworks display. Over 2,000 light bulbs are used on the Fourth of July barges in New York City. Between 10,000 and 20,000 fireworks shells are fired in a typical Fourth of July celebration in New York City.

Q: What is the height at which they explode?
A: 1,000 feet.

Q: How many elephants would it take to equal the weight of explosives for one of the city's Fourth of July celebrations?
A: 20.

1995

Q: How many women were in Titi Liberation, a group whose members believe women should be able to appear in public bare-breasted?
A: 11.

1995

The price of admittance to Barbra Streisand's performance at Madison Square Garden was $50, $125, or $350. Undercover investigators paid two separate ticket scalpers $300 and $350 per ticket for the $125 seats.

Q: How many tours had Barbra Streisand taken before 1995?
A: None.

Q: How many hours did it take to sell 65,000 tickets?
A: 1.

1995

Q: How many prime-time television shows were set in New York City?
A: 8.

Q: How many people attended a movie at the Anjelika Film Center on Houston Street on an average day?
A: 2,200. During the July and August heat wave, the number was 3,600.

THE NEW YORK SCREEN SCENE

*I like New York at dawn. . . . It's something like watching a movie
with the sound track off.*

KIM NOVAK

New York is one big location. Everyone is an extra.

JOHN GUARE

*What can you say about a profession where you can be anybody
and do anything?*

AL PACINO

- It costs $100,000 extra to shoot a 1-hour television episode on a
  Manhattan street, as opposed to on a back lot or in another
  city.
- More than 40 Ingmar Bergman films were shown over the
  course of 40 days at the Film Society of Lincoln Center.
- Film and television industries bring, on average, $3 billion
  annually to New York City in the 1990s.
- Since 1990 New York City has become the independent film
  mecca of the country. The Mayor's Office of Film, Theater, and
  Broadcasting issues permits to movie crews; two-thirds of the
  feature films granted permits since 1990 were for independent films.

1996

There were two club parties in Manhattan that catered to
women size 14 and over. The club's organizer is responsible for
inspiring at least seven weddings. There was also a singles club in
the city for people over six feet tall.

1996

Twenty-eight people posed nude in front of the United Nations
Building for photographer Spencer Tunick. He photographed at
least 100 nude scenes in New York City.

1996

David Ingram was head of the personal shopping division at
Barney's Downtown.

Q: What was his annual salary?
A: $150,000.

He sent Elizabeth Taylor a lavender porcelain candy dish encased in 20 pounds of lavender jellybeans.

Q: How much did the gift cost?
A: $3,000.

He sent also Michael Jackson a $4,000 Lalique crystal whale, since he had heard that the singer liked the movie *Free Willy*, and inserted it in a child's $27 bear-shaped backpack with a note that read, "Unzip me for more treasures." Most of his job was centered around choosing a wardrobe for his clients, most of whom spend more than $50,000 (and as much as $400,000) a year on clothes.

1996

There were 150 people in the Queens Psychic Club, and there was a Vampire Institute located in Queens.

1996

Six hundred hosts and hostesses were hired by the Disney Company for the premiere of *Pocahontas* in Central Park, along with 1,500 staffers. One hundred thousand people watched the movie on the Great Lawn, and $150,000 was spent on police overtime for the event. Total cost to the Disney Company was $1 million. Eighteen thousand square yards of artificial lawn carpet were purchased for $50,000, and 350 trucks motored over Central Park to prepare for the event. Two-and-a-half-million feet of phone lines were laid.

Q: How many pages were in the Disney Employee Guest
    Relations Handbook for the event?
A: 24.

Q: How much would it have cost the Disney Company to
    rent the Goodyear Blimp for the evening?
A: $100,000.

1997

Q: How many people were in New York City's Barbie and Ken Doll Collector's Club?
A: 30.

1998

Arnold Diaz of WCBS-TV presented about 100 "Shame on You" reports each year. He received approximately 150 calls and 30 letters every day.

1997

The concept of the cocktail was revived with the popularity of drinks called "the Cosmopolitan" and "the Metropolitan" in bars and restaurants across the city. The Cosmopolitan is equal parts premium citrus vodka and Cointreau, with a dash of cranberry juice and fresh lime. The Metropolitan is the same, except currant vodka is used instead of citrus-flavored vodka.

1997

Philosophy debates were scheduled every two weeks at the Northside Cafe in Brooklyn's Williamsburg area to ponder topics like "What Is Love?" or "What Is Beauty?" About 30 people attended the discussions.

1998

Q: What percent of the animals at the Bronx Zoo are on display at night?
A: 25%. At Christmas time, 300,000 lights are strung along the zoo's trees, in exhibition halls, and around animal sculptures for nighttime visitors.

1998

The two Hungarian brothers who own Klavierhaus, a piano-restoring company near Lincoln Center, and their 13 employees currently restore between 40 and 50 pianos a year for customers, and buy, restore, and resell 25 to 30 pianos for themselves. "Klavierhaus" is German for "Keyboard House." The company's illustrious clients include Frank Sinatra, New York Philharmonic music director Kurt Masur, fashion designer Isaac Mizrahi, and David Letterman's Late Show orchestra. Klavierhaus charges between $10,000 and $20,000 per restoration. A full restoration can take from three to six months. Frank Sinatra's concert grand is worth $110,000 and is nine feet long.

Q: What type of wood is always used for the soundboard of a piano?
A: Spruce.

Q: How many parts does a piano have?
A: 12,000.

1998

There are between 4,000 and 5,000 street fairs each year in New York City. The Upper West Side's Greenflea market attracts about 350 vendors and 10,000 visitors.

Q: How much does it cost per day to rent a portable toilet in New York City?
A: $75.

1998

Q: How many New Yorkers, on average, visit Atlantic City each year?
A: 10 million.

Q: How many slot machines are in Atlantic City?
A: 28,000.

1999

The International Jazz Museum is slated to open in New York City.

CHAPTER 9

Sports & Games

I love New York City. I've got a gun.
CHARLES BARKLEY, BASKETBALL STAR

Colonists spent their leisure time pursuing tavern sports, which sometimes included gambling, as well as outdoor games such as lawn bowling and ice-skating. The English introduced horse racing to the city in 1665. By 1885 there were seven trotting tracks in the New York City region, and rowing and cricket were also popular sports. The first organized baseball club was formed in 1845. New Yorkers developed an interest in tennis after the Civil War and the New York Athletic Club was formed in 1868. College football and boxing grew in popularity, and in the 1880s New York City was considered the country's center for boxing.

Babe Ruth joined the New York Yankees in 1920 and broke records both in attracting game attendance and game performance. Jackie Robinson joined the Brooklyn Dodgers in 1947 as the first black player in the major leagues, and the New York Mets were formed in 1962. The New York Giants football team was formed in 1925 and the New York Rangers hockey team was formed in 1926.

Boxing made a comeback featuring Jack Demsey in the 1930s, but was largely controlled by organized crime figures such as Frank Carbo until 1955. Six-day bicycle races were held in New York City in the 1920s, and basketball first made an appearance at Madison Square Garden in the late 1920s and early 1930s. The New York Knickerbockers were formed in 1946.

Running became a popular sport in the city after the 1960s, and the first New York City Marathon was staged in 1970 with 127 entrants. The race currently attracts more than 20,000 entrants. Gyms and enormous health clubs flourished in the city after the mid-1980s, as did various types of aerobic exercise classes, kickboxing, rollerblading, yoga, skateboarding, mountain biking, snowboarding, and "extreme sports" activities.

Warner Wolf, a local New York City sports reporter for WCBS from 1972 through 1992, was a pioneer of the upbeat, enthusiastic style of sports announcing. He left the city after a contract dispute to work in Washington, D.C., and returned to WCBS-TV in New York City in 1997.

If it was up to me, I'd never leave New York again.
WARNER WOLF TO THE *NEW YORK TIMES*

New York is a galaxy of adventure at once elegant, exciting, and bizarre. It's a city that moves so fast, it takes energy just to stand still.

BARBARA WALTERS

1600

Local Indians held the Bowl Game each autumn, a sacred game of chance in which each team tried to win all of 102 beans.

1609

Henry Hudson's *Half Moon* crew cast their nets into local waters and caught "ten great Mullets . . . and a Ray as great as foure men could hale into the ship."

1624

The Dutch and other settlers enjoyed ice-skating on the many ponds throughout New Amsterdam. At the foot of Broadway at Bowling Green Park, settlers played lawn bowling, which remained popular for over a century.

1635

Settlers fished at Collect Pond just north of the Wall Street area. They also enjoyed rounding up cattle in City Hall Park.

1648

Tradesmen, merchants, and mariners enjoyed the pastimes of both city and country life in New Amsterdam. In winter they went fishing and ice-skating. During the spring and summer they went horseracing, bowling on the green, and fishing. During any type of weather, they savored the conviviality of the local tavern.

1665

The English introduced horse racing to New York City (New Amsterdam had become New York City a year earlier). The first English governor, Richard Nicolls, offered a silver cup for a race to be held each spring and autumn. The blossoming of a wealthy upper class with ample leisure time contributed to the growth of sports, especially horse racing.

1730

New York City residents first began playing billiards.

1776

During and after the American Revolution sporting activities declined, partially because people were preoccupied with politics and partially because they were symbolic of the colony's English "aristocracy." Sporting and drinking were also considered to be a violation of the Sabbath, but police records indicate that few colonists cared about the drinking portion of the violation.

1776

Bill Richmond, a slave belonging to the Staten Island-based Duke of Northumberland from England, astounded three ruffians who had picked a fight with him by soundly trouncing them. Soon after, the Duke took Richmond back to England with him when the British left the city. Richmond attended school in England and at the ripe old age of 42 became a professional boxer. He was undefeated until 1805, when he sparred against Englishman Tom Cribb for 90 minutes; Cribb was known as the best bare-knuckle boxer in boxing history. Richmond opened an inn in England called the Horse and Dolphin, which was visited by landed gentry and sportsmen. He also ran a boxing school and counted among his pupils Lord Byron and a black man named Tom Molineux—who later became America's heavyweight champion.

1802

Thoroughbred horse racing was banned in New York State, but harness races were still held on Third Avenue.

1817

Two private marine baths for swimming were anchored off the Battery.

1820

Thoroughbred racing was deemed legal again in New York State and racing enjoyed another renaissance in the city. New York City residents began to rely on organizations and sporting entrepreneurs to supply venues for races and games, as opposed to creating informal sport outings.

1821

Saloons such as the Rat Pit and Kit Burns's Sportsmen Hall near the Bowery featured betting fights between rats and dogs. These fights were previously played out in alleyways and farmyards and attended by a rough crowd, but when they moved to the saloons, even part of the city's merchant class began participating.

1821

Wealthy residents formed the Jockey Club and built Union Course in Queens. New York City was the national center for horse racing until 1850 and almost all of the significant races were held at the Union Course.

1825

The New York Trotting Club was formed and a racing course was built in Centerville on Long Island.

1835

Boats were first sailed and raced for sport, and the first pleasure crafts were built in the city. New York City soon became the nation's premier location for boating and boat racing.

1844

Lauded sportsmen John C. Stevens, John Jay, George Schuyler, Hamilton Wilkes, and five others founded the New York Yacht Club. The club's annual regatta soon garnered extensive press coverage because of the elevated social standing of the club's members and the multitude of spectators who turned out for the event.

1845

Harness racing was more popular than thoroughbred racing because the wealthy who controlled thoroughbred racing were unable to appeal to the city's burgeoning middle class.

Franconi's Hippodrome was a popular venue for equestrian events in the 1880s.

1845

A club called The Knickerbockers was formed as the first organized baseball club in the city, and New York City was considered the national center for boxing.

1850

A survey was taken by the New York Association for the Suppression of Gambling to determine the extent of gambling and gaming houses in Manhattan. Six thousand gambling houses existed in the city, 200 of them "of the first class," excluding lotteries and raffles. The figure averaged one gambling house for each 85 residents. It was estimated that 25,000 men, or one-twentieth of the city's population, relied upon gambling for their livelihood.

1850

The first billiard table was manufactured in the city. Within 50 years there were 13 billiard manufacturers based in New York City.

Q: In which decade did the most pool halls exist in New York City?
A: The 1920s.

DOWN AT THE POOL HALL

Number of pool halls in the city in:

1850	60
1900	130
1920	4,000
1961	257
1997	220

1852

The Union Bay Boat Club was founded.

Q: What was it renamed in 1861?
A: The Brooklyn Yacht Club.

1853

There were seven trotting tracks in the New York metropolitan area and clubs had formed in the city for those who enjoyed cricket, yachting, rowing, gymnastics, target shooting, and racquet sports.

1857

There were a hundred baseball teams in New York City, so players formed the National Association of Baseball Players to create clear-cut rules and codes for playing the game.

Q: What did people in Manhattan call residents in Brooklyn in the 1880s?
A: "Trolley Dodgers" or simply "the Dodgers."

1857

The first national chess tournament was held in New York City as part of the First American Chess Congress. The winner was a 20-year-old man named Paul Morphy from New Orleans. In 1858 he defeated European masters; in Paris he played blindfolded against eight opponents, defeating six of them and drawing with the two others. His impressive round of victories sparked an interest in the game of chess in New York City and across the country. He returned to New York City in 1859 much lauded, but decided he disliked the game. He returned to New Orleans in 1860 and never played chess again (in public, at least).

The next chess three world champions resided in New York City. They were: Wilhelm Steinitz of Prague, Emmanuel Lasker of Barlinek, Poland, and Jose Raul Capablanca of Havana, Cuba. Capablanca was a student at Columbia University and later held a position in the Cuban Diplomatic Service.

1858

The first official ice-skating rink was opened at Central Park South,; a year later the *New York Times* estimated that 60,000 pairs of ice skates had been sold in the city.

1860

A woman dared to skate on the men's ice-skating rink in Central Park. Ten years later, separate areas for men and women were eliminated.

1863

"Blood sports" were at the peak of their popularity and would continue in popularity through the 1870s. These sports included cockfighting, ratting (pitting man against rat), dog fighting, bull baiting, gander-pulling, and bear baiting

1865

The Atlantic Yacht Club in Brooklyn was established, followed by the Columbia Yacht Club at West 86th Street in 1867.

1866

The New York Yacht Club sponsored the first transatlantic race. This race and another in 1870 were received with unbridled enthusiasm across the city and with glowing press coverage.

1868

The New York Athletic Club opened for those who enjoyed playing tennis, running around a track, and swimming. Athletic clubs in New York City would grow increasingly more exclusive until the 1880s, when members were recruited outright by social standing alone. Membership in a club became a means of proclaiming wealth and for forging beneficial social ties.

1873

Columbia College adopted English soccer rules for collegiate play. The school was a founding member of the first Intercollegiate Soccer Association in 1905.

1876

The Polo Grounds, a complex of sporting facilities, was built on 110th Street (stretching to 112th Street) between Fifth and Sixth

Avenues. Originally opened for polo matches, the complex was used for the baseball games of the Giants and the Metropolitans in 1883. The complex moved to 157th Street at the Harlem River in 1891, was razed by fire, and then was replaced at the same location in 1911 with a new structure made of concrete and steel.

THE GARDEN

The first structure called Madison Square Garden was built by William Vanderbilt and opened on May 31, 1879 at 26th Street and Madison Avenue. The sporting hall was drafty and dirty and primarily featured boxing matches (boxing champion John Sullivan drew massive crowds to the arena). Ten years later, in 1889, Vanderbilt razed the structure because it was losing money.

Horse Show Association officials replaced the building with another Madison Square Garden—a Moorish-style building designed by Sanford White that cost $3 million to build and was the second tallest structure in the city. The facility was used for bicycle races, horse and dog shows, long-distance foot races, boxing matches, and political rallies. The building continued to lose money until 1920, when Tex Rickard leased the building for boxing matches. He brought in $5 million in five years (his lease was $200,000 a year) and featured rodeos, the circus, foot races, and bicycle races.

Rickard moved Madison Square Garden to 50th Street and Eighth Avenue in 1925 with new features such as New York Rangers hockey games and ice capades; the building remained profitable in spite of the depression. Madison Square Garden was moved to Pennsylvania Station at West 34th Street and Eighth Avenue in 1968 at a cost of $116 million.

1881

Bare-knuckle boxing champion John Sullivan fought his most memorable matches in Manhattan and Brooklyn between 1881 and 1884. New York City was noted for being a center of both bare-knuckle and gloved boxing.

1883

The first Brooklyn Dodgers baseball game was played, and the Harlem Yacht Club was established at West 123rd Street.

1885

There were 200 tennis courts in and around Prospect Park, and the popularity of watching college football increased. Princeton and Yale played at the Polo Grounds in New York City to crowds of more than 30,000 each Thanksgiving Day, a tradition that started in the early 1880s. Around the turn of the century many people began criticizing the games for being too commercialized to meet the needs of the students, so the games moved back to the college towns in the early 1900s. Other college football games held in the city included those between Notre Dame and Army (West Point's U.S. Military Academy); these games were especially popular because of the city's enormous Catholic population.

1886

Gaming—or gambling—houses on the Bowery featured Chuck-a-luck (also known as Sweat or Sweat Sloth), a dice game that was eventually replaced by craps in the early 1890s. Card games included Hearts, Euchre, Seven-Up, Loo, All-Fours, Écarté, Keno, Faro (especially popular throughout the 1800s), Monte, Pitch, Boston, Casino, and Rouge et Noir. The upscale and expensive gaming houses were centered around Park Row, Park Place, Liberty Street, Vesey Street, Barclay Street, and Lower Broadway.

1887

The Canarsie Yacht Club was founded in Brooklyn.

1889

Bicycles appeared for the first time in Central Park, although people in the city had been riding them elsewhere before 1889.

1890

Fifteen free-floating swimming pools, also used as baths, were installed in rivers around the city. Dozens of public bathhouses were built by 1912, fusing public health and cleanliness with swimming. Swimming became a competitive sport between 1900 and 1925 in the city, with many of the sports clubs offering pools for teams.

1892

Nearly all of the owners of baseball teams in New York City had connections with the Democratic Party and the infamous Tammany Hall. Owners could receive prepublicized information on mass transit developments and keep competitors at bay with the help of the city's politicians.

1902

John McGraw became the manager of the New York Giants.

HOW 'BOUT THEM APPLES?

From 1902 until 1990 there was never a span of more than four years during which a baseball team from New York City failed to play in the World Series.

1903

The Public School Athletic League was formed. Education reformers believed that sports and regular exercise contributed to the well-being, character, and morality of a student. One hundred thousand New York City students enrolled in the league, which was supported by sports figures, prominent businessmen, and educational funds.

1913

The first U.S. Open (or U.S. Lawn Tennis Championship) was held at the Forest Hills Tennis Stadium in Queens.

1913

The United States Soccer Association was formed and presented its first tournament for the U.S. Challenge Cup in Brooklyn between two local teams of Irish immigrants.

1914

There were more than 700 athletic clubs in the city, catering to all backgrounds and preferences.

1919

Sunday baseball games were legalized; local ball clubs had fought the city's "pro-Sabbath-day-rest" faction for two decades in order to present public ball games on Sundays. The legalization of Sunday sports translated to larger baseball crowds (usually more than 20,000 people) and a more diverse array of fans.

1920

The New York Yankees purchased the contract of Babe Ruth from the Boston Red Sox for $125,000. The New York Yankees and Babe Ruth attracted almost 1.3 million fans in 1920, which broke attendance records and was double the figure for 1919.

Q: Why were the New York Yankees evicted from the Polo Grounds in 1920?

A: The owner of the New York Giants, Charles Stoneham, had shared his stadium with the Yankees since 1913, but the team's growing popularity because of Babe Ruth threatened to overshadow the Giants on their own turf. The Yankees decided to build their own ballpark.

1920

Q: What was the Walker Act?

A: Its passage in 1920 rendered boxing legal again after a 20-year ban. Unlike boxing's 1880s fans, the renewed interest in boxing in the 1920s included the upper and middle classes.

Q: Which boxer drew the largest crowds at Madison Square Garden in 1920?

A: Jack Dempsey.

BOXED IN

Boxing became increasingly controlled by organized crime in the 1920s just as it was being embraced by the mainstream. Championship fights were no longer athletic events, they were also social events.

1921

The New York Yankees made more than $3 million in profit between 1921 and 1930.

1921

The world heard the first World Series broadcast. The New York Giants played the New York Yankees while Newark-based radio station WJZ featured a play-by-play account of the eight games.

Q: Who won?
A: The Giants won 5, the Yankees won 3.

Q: How did the radio announcer glean the facts of the game?
A: The announcer relayed details he received by telephone from a reporter at the *Newark Star.*

1922

Yankee Stadium was built in the Bronx; it boasted the largest seating capacity in the country for baseball viewing with 67,224 seats and three decks. More than 74,000 fans attended its opening day ceremonies and 24,000 were turned away.

Q: What phrase was coined by Fred Lieb of the *New York Evening Telegram* to describe the new stadium?
A: "The House that Ruth Built."

Q: That phrase summed up the immense popularity and talent of Babe Ruth. What were 2 of his best-known nicknames?
A: "The Sultan of Swat" and "the Bambino."

Q: How many home runs did he hit for the Yankees?
A: 659, between 1920 and 1934.

1922-23 YANKEE STADIUM CONSTRUCTION OVERVIEW

Working days required to complete the stadium 284
Number of workers required to complete the stadium 500
Amount of dirt excavated at stadium site . . . . .25,000 cubic yards
Amount of steel required to complete the stadium . . .2,500 tons

Materials used for the original
stadium bleachers ....2 million board feet of fir
The cost of constructing the stadium ....$2.5 million
The cost of renovating the stadium in 1975-76 ......$100 million

The original distance to the fence down the left field line was
281 feet—now the distance to the fence is 318 feet. Mickey
Mantle hit a ball 620 feet on April 22, 1953, which hit the facade
over right field.

The odds of winning the New York Lotto jackpot are 1 in 12.9 million.

Q: What are the odds of getting hit by a baseball during a game in Yankee Stadium?
A: 1 in 300,000.

1923

The New York Yankees won their first World Series. The Yankees won six American League pennants and three World Series titles in the 1920s.

Q: What was the nickname given to Babe Ruth and his team-mates?
A: "Murderer's Row."

1923

The first professional soccer league in the country, the American Soccer League, included a team from New York City.

1925

Tim Mara formed the New York Giants football team. More than 70,000 fans went to see the New York Giants play against Red Grange and the Chicago Bears at the Polo Grounds at 110th Street and Fifth Avenue in December 1925.

1926

The New York Rangers hockey team was formed.

1927

The Yankees won 110 games and lost 44, which was one of the best records in the history of baseball.

1928

Basketball, which had been popular with youth groups in ethnic neighborhoods throughout the city since the turn of the century, began to garner more attention. Professional teams had formed by 1928, but they remained community-based.

1931

Local sportswriters organized college basketball games at Madison Square Garden and the games were sold out. Mayor James Walker had requested the games to benefit the city Relief Fund.

Since its creation in 1879, the Garden has never been closed.

1933

New York Yankees pitcher Vernon "Lefty" Gomez was asked to take a cut in pay—from $20,000 to $7,500—after a poor year.

"Tell you what," he said, somewhat shocked, "you keep the salary and pay me the cut."

1934

Sportswriter Ned Irish became a promoter for college games at Madison Square Garden between local teams and formidable opponents across the country.

1934

Babe Ruth retired from the New York Yankees.

1935

Gangster Frankie Carbo controlled the outcome of some (if not all) of the major boxing matches in the city through intimidation and sheer brute force. He also determined who would fight.

1936

The New York Yankees won seven pennants and six World Series between 1936 and 1943. Team members included Joe DiMaggio, Charlie Keller, Tommy Henrich, and Bill Dickey. The Yankees were dubbed "the Bronx Bombers."

1938

A group of sportswriters formed the National Invitation Tournament (NIT) at Madison Square Garden.

1945

Q: Which baseball player was signed with the Brooklyn Dodgers—to a minor league contract?

A: Jackie Robinson. He became the first black player in the major leagues in 1947, and was synonymous with a Dodgers victory for the next 10 years.

1946

The New York Knickerbockers were formed and the basketball team played at Madison Square Garden. The New York Rangers and the New York Americans also played at the Garden.

1947

Jackie Robinson signed with the Brooklyn Dodgers as the league's first black baseball player.

Q: What kind of team was the New York Americans?
A: A hockey team.

1947

Kareem Abdul-Jabbar was born Lew Alcindor in New York City. He would later play basketball for Power Memorial High School in the city. Other high school basketball players from the city who became prominent in college and as professionals are Julius Erving (b. 1950), Albert King (b. 1959), Connie Hawkins (b. 1942), Roger Brown (b. 1942), and Nate "Tiny" Archibald (b. 1948).

1949

The New York Yankees won the World Series each year from 1949 to 1953. Between 1954 and 1964 the team won four World Series and nine pennants. Team members included Phil Rizzuto, Mickey Mantle, Roger Maris, Yogi Berra, and Whitey Ford.

1951

Q: Which famous player was signed to the Giants in 1951?
A: Willie Mays.

1951

Manhattan District Attorney Frank Hogan decided to investigate rumors that the college basketball games at Madison Square Garden were rigged. The games drew more than 600,000 fans in 1950, and the City College of New York team won both the NIT and the NCAA championships. Hogan discovered that the games were rigged, with players deliberately reducing the margin of victory in their games for the benefit of bettors (or "point shaving"). Thirty-two players from seven schools in New York City's metropolitan area were arrested. The effect was devastating to the image of professional games and to Madison Square Garden's ability to draw fans. The NIT became a tournament of little importance and the Garden suffered financial setbacks. Other players around the country were also found to be rigging games.

1955

Q: Who became the first black player on the New York Yankees team?
A: Elston Howard.

1956

To underscore football's growing popularity in the city, the Giants football team moved to Yankee Stadium from the Polo Grounds and won the NFL championship for the first time in 10 years.

Q: Who were 2 of the team's more colorful players?
A: Frank Gifford and Sam Huff.

1958

Q: The president of the Brooklyn Dodgers, Walter O'Malley, moved the team to another city. Which city?
A: Los Angeles.

Q: Why did he move the Dodgers out of New York City?
A: New York City refused his request to rebuild Ebbets Field and include more parking spaces and better access to subway lines. The city offered to build a ballpark in Queens Flushing Meadow for him, but he refused the offer.

Q: Which team defected to another city next?
A: The New York Giants baseball team moved to San Francisco shortly after the Dodgers left.

1960

The American Football League established a franchise in the city first known as the New York Titans.

Q: What was the team's name changed to in 1963?
A: The New York Jets. The team moved to Shea Stadium from the Polo Grounds in 1964.

1962

The New York Mets baseball team was formed; the team moved to Shea Stadium from the Polo Grounds in 1964. A new factor in the placement of teams with stadiums was the suburban draw: fans from Long Island and the far reaches of the outer boroughs could drive to Shea Stadium in Flushing Meadow while city-based fans could reach the stadium by subway.

1962

Q: Which Baseball Hall of Fame athlete was the CEO of the Chock Full O' Nuts fast-food chain in New York City?
A: Jackie Robinson.

1964

The Polo Grounds were destroyed to make way for apartment buildings and CBS bought the New York Yankees for $14 million.

1967

The Mayor's Cup for yacht races was established, sponsored by the South Street Seaport Museum. Only yachts built before 1960 were eligible and most entrants lived in New York City.

1968

Madison Square Garden's new facilities on top of Pennsylvania Station could seat 20,000 fans.

Q: What is a ticket scalper's average spring markup at Madison Square Garden?
A: 30%.

Q: What is the average winter markup?
A: 5% to 10%.

1970

The first New York City Marathon was held in Central Park.

Q: How many entrants were there?
A: 127.

1971

The New York Cosmos soccer team was formed as part of the North American Soccer League. The league also moved its headquarters to Manhattan in 1971.

Q: Where did the team play its home games?
A: On Randall's Island at Downing Stadium. Randy Horton was part of the team and is widely considered to be the most popular American soccer player. The team won the league championship in 1972.

1973

A syndicate controlled by George Steinbrenner bought the New York Yankees from CBS for a reported $10 million.

Q: Where was Steinbrenner originally from, and what did he start out doing for a living?
A: Cleveland; he began his career as a shipbuilder.

1974

Yankee Stadium was renovated from 1974 until 1976. Renovation costs were estimated at $24 million but ended up being more than $100 million.

1975

Brazilian soccer star Pele was signed to the New York Cosmos; he drew enormous crowds, and the team moved to Yankee Stadium the following year.

Q: What year did Pele retire?
A: 1977.

The Cosmos qualified for the playoffs each year between 1975 and 1984.

1976

The Giants moved to New Jersey to a new coliseum called the Meadowlands Complex that had been built for the team in East Rutherford. It was then renamed Giants Stadium. New Rutherford was located only five miles from midtown Manhattan so it presented fierce competition to the city. The new facilities also offered a basketball arena and a racetrack.

1976

The New York City Marathon was extended to encompass all five boroughs, which rendered the Marathon the only sporting event in the city to link all of the boroughs together.

1977

The New York Yankees won the World series in 1977 and 1978 and pennants in 1978 and 1981. Team members included Reggie Jackson, Catfish Hunter, Thurman Munson, Ron Guidry, and Sparky Lyle.

Q: How many times did Steinbrenner fire manager Billy Martin in the 1980s?
A: 5.

1978

The National Tennis Center opened near Shea Stadium to replace the Forest Hills Tennis Stadium as the site of the U.S. Open.

1994 U.S. OPEN

- 1,405 accredited journalists covered the U.S. Open.
- Box seats cost $55 to $160.
- 529,687 people attended the Open.
- 137 countries televised the event.
- 900 tons of garbage were produced by the event.
- There were 50 different items for sale in the event's souvenir shop.

1978

Q: Who won the women's division of the New York City Marathon?

A: Grete Waitz, a Norwegian runner who won the women's division of the race 9 times between 1978 and 1988.

1980

The New York Mets team was bought by Nelson Doubleday and the real estate executive Fred Wilpon. A new general manager, Frank Cashen, assembled a new team that included Dwight Gooden, Daryl Strawberry, Wally Backman, and Keith Hernandez.

1982

Approximately 11,000 athletes from around the world competed in the New York City Gay Games, and 500,000 to one million people viewed the events. The estimated amount of money that visitors to the Gay Games spent was $400 million.

1983

The city spent five years and $12 million renovating Wollman Memorial Rink in Central Park. Donald Trump took over the reins of the rebuilding effort and reopened the rink within a few months.

1983

In 1983 and 1984 Spalding sponsored a stickball exhibition on West 60th Street.

1984

The Liberty Cup, sponsored by the Harbor Festival Foundation, was founded as an annual race in New York Harbor. The race drew competitors from around the world.

1985

Q: Another New York City team moved to New Jersey's Meadowland Complex (renamed Giants Stadium) in 1985. Which one?

A: The New York Jets. The president of the Jets, Leon Hess, didn't want to share Shea Stadium with the Mets. Even after the Jets and the Giants defected to New Jersey, they still retained the word New York in their titles and were still perceived by city residents as being their home teams.

1985

The New York Cosmos withdrew from the soccer league and disbanded.

1986

The Mets won the World Series.

1987

The Manhattan Yacht Club was formed at 207 Front Street.

1988

Seventy-seven spectators at a cockfighting festival in the Bronx were arrested.

1988

Q: What is the Yankees record for home attendance for a season?
A: 2,633,710 in 1988.

With such a selection of New York City teams about which to become fanatics, enterprising sports stores are sure to make a profit.

PHOTO BY ERIC CAPSTICK

1989

An illegal Cuban social club in the Bronx was raided for cock-fighting.

1989

Off-Track Betting (OTB) was netting $33 million annually for the city.

1989

Juma Ikangaa won the New York City Marathon's Men's Division at 2:08:01, representing the fastest finish time between 1970 and 1994.

1990

There were more than 20,000 entrants in the New York City Marathon. The Marathon had evolved to include prize money, a television contract, and impressive corporate sponsors.

1990

By 1990 the New York Yankees had won 22 World Series and 33 American League pennants, a record in the game of baseball.

1992

Lisa Ondieki won the New York City Marathon's Women's Division at 2:24:40, representing the fastest finish time between 1970 and 1994.

1993

The Mets won 59 games and lost 103, finishing last in their division. By 1994 Dwight Gooden was the last remaining player from the championship team of 1986.

1994

The New York Rangers won the Stanley Cup.

Q: In which other years did the team win the Stanley Cup?
A: 1928, 1933, and 1940.

1995

About 600 people waited to see infamous boxer Mike Tyson appear briefly in front of the Apollo Theater.

1995

Eighteen people were arrested for drag racing in Queens in the month of August.

1995

There were 20 competitors in a race to swim around Manhattan.

1996

The Yankees won the World Series.

1997

The Arthur Ashe Stadium opened at the National Tennis Center in Queens in time for the 1997 U.S. Open, with improved construction to stave off winds and lighting with less glare to distract players. The Arthur Ashe Stadium has 1,500 general public seats and 90 luxury boxes.

Q: Who was inconspicuous by his absence at the stadium's ribbon-cutting ceremony, claiming ticket prices were too high and tennis was for the wealthy?
A: Mayor Giuliani.

TODAY'S CATCH

Bluefish and striped bass are found in the East River. Under the State Department of Environmental Conservation's rules, bluefish of any size may be taken year-round, but the daily limit per person is 10. The season for striped bass is May 8 through December 15, and bass under 28 inches long must be released. The limit on striped bass is one fish per day. The state's Department of Health issued a general health advisory suggesting limited consumption of sport fish caught in the waters around Manhattan—including the East River to Throg's Neck Bridge. Some fish, especially the larger ones, may be contaminated with polychlorinated biphenyls, heavy metals, or industrial pollutants.

1997

There were 19 chess tables for speed-chess in the southwest corner of Washington Square Park. The average cost to bet on a game is $5.

Q: How many of the 41 American chess grandmasters live in or around New York City?
A: 22.

1997

There are 890 playing fields, 2,000 basketball courts, and 1,885 handball courts in New York City.

1998

Q: How many people, on average, can be found fishing on the Lower Queens riverfront in Long Island City on Saturday morning?

A: 25 to 30.

PHOTO BY LARRY JOHNSON

BIBLIOGRAPHY

Ambulando, Solvitur. *In The Hudson Highlands.* New York: Walking News Inc., 1945.

Auchincloss, Louis. *The Hone & Strong Diaries of Old Manhattan.* New York: Abbeville Press, 1989.

Bender, Thomas. *New York Intellect: A History of Intellectual Life in New York City from 1750 to the Beginning of Our Own Time.* New York: Alfred A. Knopf, 1987.

Bloom, Alexander. *Prodigal Sons: New York Intellectuals and Their World.* New York: Oxford University Press, 1986.

Brown, Francis and Roucek, Joseph S. *One America: The History, Contributions and Present Problems of Our Racial and National Minorities.* Englewood Cliffs, NJ: Prentice Hall, 1952.

Cirino, Linda D. and Edmiston, Susan. *Literary New York: A History and Guide.* Boston: Houghton Mifflin, 1976.

Condit, Carl W. *The Port of New York: A History of the Rail Terminal System.* Chicago: Chicago University Press, 1981.

Deutsch, Albert and Schneider, David M. *The History of Public Welfare in New York State, 1867-1940.* Chicago: University of Chicago Press, 1941.

Duffy, John. *A History of Public Health in New York City.* New York: Russell Sage Foundation, 1974.

Eastman, John. *Who Lived Where: A Biographical Guide to Homes and Museums.* New York: Bonanza Books, 1983.

Egan, Robert. *The Bookstore Book: A Guide to Manhattan Booksellers.* New York: Avon, 1979.

Fadiman, Clifton. *The Little Brown Book of Anecdotes.* New York: Little, Brown and Company, 1985.

George, Michael. *New York Today.* New York: Harry Abrams, Inc. Publishers, 1988.

Goldberger, Paul. *The City Observed: A Guide to the Architecture of Manhattan.* New York: Random House, 1979.

Graham, Frank. *The New York Yankees: An Informal History.* New York: G. P. Putnam's Sons, 1948.

Grashow, Mark. *How to Make New York a Better Place to Live.* New York: City & Company, 1994.

Henderson, Mary. *The City and the Theater: New York Playhouses from Bowling Green to Times Square.* Clifton, NJ: James White, 1973.

Honig, Donald. *The New York Yankees.* New York: Crown, 1981.

Jackson, Anthony. *A Place Called Home: A History of Low-Cost Housing in Manhattan.* Cambridge: MIT Press, 1976.

Jackson, Kenneth. *The Encyclopedia of New York City.* New Haven: Yale University Press, 1995.

Jennings, Gary. *Parades!: Celebrations and Circuses on the March.* Philadelphia: J. B. Lippincott, 1966.

Kammen, Michael. *Colonial New York: A History.* New York: Charles Scribner & Sons, 1975.

Kisseloff, Jeff. *You Must Remember This.* New York: Harcourt, Brace, Jovanovich, 1989.

Kwong, Peter. *The New Chinatown.* New York: Hill and Wang, 1987.

Moscow, Henry. *The Book of New York Firsts.* New York: Collier Books, 1982.

Museum of the City of New York. *Modern Metropolis: Artists Images of New York.* New York: The New Press, 1993.

New York City Landmarks Preservation Committee. *Guide to New York City Landmarks.* Washington DC: The Preservation Press, 1992.

New York Public Library. *The New York Public Library Desk Reference.* The Stonesong Press, 1989.

Rink, Oliver A.. *Holland on the Hudson: An Economic and Social History of Dutch New York.* Ithaca: Cornell University Press, 1986.

Still, Bayrd; Mirror for Gotham, New York: New York University Press, 1956.

Robson, John William. *A Guide to Columbia University.* New York: Columbia University Press, 1937.

Ross, Betty. *Museums, Historic Houses, Art Galleries and Other Special Places.* Washington DC: Americana Press, 1991.

Sante, Luc. *Low Life.* New York: Farrar, Straus, Giroux, 1991.

Smith, Steven T. *Wall Street.* New York: Columbia University Press, 1991.

————*A Timeline of New York City Park History.* New York: Department of Parks and Recreation, 1988.

Werner, M. R. *It Happened in New York.* New York: Coward-McCann, Inc., 1957.

Wertenbaker, Thomas Jefferson. *Father Knickerbocker Rebels.* New York: Cooper Square Publishers, Inc., 1948.

Wiener, Joan and Lynton C. *New York, New York.* Peter Pauper Press, Inc., 1994.

Wilentz, Sean. *Chants Democratic: New York City and the Rise of the American Working Class.* New York: Oxford University Press, 1986.

City officials contacted through the Green Book of New York City—the City Departments of Transportation, Health, Sanitation, New York Police and Fire Departments, Department of Parks and Recreation, NYC Transit Authority, and Frank Vardy of the New York City Planning Department—were used as source material, in addition to dozens of articles from the New York Times and information from the files of the Census Bureau Library in New York City. Source material was also found in the local history room of the New York Public Library at 42nd Street and at the library's newspaper annex.

ABOUT THE AUTHOR

B. Kim Taylor has written for the *New York Times, New York Newsday, New York Press, National Lampoon, Vibe, Time Out* (New York), *Manhattan File, Our Town, Special Report, Japan's AB*Road* magazine, Gale Research encyclopedias, the *Yale Press Encyclopedia of New York City,* and for Berkshire MultiMedia in Stockbridge, Massachusetts, as a CD-ROM scriptwriter. She lives in Manhattan with her husband and two-and-a-half-year-old son.